God with You

A 52-Week Devotional Through the Whole Bible for Teenagers

CAMERON COLE,
CHELSEA KINGSTON ERICKSON,
ANNA MEADE HARRIS, EDITORS

ZONDERVAN REFLECTIVE

ZONDERVAN REFLECTIVE

God with You

Published by Zondervan, 3950 Sparks Drive SE, Suite 101, Grand Rapids, MI 49546, USA. Zondervan is a registered trademark of The Zondervan Corporation, L.L.C., a wholly owned subsidiary of HarperCollins Christian Publishing, Inc.

Requests for information should be addressed to customercare@harpercollins.com.

Zondervan titles may be purchased in bulk for educational, business, fundraising, or sales promotional use. For information, please email SpecialMarkets@Zondervan.com.

ISBN 978-0-310-16903-1 (softcover)
ISBN 978-0-310-16905-5 (audio)
ISBN 978-0-310-16904-8 (ebook)

HarperCollins Publishers, Macken House, 39/40 Mayor Street Upper, Dublin 1, D01 C9W8, Ireland (https://www.harpercollins.com)

Cover design and art: Emily Weigel
Cover texture: © Busliq / Shutterstock
Interior design: Mallory Collins

Printed in the United States of America
26 27 28 29 30 LBC 5 4 3 2 1

To our children—with great love—
Cam, Mary Matthews, Hutch, and Knox
Wells and Emmett
Mac, Sam, and Ben
Wiley, Parr, and Wells
May the grace of the Lord Jesus Christ and the love of God, and the fellowship of the Holy Spirit be with you all. (2 Corinthians 13:14)

Contents

Praise for *God with You*

Finally! A devotional book that presents God's grace in a way today's teens can trust—straightforward, unfiltered, and eminently applicable for the questions and issues they face every day. *God with You* does not dumb down the gospel; instead, readers will find themselves challenged to grapple with God's promises, shape thoughts into prayers, and be transformed as their hearts and minds are made new.

JODIE BERNDT, BESTSELLING AUTHOR OF *PRAYING THE SCRIPTURES FOR YOUR TEENS*

How I wish I would have had a copy of *God with You* when I was a teenager! It brims with the wisdom and grace one thirsts for at all stages of life but especially during the singularly spiky period known as adolescence. This is the Good News, digestibly delivered day after day without a whiff of condescension—zero homework vibes, in other words. Highly recommended and urgently needed. I'll be gifting one to every teenager I know.

DAVID ZAHL, AUTHOR OF *SECULOSITY* AND *THE BIG RELIEF*

Rooted in Scripture and shaped by the real questions and pressures teens face today, this devotional offers far more than inspiration; it points young people to a hope that is practical and resilient, grounded in God's story, and strong enough to help them trust and follow Jesus in the midst of real life.

KARA POWELL, PHD, EXECUTIVE DIRECTOR OF THE FULLER YOUTH INSTITUTE AND COAUTHOR OF *FUTURE-FOCUSED CHURCH*

Today's students need resources for forming their faith in the one true God, as they are all too often deformed by a culture that consistently seeks to undermine their flourishing. *God with You* builds student faith by serving as a rich and trustworthy fertilizer to feed and energize the roots that will yield abundant fruit of great spiritual growth, both now and for the rest of their lives.

DR. WALT MUELLER, CENTER FOR PARENT/YOUTH UNDERSTANDING

Most teens are spiritually starving. They may get one spiritual meal each week at youth group, but it's not enough. Our sons and daughters need daily time with the Lord in his Word. If you want to see your children develop a strong foundation for their faith, this devotional is a great next step. Don't just give it to your child; take the journey together and be prepared for what God will do.

DR. ROB RIENOW, VISIONARY FAMILY MINISTRIES

God with You is a must-have for all youth leaders. It's useful as both a personal devotional and a resource for discipleship and preaching. The devotions here are biblically centered, theologically rich, and suitable for all contexts—for seeker and believer alike.

REV. DR. DAVID A. WASHINGTON, SENIOR PASTOR, KINGDOM COVENANT CHURCH

If you've ever hoped for a gospel-soaked resource that refreshes you, raises the bar in your life, points you to Jesus every day, and understands you as a teen, this devotional may well be the answer to your prayer.

SHELBY ABBOTT, AUTHOR OF *WHY WE'RE FEELING LONELY* AND *DOUBTLESS*; SPEAKER; CAMPUS MINISTER

God with You is an ambitious project with significant potential. With 260 short readings, five per week, the devotions trace the Christ-centered story of Scripture in ways teens can grasp. I encourage families and youth groups to work through it in sections for deeper impact. It can strengthen biblical literacy and cultivate a durable, gospel-rooted faith.

STEVE S. CHANG, PRESIDENT, SOLA NETWORK

As a teen, I remember trying to squeeze time with God in the midst of the many demands on my time. I wish I would have had this devotional then. It is gospel-centered, comprehensive, and accessible to teen and parent alike. I highly recommend it.

CHAP BETTIS, AUTHOR OF *THE DISCIPLE-MAKING PARENT*

If we want students to follow Jesus for life, we must help them engage the Bible consistently. This yearlong devotional covers the entire story of Scripture and keeps Jesus at the center. I wholeheartedly recommend it to any church that is focused on discipling the next generation.

CHRIS LI, HIGH SCHOOL PASTOR, MARINERS CHURCH

CONTENTS

CONTENTS

CONTENTS

CONTENTS

Dear Reader,

We are so glad that you picked up this devotional or that someone who loves you gave it to you. This book is meant to help you read and understand the best, most important book in the whole world—the Bible, God's own Word to us.

Maybe you've never read the Bible before, or maybe you've been reading it on your own for a long time. Either way, you may have a lot of questions about what it says, and if so, you're in good company.

Whatever you've heard or wondered about God and his Word, we want you to know that the Bible is, most of all, a story—*the true story of how God forms a people for himself so that he can be with them forever.*

The one true God who existed before all things creates human beings in his image and reveals himself to them. Sadly, the people rebel against him and his word to them. The Bible calls this *sin*. But God makes a way to rescue people from their rebellion, eventually sending his beloved Son, Jesus, into the world to bring us back into relationship with him, so he can be with us. The Bible tells the story of humanity's separation from God. Through Jesus, God moves to rescue us and restore our close relationship with him.

Is this surprising to hear? That the God of all creation wants to be *with you*? It doesn't always *feel* like he does. Sometimes God's presence seems mysterious. We question whether God notices or cares about our messed-up, broken world. We can't see him, after all, so we wonder whether he is really there at all.

The God Who Is Near

One night when one of my (Chelsea's) sons was a baby, he was having trouble separating from me at bedtime. The audio monitor was sitting on his shelf, and I took him with me to inspect it. In simple terms, I explained that he could call for me at night, and I would be sure to hear. (Then I prayed that in my sleep-deprived state, I would actually wake up if he called!) He listened intently, his bright eyes tracking from the monitor to me and back.

That very same night, I heard my infant son's tiny voice call, "Mama!" He had gotten himself into a sitting position, but couldn't figure out how to lie back down on his own. His calm voice revealed a confident trust that I could hear his call and would surely come to help him.

The Bible offers an even greater hope—that God is *always* near to us. He sees and hears and *knows* our distress (Exodus 3:7). He promises that when we seek him, we will find him (Jeremiah 29:13).

Just as I pointed to my son's monitor as a physical reminder of my not-far-away presence, God has given us his Son, Jesus, who came in a physical body to demonstrate that God is *with us* (Matthew 1:23). Although we can't see Jesus in the flesh now, God gives us his Spirit to be with us until Jesus comes again (John 14:16–17). When Jesus returns, he will make right again all that is wrong and broken in our world. And he will bring those who love him into God's presence forever (Revelation 22:3).

The storyline of the Bible comforts us in our questions because we see a God who continually comes near to the people he loves, no matter how messed up and sinful they are. As you read through the Bible from the first book of Genesis to the last book of Revelation, we pray you will come to know God personally—the one who draws near by the life, death, and resurrection of his Son *for you*.

Knowing God as a Person

Do you remember playing the game "Telephone"? One person whispers a message to the person next to him, and then that person whispers whatever they heard to the next person in the circle, and so on. By the time the message reaches the last person in the game, it's usually been hilariously butchered and contains only remnants of the original.

If we're not careful, we can relate to God as though we're playing a game of Telephone, listening to what everyone else says about him rather than going straight to the original message.

God has revealed himself powerfully to human beings through his creation and through his Word, the Bible. Faithful Bible teachers and gifted scholars help us immensely to understand God's Word; but reading the Bible for ourselves takes us straight to the source himself. Hearing from God through his Word is the most fundamental way we begin to know God as a Person. This is why we encourage you to read the Bible for yourself.

Think about the relationships in your life. If you never talk to your best friend or your cousin or your parents, you probably won't feel very close to them. Relationships require some level of communication in order to thrive. The Bible is the primary, authoritative (without question) way God communicates with us. Whatever else we think God might be speaking to us—through his Spirit living within Christians, through other believers, or through our circumstances—we must hold up their word to what God has already said in his Word, the Bible. Just as you'd be able to pick out a family member's voice in a crowd, the Bible helps us recognize God's voice.

We pray that in taking a year to read through some key passages in the Bible, you will come to know God *personally*. In fact, God's Word teaches that he is God in three Persons, one God—Father, Son, and Holy Spirit. So we pray you will know God the Father, whose love for you is greater than even that of human parents, and who sacrificed his own Son to make you his child by grace through faith (Ephesians 2:8–9). We pray you will know Jesus, the Son, our older brother who took on the sins of humanity, paying the debt we owed and giving us his own right standing with God (Romans 3:22–25). We pray you will know the Holy Spirit, who comes to live within those who trust in Jesus. The Spirit is our helper and comforter, the one who helps us understand God's Word (John 16:12–15) and who is the presence of God *with us* until we dwell with God face-to-face forever (John 14:16).

At one time, we all were separated from God because of our sin. But he brings us near to himself by the blood of Christ, shed for all who would trust him in faith (Ephesians 2:13). This one true God invites you to know him through his Word, the Bible.

How to Use This Book

The writers of the devotions in this book are all adults who love God and his Word—and they also really love teenagers. Some of us are longtime youth ministers who have taught the Bible and spent time with students for many years. Others of us are parents of teenagers, and still others are professors or pastors. All of us have been where you sit right now: We were once teenagers trying to understand God's Word and how to follow God. In fact, we're still trying to do those things as adults. We've written this book in the hope that it will help you grow in knowing God and understanding his Word. As we wrote, we imagined sitting down with you for coffee or pizza, and we hope that's how you'll experience our words—as though you're talking with an older friend who cares about you.

It's important to note that the daily entries in this book do not follow the order we find in our Bibles. This is because our Bibles are ordered by genre (the type of literature) and length of the book, *not* chronologically (how the events occurred in history). We want you to understand the Bible as a single story, so we've put the entries in order according to the timeline of history. You can find a timeline on page 287 of the book.

We encourage you to talk about what you're learning with a parent or youth minister. You might choose to read along with a youth leader and a group of friends, starting a text thread to share your questions and observations throughout the week. Perhaps you'd want to meet once a week for breakfast to talk about what you're learning. Or you could read together with your family and set a time to check in over breakfast or dinner. While we want you to grow in reading the Bible for yourself each day, we believe the best Bible learning can (and usually does) happen when we do it in community with others.

The book is divided into fifty-two weeks, with five devotions per week. As much as we would *love* for you to read the Bible every day, we wanted to provide some margin to catch up if and when you fall behind. We have had the experience of starting a new devotional, only to fall behind on Day Three, and it's not so fun to try to race through multiple days at a time. Our suggestion would be to plan to read on Monday through Friday, and then over the weekend, you could set aside time to read in greater depth some of the passages covered that week.

Speaking of the passages themselves, we hope you'll open your Bible (physical or digital) as you read this book. We've included a verse or few verses for each day, and writers have explained the broader passage as much as possible in each short entry. Still, you will get even more out of your reading if you read the section or passage recommended in the title for each day. Our devotions are based on the text of the New International Version, but feel free to read your favorite translation or any other one that may be close at hand. Comparing the different word choices and phrasing in translations is another way to slow down and notice what God is saying through his Word.

Finally, we invite you to read "How Can I Know Jesus as 'God with Me'?" and "What Now: How Can I Live as a Christian?" at the end of the book. We wish we really could sit across from you to talk about following Jesus and how

Made in the Image of God

CLARK FOBES IV

Our culture puts a lot of emphasis on image. From Instagram and TikTok to wearing the right clothes or sneakers, we care deeply about how people view us. At the same time, our culture also tells us that *no one* should determine how we present our image.

While we often feel pressure surrounding image and how we present ourselves in the world, Genesis 1 tells us that God created us in *his* image, and he calls it "very good." This tells us that God had a perfect and beautiful purpose in the way he designed us.

An "image" does not celebrate itself or create its own identity, but rather reflects a picture, or likeness, of the one it represents. When God creates human beings in his "image," he tells us about our purpose in the world he has made: to bear God's "likeness" through how we live and act and to spread his glory—his character and presence. This is what God means when he tells the man and woman to "be fruitful and increase " and "subdue" the earth.

We so desperately want to believe we are "very good" that we'll do anything to get us there. We look for peace by altering our appearances, catering to social media standards, or even trying to change our identity. But our greatest purpose in life is not to curate our own image; it's to celebrate and reflect the image of the One who created us.

After God finishes creation, he blesses humanity to enjoy all of his creation (1:29). Then he *rests* from his work (2:1–3). Both God's blessing and his rest point to the way God will one day restore the world, allowing us to enjoy him forever. The story of the Bible is about how God accomplishes this through the life, death, and resurrection of Jesus Christ, the image of the invisible God (Colossians 1:15). As long as we live on this earth, our hearts will long for that perfect world. But until that day comes, we trust that living in a way that reflects God's image is the true and better path to peace.

Prayer: God, thank you for creating human beings in your image to represent you in the world. Help me to trust your designs and purposes for my life.

Reflection Question: How have you felt pressure to create your own image or identity? How does knowing about the image of God challenge you to think differently?

Adam and Eve

CHELSEA KINGSTON ERICKSON

Marvel's Multiverse. The Lord of the Rings. The Avengers. The Chronicles of Narnia. Have you noticed a common theme running through many of the stories we tell? Whether you're into fantasy, superheroes, or dystopian novels, most of us love to cheer for a group of heroes who save the world from evil. Maybe you wished you were one of these heroes yourself. I think we love these stories because they echo the true story of the Bible.

Throughout Genesis 1, we read that God declared each part of his creation "good." But here in Genesis 2, God says that something is "not good." It isn't good for this man to be *alone*. Twice in today's passage, we read that Adam needs a helper fit for him (vv. 18, 20). At first glance, this word *helper* may sound a little bland. But in Hebrew, the word powerfully evokes an *ally* or *warrior*. The same word is used throughout the Old Testament about God himself—the warrior for his people, Israel, and the ally we all need as we face evil.

The word *helper* tells us that God is calling Adam and Eve into the fight together—a battle that is introduced in Genesis 2. You see, in verse 17, God gives Adam a single command, telling him not to eat from one tree in the garden. God knows that by himself, Adam will not be able to walk in God's ways. He needs a complement, someone to join him in representing God and keeping his commands.

In the days that follow, we'll read about how Adam and Eve—and all human beings—reject God and fail to defeat God's Enemy, the serpent. But the story of the Bible shows us that we have a powerful helper in Jesus Christ, God's own Son. Jesus is the warrior that Adam and Eve (and all of us) have failed to be. He took our sin upon himself and conquered evil on the cross (Colossians 2:13–15). He calls us into relationship with himself and with one another so that we will not be alone.

Whatever darkness you are facing in your life today, Jesus is the ally you need. As we trust in him, we recover the mission that God has given people made in his image—to stand with him against evil in the world.

Prayer: Lord, thank you that in the midst of suffering and evil, you sent Jesus to be the helper I need. Forgive me for the ways I sin against you, and help me stand for your truth.

Reflection Question: What is one difficult thing you're facing right now? How can knowing Jesus as your ally help?

Choosing Our Own Way

LIZ EDRINGTON

We all long to belong. Being left out hurts—not getting an invite to a party or not being included in a hangout with friends.

Genesis 1 and 2 teach that we are *made* to belong—to God and one another. God designed us for relational connection. So when we experience rejection, exclusion, or the pain of being forgotten, we feel a holy ache. We know this is not how things ought to be. The tightness in our gut, the heat in our throat, and our tears tell us, "Something is not right."

Genesis 3:1–7 explains why things aren't right in our world, even though God created it as a place for us to flourish. The serpent tempts Adam and Eve to doubt God's good design of his world. They make themselves into the gods of their *own* little worlds by twisting God's words to suit themselves. They take the fruit and eat it, choosing to do things in their *own* way.

This is the essence of sin. More than just "the bad things we do," sin is a disease of rebellion that runs through every human heart since Adam and Eve's first sin. It is a condition of wanting to make ourselves the center of the universe, and to rule with *our* priorities instead of God's. Sin runs deep, affecting our actions, our emotions, our thoughts, and even our wills. It isn't something we can cure ourselves of. We need rescue from outside ourselves.

Thankfully, God has always had a plan to set his world right, to see his people grow into those who love him, one another, and themselves. In his life, death, and resurrection, Jesus paid the penalty we deserve for sin and set our world on the path toward redemption. His work is the only cure for our sin (Romans 3:21–26). When we experience hurt, embarrassment, or even the guilt of our own failings, we can take all of that to Jesus. He is the one who forgives sin. He will stop at nothing to see his love infiltrate every square inch of this world and our lives. He is making all things right.

Prayer: Thank you for being our good King. Forgive me for trying to make myself the king of my own life. Help me to submit to your love when I'm tempted to give in to selfishness. Amen.

Reflection Question: Where do you see the effects of sin in yourself and in the world around you?

God Makes a Promise

CLARK FOBES IV

My first real job as a teenager was as a parking valet. I remember how proud I felt going to work in my red vest and clip-on name tag. Then I got my first paycheck, and the honeymoon period was over. I quit after just a few months, hoping to never again have to work so hard for so little.

After Adam and Eve disobey God, God pronounces curses as a consequence. He curses the tasks that are vital to being created in God's image—child-raising, work, and the relationship between man and woman. Now all of these will be difficult and even painful. The curse explains why no job will ultimately bring us contentment. It explains why romantic and family relationships are often the most difficult and broken ones, even when they should be the safest and most secure. But worst of all, the enduring consequence for sin means we no longer live in the peace and rest of God's presence.

But there is hope. God declares that Eve's offspring will one day crush the serpent's head (Genesis 3:15). God sends Adam and Eve out of the garden to prevent their eating from the tree of life; otherwise they would live forever in their sinful state. Still, he clothes them with animal skins, foreshadowing how he will cover the shame of mankind's nakedness. On the cross, Jesus accomplishes what God promised in Genesis 3:15. He deals with sin by dying in human beings' place, crushing the serpent. By becoming a curse for us, he defeats sin's hold on us and all creation. One day, Jesus will completely restore creation, removing the curse of sin and death (Revelation 22:3).

Jesus begins this work of restoring creation, first and foremost, by inviting us back into God's presence. Although we live under the miserable effects of sin, God has begun the work of covering our sin and shame. When Jesus returns, he will bring us fully into his presence, where we will enjoy him forever.

Prayer: God, I confess that I haven't lived in sync with your good design and purpose. Thank you for dealing with my sin and shame in Christ. Allow me to feel your comfort and presence. Amen.

Reflection Question: What are some disappointments you have faced? How do they reveal both the sin in the world and the longing we have for God to make things right?

The First Murder

MIKE MCGARRY

I'm the youngest of four, which means my older siblings thought I was a spoiled brat and I always felt like I lived in their shadows. If you have siblings, I'll bet you can relate to our tension.

Adam and Eve's first sons, Cain and Abel, probably had the most significant sibling rivalry of all time. When each brother brought an offering to God, he accepted Abel's, but not Cain's. But why? Why did God reject Abel's offering and accept Cain's? Two clues help us understand what's going on in this passage.

First, Cain's heart is exposed through these verses, and it doesn't seem like a godly one. He is filled with bitterness and rage to the point that he "attacked his brother Abel and killed him" (v. 8). Then he thinks he can lie to God and get away with murder. That's pretty gutsy. And stupid. And evil. This doesn't seem like someone who is approaching God in genuine faith.

Second, Cain seems to bring his offering to God as a payment rather than a gift. He has worked hard, and this is his chance to show God what he's accomplished. He is enraged when God rejects it. Sin has separated all human beings from God, and Cain and Abel both know it. But God isn't impressed with Cain's (or our) hard work. He wants us to come to him in humility and love. God's acceptance of us isn't about the quality of offering *we* bring to him. God accepts us because Jesus Christ is "the Lamb of God, who takes away the sin of the world!" (John 1:29).

Cain and Abel represent the two ways to come to God. We can be like Cain, offering the results of our own hard work and then getting angry when it's not declared acceptable. Or we can be like Abel, coming to God through the blood of the Lamb. Praise be to God that we are welcomed through faith in the Lamb of God!

Prayer: Thank you that I don't need to work to create offerings that will be acceptable to you. Instead, Jesus, the Lamb of God, offers himself for me. Show me the ways I'm trusting in my own work and give me a heart that fully trusts you.

Reflection Question: What causes you to feel that God wants you to validate your hard work for him? How could you trust Jesus' perfect offering instead?

Walking with God

MICHELLE REYES

It can be hard to know what to do when the world feels like it's falling apart. How should we respond after seeing horrible atrocities on our TV screens and reading about them on our news apps? Or even closer to home, when brokenness ripples through our family or personal relationships?

Enoch knew what to do. Enoch lived in the days before the Great Flood, when God got so fed up with the world's wickedness that he eventually destroyed it with water. Those were dark times, and yet Enoch lived his life in the conviction of one simple truth: *The darker the world gets, the more we need God.*

We don't know much about Enoch beyond the fact that he "walked faithfully with God." His story is only mentioned in the genealogy of Adam in Genesis 5 and then briefly in Hebrews 11 and Jude 14–15. The Genesis passage twice mentions that Enoch walked faithfully with God. For a man who lived in dark times, this is an incredible thing to be known for.

To walk faithfully with God means to pursue a daily relationship with God in which you trust his promises and obey his commands. This is a lifestyle, not a onetime practice. It means we pray, listen to God's guidance, align our thoughts and actions with God's character, and choose to do what is right.

Instead of fear of the world, Enoch chose trust in God. Instead of anger, he chose holiness. He didn't join the wicked or give himself over to rage. Like Enoch, we should strive to walk faithfully with God. But this is no easy task. Despite our best efforts, we will get distracted, discouraged, and pulled into the noise of the world. We don't just need to be self-disciplined (though that is an important attribute); we need a Savior who walks with us.

Hebrews 12:2 reminds us to fix our eyes on Jesus, the author and perfecter of our faith. Jesus makes the faithful walk of the believer possible. When everything around us feels like it's falling apart, Jesus doesn't ask us to have it all together. He simply invites us to stay close to him. Like Enoch, we don't have to have a dramatic life story; we just need to walk with Jesus. That's how we endure and live well in a broken world.

Prayer: Jesus, thank you that I don't have to walk through this world alone. Teach me to walk with you faithfully and hopefully. Amen.

Reflection Question: What would it look like to walk with Jesus in one difficult area of your life?

Faithfulness in the Flood

KENDAL CONNER

Little kids often ask their friends to seal their words with a pinky promise or "cross your heart" swear. We want a guarantee that even if all else fails, this person will not. We want to know that our trust is safe.

In Genesis 6, we see how God seals his words as he makes a covenant—a sacred and binding promise. The world has become violent and wicked. Human beings have become enslaved to evil. But God wants to redeem his creation from corruption.

One man has found favor with God—Noah. God shares with Noah that he plans to flood the earth. He commands Noah to build an ark—a large boat—to protect his family from drowning. Just before the flood, God makes a covenant with Noah. Later, in Genesis 9, we learn what that promise is—to never again flood the earth.

God not only speaks this promise, but he seals it—like a pinky promise—in a way you may not expect. In Genesis 7:16, we read that the Lord "shuts [Noah] in," physically sealing him into the ark. God shows Noah that he is trustworthy by keeping him safe in the midst of the flood. Noah only has to come to the ark.

Just like Noah, God asks us to come—only we come not to a boat but to Jesus. In a world full of sin and brokenness, God wants his people to know that their trust is safe in him. When we come to Jesus in faith, God seals us by his Spirit into his Son (Ephesians 1:11–14). Just as Noah was kept in the ark, we are kept in Jesus. When we come to Jesus by faith, nothing—truly *no thing*—can ever take us out of the arms of Jesus (John 10:27–29). We belong to him alone. Even when the world around us sets us up to fail, there is no safer place for our trust than in God, who through his Son has both saved us and given us the riches of his promises.

Prayer: God, thank you that through your mercy and grace, I can place my full trust in the certainty of my salvation, knowing I am sealed by your Spirit and in your Son, Jesus. Amen.

Reflection Question: How does knowing you can trust God encourage you when people disappoint you or break their promises?

Why Is Grace Amazing?

CAROL M. KAMINSKI

Can you recall a time in your life when you messed up terribly, but instead of getting in trouble with your parents, they didn't treat you as you deserved? What your parents gave you was a gift of grace rather than what you deserved at that moment. God's gift of grace is central to his covenant with Noah.

The opening chapters of Genesis tell stories about Adam and Eve's descendants. But instead of reading about a loving family that worships God, we learn about people who turn away from God. Sin leads to conflict in marriage and fighting among siblings. Cain even goes to the extreme of extremes and kills his brother, and violence fills the land.

It is tragic to read God's assessment of humanity. He sees that the human heart has turned away from him, which leads to his judgment against sin through a flood (Genesis 6:5–8). But after the flood, God makes the remarkable announcement that he is establishing a covenant (a binding promise) with Noah and all humanity. Even though sin continues, God promises that he will never again send another flood to destroy humanity and the earth. Simply put, this means God is not treating people as their sins deserve. This is called *grace*.

You may have heard someone say that the God of the Old Testament is a God of judgment. But God's covenant promises to Noah and all humanity are the first of many that point to his grace, which is at the heart of his character. God is gracious and compassionate. Yet God is also righteous and just, so one day there will be need to give an account for those sins. In the supreme act of grace, God sends his Son, Jesus, to pay the penalty for our sins. He receives our punishment, and we receive forgiveness. God does not treat us as our sins deserve because Jesus has paid our penalty (Psalm 103:10; 1 Peter 3:18).

When you see a rainbow shining brightly in the sky after the rain, remember that the rainbow is a sign of God's covenant with Noah, and it shines a spotlight on God's grace. Thanks be to God, he does not treat people as they deserve.

Prayer: Thank you, Lord, for your grace. Thank you for not treating me as my sins deserve, but for sending your Son to die in my place. Help me live in the freedom of knowing you love me.

Reflection Question: Take a few moments to thank God for his grace in your life. How can you show this grace to others?

God's Boundaries Are Love

KATIE POLSKI

When my daughter was three, she wandered away from home after unlatching a gate she was instructed never to touch. We searched for her for what felt like forever. Finally we saw neighbors walking up the hill holding our scared little girl's hand. Our daughter later told us that she was "looking for a better backyard with a pool." She didn't understand that our boundaries were put into place for a good reason. In my daughter's mind, her plan was better.

This is just what Noah's descendants think in Genesis 11 when they decide to build a tower. God tells them to *fill the earth* (9:1), but they conclude that *not* scattering is a better plan. Though God promises he will never again flood the earth (9:15), they use waterproof materials to ensure that their tower is safe from another flood.

Not only do the people fail to trust God and his instructions, but they also seek to make their name more important than God's. The words *come, let us* are God's very words when he makes human beings in his own image (Genesis 1:26). Even their words show how they inch toward taking the place of God. In their sinful pride, they cross his boundaries, moving away from following God's instructions toward positioning themselves in the place of God.

Boundary crossing began when Adam and Eve ate the fruit from the forbidden tree, and it continues in our lives today. We think our schemes and plans are better than God's, and so we cross the boundaries that God has put into place for our good and for his glory. All boundary crossing is sin, and because we sin, we are in desperate need of a Savior.

Jesus invites us to turn to him and find rescue from our disobedience through his sacrifice on the cross. Jesus knows you will need his help to obey his ways, so he readily offers his strength and his forgiveness (1 Corinthians 10:13). Love is at the heart of God's boundaries. Jesus wants you to experience the peace that comes from obeying the teachings of his Word and trusting his perfect plan, even when your way *seems* like it makes better sense.

Prayer: Lord, when I am tempted to cross your boundaries because my ways seem better, help me to remember that your boundaries demonstrate your love for me.

Reflection Question: Sinful pride is considering ourselves more important than God and others. How can pride affect our relationship with Jesus?

God Plants His Family Tree

CLARK FOBES IV

Leaving your home and family to move somewhere new can be an exciting adventure. But moving can also be scary. Once the newness wears off, loneliness may set in. In some cases, you may always feel like a foreigner, never fully understanding others or being understood yourself. If you're from an immigrant background like I am, or you have moved to a new country, chances are you're familiar with this experience.

In Genesis 12, God calls Abram (whom he later renames Abraham) to move to a foreign land. In Abraham's culture, moving away from family was not a heroic step; it was a death sentence, cutting off family ties, heritage, and security. Why would God call Abraham to do such a thing?

God makes a covenant, or a sacred, binding promise, with Abraham that includes the promises of land, descendants, and blessing. God also chooses this old man and his barren wife to bring about the blessing he intended at creation to all the peoples of the earth—that human beings would dwell with God.

Abraham fails to trust God and nearly gives up his wife, Sarai (whom God later renames Sarah), to another man (vv. 10–20), sabotaging God's promise to give the couple a child. But God will continue to make good on his plans. Where Abraham failed, Jesus has succeeded.

As with Abraham, God chose Jesus and sent him to save his people. Jesus left his Father and home in heaven, went to a foreign land, and suffered for the blessing of all peoples. In Christ, all peoples are blessed far more than Abraham could have anticipated—a better land (his kingdom), a greater offspring (the promised Savior), and a more valuable blessing (heavenly riches).

God has reached into time and history, orchestrating our lives that he might choose and call us for his purposes. We may be obscure and unknown, mere blips in world history. Still, if you have been saved by Jesus, God has personally chosen you to bless you (Galatians 3:9). Just like he did through Abraham, God desires to bless all the peoples of the earth through you. Wherever you go, you can trust that your obedience to God is greater than any blessing the world can offer.

Prayer: God, lead me to trust in your promises. Amen.

Reflection Question: How is God calling you to be a blessing for others?

God's Grace-Filled Covenant

LIZ EDRINGTON

Have you ever felt like you had to earn your belonging? I remember trying out for my high school soccer team in my freshman year. After making the varsity squad, I felt like I had to earn my place on the team by playing really well. My acceptance by the group was based on my performance.

Instead of saying, "Hey, Abram, you need to work really hard to prove that you're worthy of belonging in my family," God makes a binding promise called a covenant with Abram (later named Abraham). God makes Abraham a part of his family simply through Abraham's belief in God's word to him. Abraham is childless and grandpa-aged by this point—long past the hope of being a father. Yet God tells Abraham the impossible is about to happen: He's going to have a bigger family tree than he could ever imagine.

In the ancient world, people sealed covenants with blood. So God tells Abraham to bring him some animals, and when Abraham cuts them in two, God passes through the pieces of the animals (Genesis 15:9–18). By this act, God is saying that he will bear full responsibility for the relationship with Abraham. He requires nothing from Abraham. This is a beautiful picture of undeserved, abundant blessing. Abraham did not clean up his act or do anything to prove himself to God. He simply trusted God.

As Christians, we don't need to earn our place by scoring twenty goals in a season or dressing cool. We do not need to prove we belong. Our acceptance and belonging are *not* based on our performance; they are completely based on the performance of Jesus Christ. He lived the perfect, sinless life we could never live. Then he died as a sacrifice that he made on our behalf—all to bring us into relationship with God and his family. When we take Jesus at his word, trusting that he came that we "may have life, and have it to the full" (John 10:10), we gain eternal belonging. We are accepted into God's family completely through God's love.

When we feel the pressure to prove ourselves, we can bring to mind God's grace-filled covenant with Abraham. This same promise of everlasting inclusion comes to us through Christ.

Prayer: God, help me to believe I am perfectly loved and accepted by Jesus. Help me extend that same belonging to others.

Reflection Question: What makes you feel like you need to earn your belonging?

The God Who Sees Me

ANNA MEADE HARRIS

I stood at the back of the school gym, waiting for that cute boy to ask me to dance. I was thrilled to see him walking toward me, until he was intercepted by glamorous Valerie . . . and that was the end of that.

For a moment I knew what it felt like to be noticed, possibly admired—until I was eclipsed by someone more noteworthy. Like you, like me, the slave girl Hagar in Genesis 16 knew what it was like to be treated like she didn't matter. But our God not only sees us; he goes to extraordinary lengths to let us know that we are loved.

In Genesis 16, Hagar's mistress, Sarah, becomes impatient after years of waiting for God's promised child, and convinces Abraham to sleep with her slave. When Hagar gets pregnant, Sarah is mean to her. Hagar flees into the desert, where she is met by the angel of the Lord, who prophesies that her unborn son will grow up to be a powerful man. The angel instructs her to name him Ishmael, which means "God hears."

Awestruck, Hagar calls God *El Roi*, meaning, "You are the God who *sees me*." Hagar is a foreigner, a slave, and a girl in a culture that does not value women. She's pregnant by her boss, who is old and married to a jealous woman. She has no way to protect or support herself, much less her unborn child. As an Egyptian, she doesn't even know this God who speaks to her so kindly. Yet the God who created the universe and gives Hagar the honor of becoming the first person in history to describe God with a new name. Culturally speaking, she's the most insignificant person on the planet, but in God's eyes, Hagar is precious.

Likewise, Jesus reflects the heart of his Father when he chooses to hang out with the disrespected and disreputable. When some religious leaders called Pharisees criticize him for eating with tax collectors and sinners (considered the lowest of the low), Jesus responds, "I have not come to call the righteous, but sinners" (Matthew 9:13). Because we are all sinners, we need only accept that he died to pay the penalty for our sins (Romans 3:23; 5:8).

What makes us valuable to Jesus is not our achievements, gifts, or social capital, but his great love for us.

Prayer: Father, when I feel unseen and unheard, remind me that Jesus considers me worth dying for.

Reflection Question: Is it hard to believe that God sees you and knows you?

Abraham's Failure Didn't Stop God

MARK HOWARD

It can be hard to trust God's promises, particularly when things aren't going the way we think they should. It's tempting to take matters into our own hands. We cheat to improve our grades, gossip to look cool, or get impatient—all because we don't trust God to take care of us.

This is exactly what Abraham and Sarah did. After years of waiting for the family God had promised them, still no baby came. When Sarah asked Abraham to sleep with her servant, Hagar, in order to have a baby, and when Abraham agreed, they both showed that they didn't really trust God. But God said the promised son would come from Sarah—despite her old age.

When Abraham slept with Hagar, he demonstrated his lack of faith that the promised son would be born to Sarah. The sign of God's *covenant*, or sacred, binding promise, is circumcision—cutting off the foreskin of a man's penis, which he uses in making children. Circumcision represents Abraham's willingness to let God cut away the sin of unbelief so he may believe that God keeps his promises. Fully aware of human faithlessness and sinfulness, God is fully committed to follow through on his promises to bless and to save.

Circumcision was never merely about cutting off a piece of flesh; it was about acknowledging both human sinfulness and God's faithfulness. This is why Christians are not required to be physically circumcised (Romans 4:9–12). The promised Son has come, and he has dealt with all our sin on the cross. Now our circumcision is a spiritual one, in which our former sinful identity is cut off in Jesus' death and replaced with new life in Jesus' resurrection (Colossians 2:11).

So the next time you're having doubts or are beating yourself up for your lack of faith, remember that Abraham also had difficulty trusting—and God stayed committed to him. The next time you're living with the consequences of taking matters into your own hands, know that Abraham did too—and it didn't disqualify him from God's blessing. God knows who you are and still loves you deeply. That's why Jesus came. He will remain true to his promises.

Prayer: Thank you for being faithful even when I'm not.

Reflection Question: Which of God's promises are hardest for you to believe?

God Keeps His Promises

KENDAL CONNER

I had a friend in high school whose dad made a lot of promises but rarely came through on them. From big promises like taking her to Disney World to small ones like coming to her softball games, he was quick to break each one. When my friend's dad showed up at our high school graduation, she said, "I can't believe you're here!" After waiting for so long, she doubted that her dad would ever keep his promises.

As Abraham and Sarah waited for God to fulfill his promises to them, they were likely wondering whether God would truly come through. Remember, God had promised Abraham children who would be as numerous as the stars (Genesis 15). God had also promised that Sarah would become a mother, even in her old age (Genesis 17). God's angels had told Abraham he would have a child by the same time the next year (Genesis 18). What's more, God had promised that he would build a nation through Abraham—a nation that would bless all others (Genesis 12).

As Abraham and Sarah grew older by the day, their circumstances made it seem like God might never deliver on his promise to give them a child. But as we see time and again in the Old Testament, when God makes a promise, what does he do? He comes through!

Not only does God fulfill this promise to Abraham and Sarah, but we read that the child comes *at the very time God had promised*. The birth of Isaac shows that God was going to fulfill all of his promises to Abraham—to make him into a great nation and to bless the other nations of the earth through his family (Genesis 12).

God is always faithful to do what he says. We may have to wait for the fulfillment of the promise, but we can be certain he will come through. We can hold fast to God's word with certainty because, in Jesus, we know that all the promises of God have already found their yes and amen (2 Corinthians 1:20). Jesus saved us and sealed us through his sacrifice at just the right time (Romans 5:6).

In our own waiting, we can take courage as we look to Jesus. God will fulfill his promises, not in *our* timing, but in *his* perfect timing.

Prayer: God, thank you for always being true to your word. Help me grow in faith as I trust your promises.

Reflection Question: When do you find it hardest to trust that God will be faithful to do what he has promised?

When Faith Isn't Easy

MIKE MCGARRY

If faith were easy, we'd be a lot better at it. This story about Abraham and Isaac is a perfect example. Abraham receives God's covenant promise that he'll become the father of many people, yet decades later he and his wife are still childless. Then when he finally has this promised son, God tells him to sacrifice his son, Isaac, as an offering.

Abraham could have refused. "No way! Isaac is the promised son. This makes no sense." First, child sacrifice is obviously evil and out of character with who God is. Second, it seems cruel of God to even ask Abraham to make this sacrifice. Third, doing this, it seems, will undo God's covenant promises to Abraham.

Despite all these legitimate issues, Abraham trusts God. When Isaac asks, "Where is the lamb for the burnt offering?" Abraham replies, "God himself will provide the lamb" (vv. 7–8). Even when Isaac is on the altar and Abraham is raising the knife, Abraham trusts that God will somehow fulfill his promise. *And God does!*

The angel of the Lord prevents Abraham from sacrificing Isaac and provides a ram for the offering instead. Interestingly, this story takes place on the same mountain where the temple in Jerusalem would later be built. Centuries later, on a mountain overlooking the temple, Jesus Christ would be crucified as the Lamb of God. Jesus is the ultimate son of Abraham. Jesus' sacrifice brings salvation for all people who trust in God's provision and live by grace through faith. God's promise to Abraham's offspring is given to all who trust in Jesus rather than to only those who are biologically descended from Abraham (Romans 9:8).

Notice what Abraham called that mountain: "The LORD will provide." God has provided his Son as the sacrifice for our sins. God will provide meaning and joy through faith in Christ. God will provide for your daily needs.

When people talk about having faith and trusting God, they sometimes make it seem so simple and easy. But faith is often hard and confusing. Still, you can walk by faith because the same God who provided for Abraham, saved Isaac, and raised Jesus from the dead is the one who invites you to call him Father. Our God saves!

Prayer: Father, strengthen me to believe that you will provide for me.

Reflection Question: How does this story assure you that God can be trusted?

Playing Favorites

ANNA MEADE HARRIS

I've always wondered why we use the phrase "playing favorites," because it's not a game we're playing and no one is having fun.

In Genesis 25:28, there's a little word—*but*—that tells us the parents of twin boys are playing favorites. Esau and Jacob wrestled in their mom Rebekah's belly before they were ever born. Now that they are grown, Mom loves Jacob, who likes to hang out with her back at the tent, *but* Dad loves Esau best because he's good with a bow and arrow. Rather than appreciating both sons for who God made them to be, Rebekah and Isaac let their personal preferences dictate which son they would love best. Playing favorites hardens their hearts toward one another and destroys their family. Everyone loses.

Certainly it's all right to enjoy hanging out with people who share your interests. Rebekah is not wrong for enjoying her time with Jacob. Isaac appreciates Esau's skill in hunting. None of that is bad. What is wrong is valuing the brainy person over the brawny one, or vice versa. In our sinfulness, we find it hard to love and appreciate people who don't like what we like, who are different in some way that matters to us.

Thankfully, God does not play favorites with us. In the infinite variety of people he has created, we are all made in God's image and we all need him. "For God so loved *the world* that he gave his one and only Son, that *whoever believes in him* shall not perish but have eternal life" (John 3:16, emphasis added).

In the perfect relationship of our three-in-one God, Jesus is God the Father's only loving, obedient Son. If God's favor were to depend on how a person acted or what they were good at, Jesus would have remained God's one and only favorite child. Instead, God gave Jesus up, allowing his sinless Son to pay the penalty for our sins so that he might bring you and me into his family. Romans 8:15–17 says that God actually adopts *whoever believes in him*. Instead of playing favorites, God makes us Jesus' brothers and sisters.

God's family is full of homebodies and hunters, artists and acrobats, golfers and gardeners. The gracious heart of God is big enough to love us all.

Prayer: Father, I confess I like certain kinds of people more than others. Please help me love like you do, seeing your image in every person.

Reflection Question: How does the sacrifice of Jesus for the whole world challenge your tendency to play favorites?

Family Friction

CARL LAFERTON

You may think your life or family is a bit of a mess, but I'm guessing it's not as much of a mix of deceit, betrayal, and anger as Esau and Jacob's family was. Genesis 27 is the climax of a story of two twins who have competed since the womb. The older brother stands to inherit a privilege that he cares about less than a good meal. The younger one chafes and schemes to get what isn't his.

In ancient culture, Esau, as the eldest boy, is lined up to be blessed and receive his father's inheritance. But Rebekah helps Jacob dress like Esau and wear animal skins to seem hairy like Esau, so that her near-death, near-blind husband, Isaac, gives Jacob the blessing. This is dysfunctional, but (sadly) not very abnormal. What is unique to this story is the inheritance. Esau is Abraham's eldest grandson, and he stands to inherit God's promises to Abraham—that he would be numbered among God's people, given a good land, and employed by God to bless the world.

That's the inheritance Esau trades for a meal and that Jacob deceives his own dad to steal. It is messed up—and yet it is also God's plan. Before the birth of the twins, God had said that "the older will serve the younger" (Genesis 25:23). God had already planned to pass his promises to Jacob, not Esau. Even so, these two men are accountable for their behavior. The consequences of their choices would reverberate negatively through history.

But in all this, God is at work to keep his promises. He chooses to work through messed-up people. That's good news for us because when we're honest, we know, one way or another, that we're a mess. So get this: To be in a position to inherit God's promises, you don't need a strong moral performance; you simply need to *know* that you've messed up.

It was not the religious elites, the high-performing types, whom Jesus came to save. No, it was the "tax collectors and sinners" (Mark 2:15). Anyone can come to him. So what about you? Are things a bit of a mess, inside you or around you? God doesn't recoil from that. He has always worked in messy situations, through people who mess up, to keep his promises. Just come to him, and keep coming to him.

Prayer: Lord Jesus, you know how I've messed up. Thank you for forgiving me and blessing me anyway.

Reflection Question: What is it about your life that causes you to imagine that God might turn away from you?

Meeting God in a Dream

KATIE POLSKI

Have you ever had a life-changing encounter with God? Sometimes this happens when we slam on the brakes and God spares us from an accident, or it can happen in a worship service where we are so drawn to our Father that we can't help but lift our hands in praise.

Jacob has this kind of intense spiritual experience when he encounters God through a dream, and it literally changes his life. After tricking his family to get his brother's inheritance, Jacob leaves the only home he knows in hopes of finding a wife. As Jacob drifts off to sleep one night along the journey, God speaks to him directly. He first reminds Jacob that he is the great God of Jacob's fathers. Though Jacob is not married, God promises him numerous descendants. Though Jacob knows no one in the area where he is traveling, God promises that the land will one day be his. Though Jacob is alone, God promises to be near to him always. In his grace, God fulfills each one of these promises.

Just as the Lord promised to be with Jacob, he also promises to be with you always (Hebrews 13:5–6). God does not break his promises. We don't have to earn the privilege of a relationship with him by being good enough. This promise is yours when you put your trust in Jesus. There are no qualifications and no stipulations.

Sometimes we are awakened to God's presence through an extraordinary spiritual event, and other times God reminds us of his faithful presence in the quiet, mundane aspects of life. He speaks to us when we read his Word, the Bible, and he reminds us that he is near when we pray during a difficult situation. God is with you, whether you are out and about or at home, stressed or calm, anxious or joyful. He will meet you right where you are and provide just what you need.

Prayer: Lord, you tell me you are always with me. Remind me of your faithful presence in small and big ways, and then by your Spirit open my eyes to see you. Amen.

Reflection Question: God is not a king who rules in a far-off world; he is always near. Describe a time when you experienced God's nearness. If you haven't experienced him in that way, pray boldly that he will reveal himself to you.

Wrestling with God

MARK HOWARD

A new school, a big test, asking someone you like out on a date, parents fighting, a world in conflict—indeed, the world can be a scary place.

Scripture tells us we have a choice in how we respond to fear. When we trust the Lord and stay loyal to his ways, we can find peace even when we're scared. But when fear leads us to scheme and lie, people get hurt. Eventually, God will intervene to wake us up and teach us to cling to him, and this wake-up call isn't always gentle.

For his whole life, Jacob has seemed afraid of not having enough, causing him to choose trickery and deception to steal his brother Esau's birthright and blessing. Instead of finding peace, Jacob has to run away from home in fear of Esau's retaliation. When Jacob is about to run into his brother again almost twenty years later, Jacob sends away his wives, children, and servants "in great fear and distress" (Genesis 32:7). All his scheming for wealth and security has left him alone and afraid. Yet despite Jacob's sin and stupidity, God loves this fearful man. He has chosen Jacob to be the one through whom God's promised salvation will continue. Rather than giving up on Jacob, God wrestles him.

When even that encounter doesn't subdue Jacob, God touches Jacob's hip with such force that his hip is wrenched from its socket, leaving him limping. Now, when Jacob meets Esau, there is nothing Jacob can do. He can't fight or run away. All Jacob can do is cling to God as his past catches up with him. God, who is gracious and merciful, rescues Jacob. God gives Jacob the blessing he had planned to give him from the start.

Jacob's story encourages us to trust that we experience God's grace when we surrender to him. God's grace ultimately points to Jesus' surrender on the cross. Jesus' death for sinners secures our inheritance and blessing (Ephesians 2:13–14). So rather than living in fear and anxiety for the future, we can cling to Jesus, who promises he will never leave or forsake us in this life and in the life to come.

Prayer: God of Jacob, forgive me for all the times I scheme and hurt others out of fear. Teach me to cling to you for peace and security. Amen.

Reflection Question: What are you afraid of? What would it look like to cling to God when you are afraid?

Blind Spots

SYLER THOMAS

"The Emperor's New Clothes" is a folktale about a ruler who spends lavishly on clothes. He is conned by two men, who offer him magnificent new clothes that are invisible to incompetent people. The emperor eagerly purchases the special attire and then parades around in his new "clothes" in front of his people—when, in fact, he is wearing no clothes at all. It's a story about blind spots—parts of our lives that others can plainly see, but we can't. Today we read about Joseph's blind spots, as well as those of his brothers.

Joseph is one of Jacob's twelve sons, part of the family God is building through Abraham's line, and Joseph is the special favorite of his father. Jacob shamelessly gives him an ornate coat, revealing that he loves Joseph best.

First, let's look at Joseph's blind spot. It's clear that God is at work in the life of this precocious teenager. God is giving Joseph divine dreams, which will later prove to be true. But it's *how* Joseph chooses to share his special talent with his family that causes problems (see Genesis 37:5–11). He seems unaware of how his words can affect others. When you see God at work in your life, by all means, share about it with others, but do it in a way that exalts God and not yourself and doesn't breed resentment from those around you. Second, the brothers' blind spot shows us the dangerous trap of jealousy. Joseph's brothers are so envious of what Joseph has that they throw him into a pit and sell him into slavery.

Both bragging and jealousy reveal a lack of trust in God. He's given us everything we need by sending Jesus to die for us on the cross (Romans 8:32). When we're satisfied in how God has provided for us, we don't need anything else—others can brag all they want. As we rest secure in Jesus' sacrifice on our behalf, we can celebrate God's work in others' lives as well as in our own.

Prayer: Lord, forgive me for making either of these mistakes—not acting with humility when I speak of your work in my life, or being upset when I see you at work in another person's life. Teach me to find all I need in you. Amen.

Reflection Question: Do you know a "Joseph" type? How do you fight against the jealousy that can come when you have friends who seem more blessed than you are?

God Works in Messy Families

MAC HARRIS

Growing up with two younger brothers, my childhood was full of chippy basketball games in the driveway, arguments-turned-wrestling matches over which movie to watch, and the *continual* stealing of my favorite shirts (always on the day I wanted to wear one of them).

My brothers never plotted to kill me—to my knowledge—but the fork marks stabbed into my bedroom door reminded me that I was on thin ice! Whether it's sibling rivalries, favoritism from parents, or feeling ignored, isolated, and lonely, we all experience messy and difficult family dynamics.

Some of the most important and famous families in the entire Bible, such as Joseph's, are really, really messed up. But it's often in the messiest places that God loves to work, and he brings incredible restoration out of Joseph's traumatic story. Joseph is sold into slavery in Egypt by his own brothers, imprisoned for a crime he didn't commit, and left to rot in a jail cell—but God is with him every step of the way. More than that, God is always at work, sowing seeds to redeem even the most irredeemable parts of Joseph's story, including his broken family.

Despite all the evil and injustice, Joseph's story reminds us that God is with us and working for us in all things. Moreover, it points us forward to a greater story where God redeems the unthinkable evil and injustice of the cross.

Jesus knows what it's like to be rejected by those closest to him, even his own family (John 7:5). Jesus knows what it's like to be sold for just a few pieces of silver (v. 28; Matthew 27:3). And Jesus knows what it's like to feel completely misunderstood and alone. Jesus came so that he could put his arm around you and call you his beloved brother or his beloved sister (Psalm 22:22; Hebrews 2:12). Though our earthly families will fail us (and we will fail them), Jesus promises to be our perfect big brother. He lived and died to save *both* the sold-out Josephs of the world *and* to save the jealous, scheming siblings of the world.

Prayer: Father, thank you for my imperfect family and for bringing me into your perfect family. Redeem the brokenness of our families and comfort us with your perfect fatherly love. In the name of our brother Jesus. Amen.

Reflection Question: What are a few ways you love your siblings or parents well? When is it hard for you to love them?

When You Lose Everything

MIKE MCGARRY

Why does God allow suffering in the world? Whether we're wondering about our own suffering or the suffering around us, this is one of the most common questions people ask about religion. Thankfully, the Bible asks this question too.

The book of Job (pronounced *Jobe*) tells about a man who lost everything—his wealth, his kids, and his health. As readers, we know something he doesn't know: His suffering is because of his righteousness, not because of his sin. God holds up Job as an example of faithfulness; Satan claims that Job will deny God if he experiences suffering. God allows the test, as long as Job's life is spared.

Job's friends attempt to help him discover what he has done to deserve this kind of suffering. After the death of their children, even Job's wife says, "Curse God and die!" (2:9). Eventually, he stops trying to defend himself to others and prays passionately, asking God for a hearing in the heavenly court of law—as if he could sue God for undeserved suffering.

Remarkably, God shows up and puts Job on trial, saying things like, "Who is this that obscures my plans with words without knowledge?" and "Where were you when I laid the earth's foundations?" (38:2, 4). Even though God corrects Job's attitude, he affirms that Job's suffering isn't punishment for sin. In the end, Job's friends admit they're wrong and ask Job to pray for them. God gives back double to Job.

Some people read this story and think God did Job dirty, but they're misunderstanding the bigger picture. God isn't using Job as a pawn in a chess match against Satan, but rather as a lighthouse to display his steadfast love. Job reminds us that God meets us in the midst of our suffering and confusion. Even as he complains, Job declares, "I know that my redeemer lives, and that in the end he will stand on the earth" (19:25). Because Job trusts God's character, he still believes God will send a savior who will redeem the world from suffering. Job does not know it, but that redeemer's name is Jesus Christ, the one whose suffering outweighed even Job's.

God is good, even during your suffering. He is entirely worthy of your worship. God heard Job's prayer, and he hears yours. He sent Jesus as our living Redeemer who conquered sin and death, so you have hope and peace through faith in Jesus.

Prayer: God, you are my Redeemer. Teach me to worship you when life is painful and confusing.

Reflection Question: When you or others experience suffering, what can help you lean on God?

Small Things with Great Love

LIZ EDRINGTON

Have you ever wondered about your purpose in the world? The story of Shiphrah and Puah in Exodus 1 shows us that God loves to use our seemingly small lives to display his larger-than-the-universe greatness.

At this point, the Hebrew people are still living as visitors in Egypt. They're doing so well that they're beginning to outnumber the Egyptians. Pharoah, the king of Egypt, fears they could overtake his country if they rebel, so he orders the local midwives—who are responsible for helping women give birth—to kill the Israelites' baby boys. Horrific, I know.

But the midwives give their loyalty to God. They decide, "No way we're doing that." They fear God more than they fear Pharoah. They're committed to their work and to the dignity of the women (and babies) they serve. By refusing to follow the command of their ruler, they put their own lives in danger. They also play a beautiful, courageous role in saving God's people.

God often uses the seemingly small faithful acts of his people to do big things. He loves to reveal his kingdom in low-key and unexpected ways. We want flashy and strong. Yet he blesses and uses ordinary and weak. For me, that's a relief. Although the world tells me I need to be cool, witty, and influential, God shows me over and over again that he is at work in the average, often unnoticed acts of love and faithfulness like Shiphrah's and Puah's. Jesus came as a plain-looking guy from a small town. He chose outsiders and underdogs to be his people. He told us to pray like children, not like people with power and influence.

It's fun to think about the many ways the Lord is at work in your life right now. You may have been intentionally kind to a sibling. You may have faithfully washed the dishes after your parents asked you to. You may have invited a less popular kid to hang out with you. Or you may have prayed for a friend who has been sick. Jesus delights in seeing his love spread through the world in seemingly tiny, ordinary acts of faithfulness. This is the way his kingdom grows.

Prayer: Lord, it can be hard to trust that you are at work when I can't see it. Please open my eyes to the unexpected ways your love comes to me every day.

Reflection Question: What are some of the ordinary ways God has shown you his love, kindness, or goodness in the last couple of days?

God Is in Control

SYLER THOMAS

"Kaila, I'm sorry, but I don't think we can afford this."

Our oldest daughter had her heart set on a certain college, and as we were running the numbers, the math wasn't mathing. There were tears. Everyone was disappointed. Her dream seemed impossible. But my sister happened to mention something about a scholarship she had heard about. We then found out about a different one that hadn't been advertised. About six weeks after D-Day (Disappointment Day), we realized we *could* afford to have her apply. Thanks to God's care behind the scenes, she committed.

In today's passage, the hidden hand of God is on display. The backdrop is the horrific cruelty of Pharaoh, who requires that all male Hebrew babies be thrown into the Nile River. Moses's Hebrew mother acts faithfully out of love for her son; she puts him in a basket and trusts in the kindness of a stranger to save him. Not only does her baby survive, but she gets *paid* by Pharaoh's daughter to feed *her own baby*. God uses the cunning and courageous acts of these three women to preserve Moses's life and provide for his family.

Theologians call this *providence*, which has the meaning baked into the name—it refers to God's *providing* for his people. And not in an obvious, sea-parting way (spoiler alert!) but in an "it just so happened that . . ." kind of way.

Why is this important to you? Well, because it frequently can feel like God is *not* in control, like he has left you high and dry and everything is going to fall apart. A passage like this one reminds you that God will provide what you need when you need it, even when it seems like he *hasn't* heard. When you don't get what you want, knowing that God's providential hand is *not* providing is also helpful. It doesn't mean he doesn't care; it means he will provide what you need instead.

Jesus probably felt this way as he pleaded with God in Gethsemane to move the journey to the cross. He wanted the Father to find another way to reconcile us to God (Luke 22:42). But God was providing something else for us—his plan of salvation through Jesus' obedience to die for us.

Prayer: Lord, help me trust in you, knowing you are in control. Help me believe that nothing that happens in my life today is outside of your will for me.

Reflection Question: Can you think of a time when you saw God's hidden hand at work?

The God Who Rescues

CHELSEA KINGSTON ERICKSON

Have you ever been in need of rescue? When I was three, my mom and I were in a car accident on an icy highway in central Illinois. Our car was totaled, so while my mom talked to the police, a kind stranger kept me warm in her car.

At the beginning of the book of Exodus, God's people are desperate for rescue. As slaves in Egypt, they very likely wonder whether God has forgotten them. But in Exodus 3, God makes himself known to Moses, the Hebrew-born prince of Egypt. He speaks to Moses from a bush that is burning, but not burning up.

His message is astonishing: God sees and hears the misery of his people in Egypt. He is concerned about them; he empathizes with their plight. Best of all, God tells Moses that he has "come down to rescue" the people he loves. This is not a God who passively observes his people's distress. Instead, he powerfully enters into the story, preparing a rescue mission to get his people out of Egypt.

God has good plans for his people. He will take them from slavery to a land rich with his gifts. In the ancient world, milk and honey were precious commodities signifying God's favor. God not only rescues his people from oppression; he settles them in a place overflowing with his blessing.

In Titus 3, the apostle Paul describes how Christians, too, were once enslaved—not to human masters but to their own sin. Then he writes, "But when the kindness and love of God our Savior appeared, he saved us, not because of righteous things we had done, but because of his mercy" (vv. 4–5).

God has seen and heard our misery that comes from living in a sin-sick world. He is concerned about our suffering. He has come down to rescue us in the person of Jesus, who lived and died and rose again to deliver us from both our own sin and the sin done against us. You are not alone in your sin and suffering. God sees. He hears. He is concerned. And he has come to rescue you.

Prayer: Lord, thank you for sending Jesus to rescue me. Help me find comfort in knowing you are concerned about my suffering and the suffering of the whole world. Amen.

Reflection Question: Where do you see suffering in the world or in your own life? Can you hand over these sufferings to God, trusting that he sees you and is with you?

God's Name

CARL LAFERTON

Imagine your first day at high school or college, and in your first slightly awkward conversations with people who may (or may not) become your best friends, everyone introduces themselves like this: "Hi, I'm Human." That would be weird! They'd be telling you *what* they are but not *who* they are. To be friends, you need to know someone's *name.*

When we call God "God," we are simply saying what he is—divine. But "God" isn't his name, any more than yours is "Human." Which is why, when God reveals himself to Moses, kickstarting his rescue of Israel from Egypt, God tells Moses his name. What is God called? I AM WHO I AM, or I AM, for short. (In Hebrew, it's *Yahweh.* In our Bibles, it's usually written as LORD.)

In Bible times, your name said something about what you were like or what your parents hoped you would be like. So in Exodus 3, Yahweh (I AM) is not only inviting Moses to be his friend; he's telling Moses what he is like.

God is who he is. He does not need to grow in knowledge, wisdom, or experience. He will be exactly the same tomorrow, the next day, and for eternity. When you read about God in the Bible, even though millennia have passed, he is still exactly like that today.

God is self-sufficient. That's why he had appeared to Moses as a fire that didn't burn up the bush it had invaded (3:2). Fires cannot burn without fuel. They are not self-sufficient (and neither are we), but I AM WHO I AM is. He needs nothing outside of himself, and therefore nothing can prevent him from doing what he wants to do. He won't ever be too tired or too weak to keep his promises.

Roughly fifteen hundred years after God appeared to Moses, a man from Nazareth in Galilee named Jesus said, "Before Abraham was, I AM!" (John 8:58)—in other words, *I'm Yahweh, and I've come to live among you.*

The great God of the universe wants a relationship with you. That's why he has told you his name. Jesus is God, and his character has not changed in any way since he walked on earth. It means that, no matter how your day, week, or life goes, *nothing* can prevent I AM from keeping his promises.

Prayer: Lord, I praise you for who you are—unchanging, self-sufficient, powerful enough to do all you have said you will do.

Reflection Question: What aspect of the unchanging character of I AM will you rely on today?

Driving a Hard Bargain

MIKE MCGARRY

Ever tried to make a deal with God? Maybe you've prayed something like, "God, if you help me with this test, I promise I'll go to church and youth group for a whole month."

This is the way Pharaoh bargains with God. He confesses his sin and claims he will let Israel go, but as soon as the plague is lifted, he returns to his old ways of rejecting Yahweh. Imagine Pharaoh's position. He is among the most powerful men in the ancient world, and he is being threatened by his slaves' spokesperson.

When the plagues continue to pour out judgment on Egypt, we might expect Pharaoh to realize it's time to do what God says. But a hard heart is closed off to God. It wants to do whatever it wants to do, and it won't worship or obey anyone. Sometimes the Bible explains that "Pharaoh hardened his heart" (Exodus 8:15, 32); other times it says, "The Lord hardened Pharaoh's heart" (9:12; 10:20, 27). Here's what we know for sure: Pharaoh never exhibits humility toward God. This seems to be a case where God gives someone what that person wants—and Pharaoh wants to be his own god.

Maybe you've found yourself resisting God's will or refusing to listen to godly counsel. These things can harden our hearts toward God, even when we don't intend it to. When you find yourself trapped in sin and temptation, don't let your feelings of guilt and shame keep you from God. Instead, ask him to help you repent—to turn away from sin. Remember that Jesus described God as the Father who runs out at full speed to welcome home his prodigal kids (Luke 15:11–32) and who sent his Son, Jesus, so that sinners could receive eternal life (John 3:16–17).

Prayer: Heavenly Father, would you keep my heart soft toward you? When I am tempted to leave you, keep me close. When I fall into sin, convict me so I will turn back to you. Amen.

Reflection Question: Why do you think a hard heart is so dangerous, and how can you guard against it?

An Impossible Assignment

MIKE MCGARRY

Have you ever received an impossible assignment? Surely that was how Moses felt when the Lord told him to return to Egypt and free two million Israelites from slavery.

Since Moses grew up in the royal household, he may know the Pharaoh God sends him to defeat. But Moses is also a fugitive; he has killed an Egyptian who beat an Israelite (Exodus 2:11–12). Returning to Egypt to ask Pharoah for Israel's freedom probably felt like a suicide mission, but when God speaks to you from within a burning bush, you go!

God demonstrates his great power, not only to Moses, but also to Pharaoh, who sees himself as a literal god. Remember that the Egyptians have enslaved and abused the Israelites for generations. Now God is setting the people free so that they can serve *him*, not Pharaoh. Each of the ten plagues recorded in Exodus 7–12 sets up Yahweh versus the Egyptian gods and goddesses who were believed to control the river, earth, and sky. The plagues display the authority of Israel's God over the gods of Egypt. Our God's power is unmatched.

Many people read about the plagues and think it wasn't fair or kind of God to allow such destruction, but no one in the ancient world would have considered Egypt "innocent." This judgment is God's plan to break Israel out of four hundred years of injustice. As the plagues progress, we see that God even delivers some Egyptians who have come to trust in him (9:20–21; 12:18, 38).

The same God who showed his power against the gods of Egypt took on flesh and died on the cross to rescue us from the power of sin—a greater oppressor than Pharaoh. Jesus rose from the grave, and he will return to finish everything he started. He was powerful to deliver the Israelites out of slavery, and he rescues us so that we can serve him, our loving, kind Savior.

Prayer: Almighty God, it's easy to forget about your holiness and power. It's easy to confuse your gentleness with weakness. Help me live with confidence because you are my all-powerful God.

Reflection Question: Do you ever feel like God is too weak to fulfill the promises he has made? When is it difficult for you to see his power?

Birth of a Nation

MARK HOWARD

I share a birthday with both my dad and my son—three generations born on the very same day! So my birthday has always felt extra special.

The Israelites' exodus from Egypt is a shared birthday for the whole nation of Israel. Pharaoh has refused to let the people go, so God sends a final plague to Egypt. Every firstborn Egyptian son dies, showing Yahweh's power over the gods of Egypt. He directs Moses to have all the Hebrew families put the blood of a spotless lamb over the doors of their homes. This marks them as a people belonging to God so that the angel of death will pass over their homes and allow their firstborn sons to live.

When Pharaoh finally lets God's people go, God declares, "This month is to be for you the first month, the first month of your year" (Exodus 12:2). God calls Israel to celebrate through a kind of birthday meal called the Passover—a meal of lamb and unleavened bread rather than cake.

Many years later, during a Passover meal, Jesus announces a new exodus—the true deliverance the world has been waiting for since Adam and Eve's failure in the garden. He calls this exodus "the new covenant in my blood" (Luke 22:20). Following that meal, Jesus is nailed to a cross, revealing himself as "the Lamb who was slain," the true Lamb to whom the first Passover always pointed (Revelation 13:8). Jesus' blood delivers his followers from death to life, freeing them from their sin. Salvation marks a new start, so that Christians are born again.

We can now celebrate our new birth in Jesus every day by resting in the finished work of Jesus. As we look to him for salvation, we invite others to join the celebration.

Prayer: Saving Father, thank you for delivering me from my old life and giving me new life in Jesus. Amen.

Reflection Question: Do you remember your "birthday" in Jesus—the day you surrendered your life to him? How has your appreciation for Jesus grown since that day? If you haven't yet put your trust in Jesus, what is keeping you from doing so today?

Nothing Is Impossible with God

REBECCA LANKFORD

While hiking alone in a canyon in Utah in 2003, Aaron Ralston stepped on a suspended boulder. The boulder dislodged and pinned Aaron's right hand against the canyon wall. For five days, Aaron was literally stuck between a rock and a hard place. Until Aaron amputated his own arm and escaped to safety, survival seemed impossible. But the now forty-eight-year-old father of two would be the first to tell you that "impossible" was not the end of his story.

In Exodus 14, the Israelites find themselves in a seemingly hopeless situation. Though God has provoked Pharaoh to release the Israelites from slavery in Egypt, Pharaoh changes his mind. He sends his army to chase the Israelites, forcing them up against the Red Sea.

Understandably, the Israelites are terrified. Behind them waits Pharoah's massive army. In front of them lies a swelling sea. The situation looks as hopeless as it could be. But God makes a way for his beloved people. He brings them out of slavery into freedom. Through Moses, God parts the Red Sea, allowing the Israelites to walk through safely.

Like the Israelites, we sometimes question if God has brought us to a "hopeless" place only to leave us in despair (vv. 11–12). But the mighty hand of God always makes a way when there seems to be no way. In Ephesians 2, Paul tells us that we used to be "dead in our sins" (v. 1). And yet, through the life, death, and resurrection of Jesus, we have been "made alive with Christ" (v. 5) and released from the slavery of our sin.

Just as God made a way for the Israelites, he made a way for us to be reconciled to himself through the work of Jesus. If God can provide a way for hopeless sinners to be united to himself, he surely can provide a way out of any "impossible" situation we face. Our job is the same as that of the Israelites: Stand firm, be still, and watch to see how the Lord will provide.

Prayer: Jesus, I praise you for being my hope in hopeless situations. Thank you for delivering me out of slavery and bringing me into your marvelous light. Help me to trust and be still while you fight for me. Amen.

Reflection Question: Is there a "hopeless" situation you are currently facing? How might God be inviting you to be still and trust him in the midst of it?

What's for Supper?

ANNA MEADE HARRIS

A sign hangs over the door to our family room: "Kindly refrain from whining." It's not the mere sound of the whine that makes it so offensive. Whiners find fault where they ought to be grateful. They insult the giver by criticizing the gift.

In spite of all that God has done for the Israelites, the entire nation grumbles against him because they don't like the food. You read that right: God miraculously frees them from their bondage to cruel taskmasters, and they complain about what's for supper.

The Israelites are shockingly ungrateful, yet God graciously gives them a gift they do not deserve—daily bread. God instructs them to collect white, flaky bread called manna from the ground each morning. God knows they're going to be tempted to stockpile his provisions, but if they try to hoard the bread, it will spoil. Only on Friday does God allow the people to collect more than they need so they can rest on Saturday. Resting on the seventh day reminds the people that they belong to God (who rested on the seventh day of creation) and not to Pharaoh (who made the people work without ceasing).

God's provision shows the people his character so that they "will know that I am the Lord your God." God works astounding miracles on their behalf, even as he provides for their mundane daily needs. Most of all, God shows them how much he loves them, demonstrated by his gracious response to their whining. The Israelites are not appealing; they are annoying. They do not earn his love through good behavior or hard work. But God returns good for their evil (1 Peter 3:9), feeding them in the wilderness when they cannot feed themselves. By giving them both manna and sabbath rest, he shows that he will provide what they need, one day at a time.

The Lord loves you and me like this too. As much as we need daily food, we have an even greater need for a sinless Savior to die the death we deserve for the sins we commit. We cannot earn God's favor or affection by being good, but God already knows that, so he makes another way. In Jesus, God gives us the Savior we need. Like the Israelites, we've received a life-saving gift we could not earn and do not deserve.

Prayer: Father, thank you for showing me your patient love. Help me appreciate your grace so that I will trust you to meet every need.

Reflection Question: How might God's grace to you through Christ—even when you are ungrateful—change your whining into gratitude?

Failing to Follow Through

CHELSEA KINGSTON ERICKSON

Have you ever promised to keep a commitment, only to find you couldn't do it? Maybe you promised you'd go to a friend's gig, but your parents said you couldn't take the car. Or you told yourself you'll do better at following God's commands, but you keep messing up.

God asks the Israelites to make a commitment. After rescuing his people from Egypt, he gives Moses the Ten Commandments, which represents another part of his covenant with them. In the ancient world, a covenant is a binding promise between two rulers or nations, often with life and death consequences. The more powerful party holds all the cards, demanding whatever he wants in exchange for protecting the less powerful party.

In Exodus 20, God is the more powerful party, and he promises to be Israel's God, protecting and caring for them. The Ten Commandments are a summary of God's law—all that he asks Israel to do as their part of the covenant. The first four instructions outline what Israel's relationship with God should look like—they must worship him alone, even setting aside one day each week to rest from their work, showing that he is Lord. The last six show how Israel should treat everyone else—their actions must show that all people are made in God's image.

There's just one problem: *The Israelites don't seem to be able to keep the law.* Like you and me, the people often fail to do what God has asked. No wonder God's people are terrified by the thunder and lightning from the mountain that are signs of God's presence with them!

But unlike other covenant makers, God doesn't bow out of his commitment when we fail. Even when we repeatedly sin, he continues his promises to us. God is so committed to us that he sent Jesus to perfectly uphold the law that Israel—and you and I—have failed to keep (Matthew 5:17; Romans 8:3).

The apostle Paul explains that the law—all those things we ought to do but don't do—will be accomplished in our lives through the perfect life Jesus lived in our place (Romans 8:4). Wow! If you are in Jesus, God looks at your life and sees something other than failure and sin. He sees *Jesus* upholding your end of the covenant.

Prayer: Father, I often feel frustrated by my lack of progress in keeping your commands. Forgive me.

Reflection Question: When is it hardest to obey God's commands? How can looking to Jesus' perfect obedience help you trust God more?

Substitutes and Go-Betweens

DANNY KWON

Dogs make good pets. They grow to a manageable size. They can be trained and taught tricks and become tender companions. A bull, on the other hand, would make a strange and terrible pet.

In Exodus 29:10, Moses's cousin Aaron and his sons are told to lay their hands on the head of a bull. But this is no petting zoo. God is setting aside Aaron and his sons as priests, which means he is dedicating them to serve as representatives to go between God and the rest of his people.

God's holiness, his spiritual and moral perfection, means that he cannot accept human sin. Because they belong to God, his people are to be set apart as holy too—only we know that from the beginning of the Bible, God's people repeatedly sin against him. Still, God is committed to being with his people, so after he gives Moses the law, he dictates plans for the *tabernacle*, a transportable tent in which his own presence will dwell among them. The only problem is, God knows that his people will not obey his law. They will continue to sin.

So God establishes the priesthood through the tribe of Levi, with Aaron as its head. The priests serve as mediators, or go-betweens, for God and his people. They offer various sacrifices to deal with the people's ongoing sin. God designates ornate clothing for the high priest to wear, including a breastplate with the names of the tribes of Israel engraved on precious stones so the priest can carry the people into God's presence. But even these priests are not holy enough to be in the presence of God. When Aaron and his sons place their hands on the bull, they transfer their sins onto the bull as their substitute. The bull's blood temporarily cleanses them and pays for their sin.

For Christians today, the gospel tells us that "there is one God and one mediator between God and mankind, the man Christ Jesus, who gave himself as a ransom for all people" (1 Timothy 2:5–6). Now Jesus is the only great high priest, who makes us holy by shedding his own blood in a once-for-all sacrifice for sin (Hebrews 10:10). Today we have the assurance of God's presence through the priestly work of Jesus Christ.

Prayer: God, thank you for the sacrifice of Jesus. Give me assurance that your presence is eternally with me as I place my trust in Jesus.

Reflection Question: What is one benefit of knowing that Christ is our ultimate sacrifice on the cross on our behalf?

What Do I Worship?

REBECCA LANKFORD

I couldn't wait to turn sixteen. I pictured myself cruising down the road, windows down, Taylor Swift's "Fearless" on full blast. I was elated to get my license . . . but a week later, I backed into a pole and ruined my new (to me) car. I was devastated. The very thing I thought would bring me satisfaction and freedom let me down seven short days later.

My relationship to my first car isn't so different from the story of Israel and the golden calf: both are tales of *idolatry*, which simply means choosing something above God.

Don't miss the timing of this story: Just before this, God has shown his people how they can enjoy a relationship with him within the good boundaries of his law. Commandments one and two make it quite clear how God feels about idols: (1) The people of Israel are to have no other gods before him, and (2) they are not to make images of created things.

But before Moses has time to descend the mountain with the commandments, the Israelites grow impatient and make their own god. They ask Aaron to construct a golden calf and wrongfully worship this created thing, claiming that *it* has brought them out of Egypt (v. 4), not God.

Just like the Israelites, you and I tend to offer ourselves to false gods that can't truly satisfy. Idolatry is on display whenever we look to a created thing to do for us what only the Creator can do (Romans 1:25). We elevate things to a godlike status—grades, relationships, human approval, security. Eventually, these idols will let us down. Relationships will end, our GPAs will slip, we'll wreck our new cars.

But Jesus can forgive idolatry. Whenever we forget God's good commands and worship false gods, he is ready to offer forgiveness and grace—an act no created thing can do. Just as Moses pleads for forgiveness on Israel's behalf (Exodus 32:31–34), Jesus died to guarantee this forgiveness for sinners (see 2 Corinthians 5:21). His sacrificial work on the cross moves us to worship him as the true God. The more we recognize his compassion, the more we will be drawn away from our idols and toward Jesus, the ultimate source of satisfaction.

Prayer: Jesus, I want to worship you above all else. But I desperately need your help. Please move my heart away from worthless idols.

Reflection Question: What are you hoping your idols will do for you? How is Jesus God so much better?

"Seeing" God

CONNIE LEUNG NELSON

Nothing compares to your first concert by a favorite artist. You are transported to a whole new world where all your senses are engaged and you're bursting with wonder. You know the melodies and lyrics by heart, yet somehow it all feels brand-new. Even after the concert has ended, you're left with a kind of awestruck glow. It's a glorious, mountaintop experience.

In Exodus 33–34, we read that Moses saw God's glory on a literal mountaintop—Mount Sinai. God's glory refers to his infinite beauty and power and presence, his supreme worth made visible. God's glory is tied to his character—he loves abundantly, punishes sin, and shows mercy (vv. 6–7).

Imagine what Moses must have felt as God revealed himself. His senses must have been lit on fire, every fiber of his being exploding with awe. Moses went away with a glow on his face that lasted for days. Seeing God's glory changes people profoundly, even today.

When we read Scripture or hear it preached, we "see" God's glory in his Son, Jesus. Jesus is fully God, yet he dwelt among us as a human being; he is "the radiance of God's glory" (Hebrews 1:3). God's glory—the same glory Moses saw on the mountaintop thousands of years ago—is expressed visibly in the person of Jesus.

The words Jesus spoke, the actions he took, and the ways he engaged people all embody God's glory. We look at Jesus and see not only his life in historical facts; we see *God's glory* in what he did for us on the cross. Indeed, God did not let sin go unpunished, and he showed mercy to his beloved people by sending Jesus to take the punishment for their sins. Everything about Jesus is stamped with God's glory and displays God's character. When we behold God's glory in Jesus, God changes us "into his image with ever-increasing glory" (2 Corinthians 3:18).

Keep looking at Jesus. He will become not only necessary but also beautiful to you. Keep looking, and the Holy Spirit will help you see the wonder of your Savior's love for you.

Prayer: Father God, awaken my heart to see your glory more clearly in Jesus. Thank you for giving me the Holy Spirit, who helps me see your goodness.

Reflection Question: What one wonderful thing about God amazes you?

A Place to Meet with God

MARK HOWARD

There are nearly 8 billion people on Earth. Earth is just one of 100–400 billion planets in our galaxy, and our galaxy is just one of 100–200 billion galaxies in the observable universe.

With numbers like this, it's easy to feel insignificant. But if we're honest, we don't need statistics to feel unimportant. Something as simple as being ignored by someone we is enough to make us feel small.

Despite our seeming insignificance, we are remarkably special to the God of the universe. In fact, God goes to extraordinary lengths to be with his people.

God instructs his people to build a moveable tent called the tabernacle ("dwelling"), where he will live with his people. The tabernacle's design echoes back to Eden, where God walked with human beings in a place where heaven and earth seemed to overlap. The lampstand in the tabernacle looks like a tree, and the basin is filled with life-giving water. The Most Holy Place contains the ark of the covenant, a wooden chest that holds the Ten Commandments. In front of the Most Holy Place hangs a curtain embroidered with cherubim, just like those that stood at the entrance to Eden (Genesis 3:24). God brings his presence through fire and cloud to this mini-Eden, heaven-on-earth place.

But there's a problem. In their sin, human beings cannot get close to God. He wants to be near us, but we can no longer survive the fullness of his presence. So to enter the heart of the tabernacle, the Most Holy Place, an animal without blemish must be sacrificed for Israel's sin. Even then, only one person—the high priest—can enter, and only once a year on the Day of Atonement. The tabernacle points forward to Jesus, the "Word [who] became flesh and made his dwelling among us" (John 1:14). Jesus' death has made a way for sinful people to be in God's presence.

But God wants to be even closer to us. So Jesus sends the Spirit to live *within* us. One day, Jesus will return to make all things new. Then it can be said, "God's dwelling place is now among the people" (Revelation 21:3). So remember who you are to God and draw near to him.

Prayer: God with us, thank you for loving me enough to rescue me from my sin. Renew me in the hope of Jesus' return to make all things new.

Reflection Question: What makes you feel closest to God? How would our world be different if everyone was more aware of God's presence?

Restoring the Peace

CONNIE LEUNG NELSON

Friendships can develop effortlessly, sometimes just by sitting next to someone in class. But relationships are not bulletproof. When your friend talks about you behind your back or you forget your promise to work with her on a group project, the relationship is strained. You and your friend must make up to restore peace.

Our default relationship status with God is separation. Ever since the fall, all people live in rebellion against God. We have lost peace with him because of our sin.

Throughout the book of Leviticus, we see that God's *holiness*, or his set-apartness, will not tolerate sin (10:3). For this reason, God's holy presence inside Israel's camp is dangerous. In the same way that the sun's power incinerates any object that comes too close, a sinful, unprepared human being trespassing into God's holy presence will die (16:2). Sin must first be dealt with in order for a holy God to dwell with Israel.

God mercifully ordains a system of sacrifices for Israel to deal with their ongoing sin (Leviticus 1–7). The system enables them to live with the presence of the holy God in their midst. Burnt offerings, grain offerings, and fellowship offerings allow people to worship God (Leviticus 1–3), while sin and guilt offerings serve to deal with sins (Leviticus 4–7).

An offense against a holy God requires a life poured out (Leviticus 17:11). Over and over again, the priests offer animal sacrifices so that the people can live with God in their midst. This system of sacrifices could not provide lasting atonement. Jesus gave his own life as the one true, unblemished sacrifice, standing in as our substitute to make payment for our sins through his blood on the cross (Hebrews 9:12–14). Because of what Jesus has done, God will always welcome you as a closest friend, no matter what you've done or how you feel. In Jesus, our peace with God is truly bulletproof.

Prayer: Almighty God, help me remember that peace between us is as sure as Jesus' sacrifice for me. I confess my sins, knowing you have already forgiven me and always will. Help me know how much you love me through Jesus.

Reflection Question: What are some sins or feelings you've hesitated to bring before God, and why? If Jesus' work has granted you permanent peace with God, how do you think God will react to these things?

A Thorough Cleaning

REBECCA LANKFORD

Airport security involves following seemingly endless precautions. You show your ID, empty your pockets, and make sure your liquid items are the appropriate size—all before you get to your gate!

Leviticus 16 describes a process even more thorough than navigating the TSA experience—the Day of Atonement. Aaron, the high priest, was to follow detailed directions to *atone*, or cleanse and pay for, the Israelites' sins once a year. These detailed instructions for the Day of Atonement remind us of the seriousness of sin. Because God is holy, he cannot ignore the sin of his people. Every iniquity must be wiped clean and paid for in order to reconcile sinful people to a holy God. So one day a year, the high priest enters the Most Holy Place in the center of the tabernacle, where God's presence dwells. There he offers sacrifices to cleanse himself and the people from defilement because of sin. The high priest's animal sacrifices worked temporarily so the Israelites could continue to live in God's presence. But God's people needed a more thorough and permanent cleansing than what the high priest could offer.

The sacrifices made on the Day of Atonement serve as a blueprint for the greater and final sacrifice Jesus would make on the cross—the ultimate Day of Atonement when the blood of the spotless Lamb of God was shed in order to take away the sins of the world (John 1:29). Because of Jesus, we don't have to complete a long list of steps to be made right with God. The checkpoint that stood between us and God has been removed, and we can now enjoy full access to the Father.

The next time you feel like you must follow a certain set of rules before you go to God, remember that Jesus shed his blood for you so *nothing* could separate you from his love. Both the sins you didn't even know you committed and the ones that keep you up at night have been atoned for by the perfect sacrifice of Jesus (Hebrews 10:1–4; 11). You can run to him with confidence, knowing that his blood has washed you clean.

Prayer: Jesus, thank you for being the final sacrifice on the cross. Help me run to you in repentance, trusting no sin can keep me from you.

Reflection Question: Do you ever feel like you have to clean yourself up to get to God? How does Jesus' atoning work on the cross bring you comfort in the midst of those feelings?

Spying on the Enemy

KENDAL CONNER

Disney's *The Lion King* opens with Simba as an overconfident cub who "just can't wait" to rule the Pride Lands. But when his father dies, Simba no longer believes he has what it takes to be king. Only when he remembers who his father is does Simba find the courage to claim his rightful place as king. This time, however, his confidence is not in himself, but in his father.

Ultimately, this is what happens with the Israelite spies in Canaan. They scout out the land that God had already promised to give them—a land flowing with milk and honey—but there's one problem: The land is filled with men twice their size. In comparison, the Israelites look like an army of ants, causing the spies to lose their confidence and run away as fast as they can—all of them except Caleb and Joshua (Numbers 14:6–10). Caleb speaks out and encourages the people to continue to pursue God's blessing.

Just like Simba's, Caleb's confidence ultimately does not come from his abilities; it comes from knowing who his father is—the King of kings and Lord of lords. If God has promised the Israelites this land, then God will give it to them. Yes, the truth is that they could never face the Canaanites in their own strength, but Caleb knows they will never have to. So while it may be true that you do not have the strength to face your giants alone, the promise you have in Jesus is that you never have to again.

No matter what our circumstances may be, our confidence is not in our own abilities but in our Father God. Even in the face of failure or anxiety, we can rest in the comforting arms of our Father, who loves us and will meet our greatest need. Because he has already done so much for us through Jesus, we can have confidence as we approach God's throne, knowing he will pour out his mercy and grace (Hebrews 4:15–16). God is good, and he hears anything we ask in accordance with his will (1 John 5:14). God has entered the land before us and provided unwavering hope in Jesus. There is no failure, trial, or fear that God has not already made a way for us to walk through.

Prayer: Father, thank you for being the God of the promise. Help me trust your word more than my circumstances. Amen.

Reflection Question: Where are you trusting in your own abilities more than in God's promises?

People Rebel, God Remains

CONNIE LEUNG NELSON

Fear is an intense emotion that seems to overtake your whole body and crowd out everything else. It's hard to think clearly when you're in this state. You might be inclined to a "fight, flight, or freeze" response, meaning you're responding without a lot of rational thought.

Maybe that's how the Israelites feel when they hear the report about the inhabitants of the promised land. Their fear of an intimidating enemy clouds their judgment, and they have no interest in listening to leaders who love them and who only want the best for them.

But fear does not excuse what Numbers 14 calls a rebellion against God. And it is a full-on coup. The Israelites are ready to execute their leaders, set up new ones, and head back to Egypt to resume their lives of slavery.

God's anger against them is justified. Yet Moses does not want the Israelites destroyed. He appeals to God on their behalf, reminding God that he is "slow to anger, abounding in love, forgiving sin and rebellion" (v. 18). Moses asks God to forgive the sin of his people, and God does forgive them. He remains Israel's God, even as he punishes the people justly by barring those guilty of rebellion from entering the promised land.

I often wonder if the Israelites realized how close they were to being disinherited. Because of Moses's prayers for them, that group of Israelites gains forty years of God's patience and the opportunity to turn to God. Although they deserve to be cut off, God remains their God.

Moses's prayer of intercession foreshadows what Jesus did for us. In our sins, we have rebelled just as gravely against God as the Israelites did. Yet we do not have to fear that God is mad at us. Jesus gave his life to pay for our sin.

Jesus prays for our good on the basis of *his* own sacrifice, the righteousness and perfection of *his* life, which is the surest, most fail-safe basis of all (Hebrews 7:25–27). Because of Jesus, God will always remain our loving Father. We never have to fear that our requests for forgiveness will go unanswered.

Prayer: Father, help me understand just how close I was to being separated from you forever because of my sins. Help my heart to be in awe of how utterly loved I am, based on the firm foundation of Jesus' work on the cross.

Reflection Question: How does it make you feel to know that Jesus is praying for you?

Wilderness Wandering

CHARLOTTE GETZ

Have you ever found yourself in a wilderness—not a literal one, but the kind that makes you feel lost, empty, and afraid? Maybe your friends turned against you, your family is falling apart, or anxiety won't let you breathe. In such times, it's impossible to imagine happy endings.

The book of Numbers tells of "wilderness wanderings." After God frees the Israelites from their slavery in Egypt, you'd think it would be the happy ending to the story. Surely they have suffered enough! But no. They're under the threats of starvation, dehydration, and even death. In Numbers 20, the people find themselves at their wit's end. In essence, they ask, "Did God free us from the Egyptians just to bring us into the wilderness to die?"

God responds with one of the great and strange miracles of the Old Testament. He asks Moses to summon water out of a rock. A rock! And in doing so, God gives his people what they need—not just water, but the knowledge that this mighty God will provide a way through.

Like the Israelites, you may be asking hard questions in your wilderness wanderings. *God, what is the point of all this? Is it ever going to end?* Throughout the Bible, God allows his people to reach points of desperation. For it's in wilderness places—those times we are out of options—when he most profoundly shows himself and his glory. Look no further than the cross of Jesus Christ to see that this is true. What seems to be death and catastrophic failure turns out to be resurrection and salvation for all who trust in him (1 Corinthians 1:18). In those rock-bottom moments, we see that only God can make life come from death and water gush from a rock. He delights to do so in often strange ways that are just what we need as we journey through life's difficulties.

Friend, you can expect that God has made a way through your wilderness. God has written his plan for you since the beginning, and the journey may surprise you. While you are hungry and thirsty, sad and afraid, God has you in the palm of his capable hand. He is there with you, as close as the rain that falls on your head, as near as the dirt beneath your weary feet.

Prayer: Lord, as I encounter painful seasons, rekindle my hope that you will make a way through it. Amen.

Reflection Question: John 14:6 tells us that Jesus is the way in the wilderness. What comfort does Jesus' life and death bring to your own wilderness?

Another Weird Snake Story

MAC HARRIS

Roughly two-thirds of all venomous snakebites happen to men and boys. Even crazier? For the snakebites that happened when a snake was *intentionally* engaged, more than 90 percent of the bites were inflicted on guys, and nearly all of them were on the hand, wrist, or arm![1] Fellas, quit trying to grab snakes!

But what do snakes and silly statistics have to do with this strange story in the Bible? It has been forty years since the Israelites crossed the Red Sea to escape slavery in Egypt. After many ups and downs, they find themselves, once again, headed back toward the Red Sea. They complain about God's provision and wonder if it would have been better to stay in Egypt.

God is not happy with their grumbling, and he sends venomous snakes to bite people! Why? For one, the snake symbolized the power of Egypt, the place to which the Israelites longed to return. More than that, these serpents remind us of *the* snake—Satan—the ultimate enemy that led Adam and Eve into sin.

It's not that God has brought Israel into the wilderness to die. Their death in the wilderness is the result of their own sin, and the solutions they desire will bring more harm than good. When the people confess their sin, Moses prays, and God presents a strange solution: Put a bronze snake on a pole and look at it (v. 9). This wasn't because a bronze snake magically cured venomous bites; it was a reminder that salvation requires faith in God.

This bronze snake hints at a future day when God's people will be delivered from death by lifting their heads and looking at Christ on the cross. Jesus himself declares the deliverance he offers: "Just as Moses lifted up the snake in the wilderness, so the Son of Man must be lifted up, that everyone who believes may have eternal life in him" (John 3:14–15).

Prayer: Father God, help me see the sin in my life, and give me the courage to believe. Help me fix my eyes on Jesus as my Savior and Sustainer. Amen.

Reflection Question: What does it mean to set your eyes on the cross of Christ? What may be drawing your attention away from him?

---

1. Joshua D. Jaramillo et al., "The 'T's' of Snakebite Injury in the USA: Fact or Fiction?," *Trauma Surgery and Acute Care Open* 4, no. 1 (October 2019), doi: 10.1136/tsaco-2019–000374.

Lost and Found

CHARLOTTE GETZ

Since my teen years, I've struggled with intense, scary seasons of depression and anxiety. Several years ago, I experienced an extended season of severe panic. I felt trapped in this wilderness with no way through it. I struggled to see God anywhere, and I certainly couldn't see how he would rescue me.

In Deuteronomy 1, God tells the Israelites to go into the hill country of the Amorites and claim it. But instead of obeying, they give in to their fear. "The people are stronger and taller than we are," they grumble (v. 28). Yet again they worry that God has led them out of Egypt just to die in the wilderness.

Moses responds to the Israelites' fear by reminding them what God has done before. *Don't you remember?* he seems to urge them. Not long ago, God had rescued them out of the cruel and violent hands of the Egyptians. Not long ago, he'd set their escape straight through the center of a raging sea. All this time when they were thirsty, he'd given them water. When they were hungry, he'd sent them manna. *Don't you remember?*

These Scriptures were essential to me during my own wilderness wanderings. Because even when I was facing the dark and terrifying ocean of fear, God was reminding me, *I have you, Charlotte. Remember how I fought for you before? I've already gone before you; I'll carry you as a father carries his daughter—all the way, until you reach the other side.* God gave me this sense of the presence of Jesus in a way that's hard to explain without sounding a little silly. I could envision him beside me. He was there *with me*.

Years later, I can confirm that God brought me through. Not nearly as quickly or as smoothly as I would have liked. And while I wouldn't want to live through it again, I also wouldn't rewrite the story. It stands now as proof: *Don't you remember?* Jesus, our in-the-flesh Immanuel ("God with us"), was there with me, just as he promised his first disciples that he'd be with them—and us—always (Matthew 28:20). He carried me through. He did. Friend, he's carrying you through right now.

Prayer: God, remind me of how you've carried me through the wilderness in days gone by. Help me experience every day the there-with-me comfort of your presence.

Reflection Question: Can you remember a difficult time and see how God faithfully brought you through it?

Passing the Baton

ISAIAH A. MARSHALL

Standing on the line, waiting for the baton from my teammate, my heart pounds. In a relay, each runner has a critical role, and our team's success depends on how well each of us executes our leg. My teammates have given me a lead, and now it's my turn. I don't want to let them down. I receive the baton, and now I face the uncertainty and challenge in front of me.

Life can feel overwhelming, especially as you face new challenges. How do you handle uncertainty? Do you let fear win, or do you run with courage?

In Joshua 1, we see Moses hand off the baton. Moses has fallen short in leading the Israelites into the promised land. Now Joshua receives the handoff and assumes leadership responsibility. I imagine Joshua is thinking to himself, *If the mighty Moses couldn't do it, I don't stand a chance!* Joshua probably feels like you and I do when we face uncertainty: *Do I have what it takes?*

We learn what Joshua learns: When God is with you, you can face any challenge with courage. If we ignore God's presence, we will face new responsibilities with fear, relying on our own strength rather than God's guidance. Sin will cause us to take our eyes off God, who promises to be with us. Through the gift of the Holy Spirit given to all who believe in Jesus for salvation, God's presence strengthens us and gives us courage.

Like Joshua, you have your own race to run. You aren't leading the Israelites into the promised land, but as a follower of Christ, you are invited to lead others to the Promise Keeper. There will be challenges and uncertainty throughout your race. So as you have received the baton of faith, run with endurance the race that is set before you by fixing your eyes on Jesus (Hebrews 12:2).

Jesus ran his race with courage, enduring the cross on your behalf (Hebrews 12:2). Don't grow weary or lose heart. Jesus promised God's presence to all his disciples, including you: "I will ask the Father, and he will give you another advocate to help you and be with you forever—the Spirit of truth" (John 14:16–17). Run with courage, knowing that because Almighty God is with you, you can face any challenge.

Prayer: God, help me experience your presence as I face challenges, looking to the cross, where you took on my sin and died for me.

Reflection Question: In which area of your life do you need to be strong and courageous?

Risk and Reward

SYLER THOMAS

Field of Dreams is a movie about a man named Ray who hears voices instructing him to build a baseball field in his cornfields. After he does, the ghosts of former players come to play there, but only Ray and his family can see them. When Ray experiences financial trouble, his brother-in-law pleads with him to sell the farm, until suddenly he can see the players *for himself.*

In Joshua 2, we meet Rahab, a prostitute in Jericho. Rahab has heard stories about Yahweh's mercy in rescuing the oppressed Israelites. When two Israelite spies arrive on her doorstep, Rahab begins to experience God's power *for herself.* Joshua sent the spies to investigate Jericho, and Rahab protects them. When Jericho's king learns the spies are in Rahab's house, Rahab helps them escape.

Rahab's hope in God's goodness proves greater than her fear of Jericho's king. Rahab risks everything, believing in faith that God will rescue her. The spies tell her to hang a scarlet cord in the window—a subtle reminder of the Passover, when God rescued his people from Egypt. When the city is destroyed, the Israelite army will see the cord and spare her family.

That's just what happens in Joshua 6—God rescues Rahab and her family (v. 18) when Israel takes over Jericho (v. 25). But that's not all. Rahab, a Canaanite woman of questionable reputation, is remembered *three times* in the New Testament (Matthew 1:5; Hebrews 11:31; James 2:25). She becomes King David's great-great-grandmother in the family line of Judah, which leads to Jesus.

Rahab's story shows us that God intends to draw people from all ethnic and social backgrounds into his family. When Jesus is born to an unwed mother in the boondocks of Bethlehem, that story continues. In fact, Jesus himself welcomes tax collectors and prostitutes to become his friends (Luke 7). Jesus paid for the sins of all who would trust him in faith when he went to the cross.

Have *you* experienced the kindness, mercy, and power of the God of Israel? This God invites you to have a brand-new life through his grace given you in Jesus. Don't just take my word for it, but look to his Word to see *for yourself.*

Prayer: Lord, I want to believe all that your Word says about you. Give me again an experience of your grace and power in my life. Amen.

Reflection Question: Is it difficult to believe that God would rescue someone like Rahab? Is it hard to believe he could rescue you?

God Goes Before You

DANNY KWON

One of the great traditions in college football happens before the game. The teams run onto the field like a thundering herd, led by their captains, excited and emotional. Then as each team forms a huddle, the captains give a fiery speech to pump up the team.

In Joshua 3, God's people, the Israelites, are marching into a real life-and-death battle. They are about to cross into the land God has promised to them after forty years of wandering in the wilderness. Like the captains of a team, the officers rally the people to wait three days and then to follow the Levitical priests who will carry the ark of the covenant across the Jordan River.

One may wonder what God's people are thinking during these days as they are about to embark on a battle. Even though God promised them victory, they must be filled with worry and fear. Joshua 3 is not a story of mere men leading men into battle, however. It's not even the story of extraordinary men leading regular people into battle. The priests are carrying the ark of the covenant, which contains the most sacred objects, including the place of God's presence with Israel known as the mercy seat, or atonement cover. God himself leads his people into battle to secure the inheritance he had promised them many years before. Just as God parted the Red Sea, allowing his people to flee slavery in Egypt, now he parts the Jordan River so they may cross into the promised land (vv. 15–17).

Even though you know God's promises, you may have worries, fears, or even doubts about who God is. Like the Israelites, we have the sacred assurance of God on our side—Jesus Christ. God's people no longer need the ark of the covenant to lead them. The Spirit now lives in us, leading and guiding us. In the full assurance of God's love, you can embrace his promise to be with you (Hebrew 13:5), to go before you, no matter what you face.

Prayer: Heavenly Father, give me peace and assurance, despite my doubts and fears. Help me believe that Jesus died for me and that you are my Father who goes before me.

Reflection Question: Is there a situation in your life in which you need assurance that God is with you, that he goes before you?

The Shout That Didn't Make Sense

ISAIAH A. MARSHALL

Have you ever been told to do something that didn't make sense? As a kid, I remember my mom saying, "Eat your vegetables so you can grow big and strong." When you think about it, how can a piece of some leafy thing put meat on your bones?

Now that the Israelites are in the land of Canaan, which God promised to give them, their challenge is to conquer the land. But they face an obstacle—an impenetrable wall around the city of Jericho. God gives Joshua specific instructions as they go into the city: To knock down this wall and take the land, you must march around, blow a trumpet, and shout.

Do what now? This makes no sense at all.

Because of our bent toward sin, we often try to rely on our own understanding and abilities, doubting God's infinite power. Sin limits our faith. It prevents us from fully trusting the power of God. The Israelites' victory over Jericho does not come out of their own might and abilities, but through a seemingly strange plan given by God. God's power working through their obedience breaks down the wall of Jericho.

Our faith is rooted in an unconventional plan that even Jesus' twelve disciples did not understand (Mark 16:14). God's power is on full display through Jesus' resurrection from the dead, which solidifies victory over sin and death and provides forgiveness of sin. The God whose power raised his dead Son from the tomb is the same God whose power smashed the wall around Jericho. God's power can accomplish what we cannot.

So trust the Lord and submit to him. Pray even when you don't feel like it. Share the gospel with your friend who rolls his eyes at you. Be patient with your pesky little sister. And of course, eat your vegetables.

Prayer: Sovereign God, help me trust in your great power and submit to your perfect will, even when I don't understand. Thank you for Jesus, whose triumph over sin and death leads us to victory.

Reflection Question: Has God ever asked you to do something that didn't make sense? How did you respond?

You Share What You Love

KATIE POLSKI

During his Hall of Fame speech, NFL quarterback Peyton Manning suddenly became emotional about his relationship with his father. Choking back tears, he said, "Football carved out a place for my favorite quarterback, my hero, my role model, my dad—Archie Manning—to pass on something he loved to me."[1]

The nation of Israel went through a very dark period during the time of the judges, in part because one generation did *not* pass on to the next a love for God and an understanding of all that God had done for them. When a generation doesn't grow up hearing stories of God's miracles or learning of God's great love, they turn to idols for comfort and direction. These young Israelites do not have a personal relationship with God like their mothers and fathers had, and therefore they completely reject the worship of the one, true God.

This way of living does not lead to happiness or prosperity; in fact, a few verses later, we learn that Israel is in "great distress" (v. 15). In his grace, the Lord raises up judges to lead the Israelites, but time and time again, they turn away from God and forget to remind each other what God had done for his people.

It can be easy to become annoyed with parents or youth leaders when they tell you the same messages about God over and over. But God charges adults to teach children who he is and why he matters. When adults talk about God, they are doing their best to pass on to you their greatest love—Jesus—because they know that a personal relationship with him will change the course of your life in every way. How is this relationship life-changing? Jesus offers hope by rescuing us from our sin. He sacrificed his life to save us, and through his death and resurrection, we can have a personal relationship with a loving God who guides, heals, and calls us his children (1 John 3:1).

You, too, can pass on your faith. If you love Jesus, there is nothing greater than showing this love through your words and actions. God can use you, no matter how inadequate you may feel, to pass on to someone else the great love of Jesus.

Prayer: Lord, help me be quick to listen to those who tell me about you and gracious toward those who share your love.

Reflection Question: Who has influenced your relationship with Jesus, and how?

---

1. Mark Chalifoux, "Peyton Manning Gets Emotional Talking About His Dad During Hall of Fame Speech," The Dad, August 9, 2021, www.thedad.com/peyton-manning-dad-hof/.

The Secret Superheroes Know

ISAIAH A. MARSHALL

As I was growing up, I saw my mom be a real-life superhero. Instead of fighting imaginary villains, she was a single mom going to school full-time and working full-time—all while raising two boys. She had real challenges to overcome that must have felt insurmountable at times. I once asked her how she did it all. Her answer was simple: "It was God."

In the book of Judges, we read about Deborah, who was also a real-life superhero. Because Israel does what is evil in the sight of the Lord (4:1), God allows Jabin, king of Canaan, to conquer them (v. 2). In a culture ruled by men, God calls Deborah, a woman, to lead them against the king's army as Israel's fifth judge.

When the people cry out to the Lord for help in their captivity, Deborah devises a plan. She summons Barak the warrior to gather his troops against Sisera, the commander of the king's army. Barak accepts under one condition: Deborah must go with him. Deborah goes, knowing that there is someone much more powerful than she who will go before them. God allows Barak's army to conquer Sisera's troops through Deborah's leadership, and he later uses another woman to kill Sisera.

Like Barak, we often feel fearful as we venture into uncharted territory. Did you know this was also true for Jesus? In Gethsemane, Jesus' soul is sorrowful because of what he will soon experience (Matthew 26:36–46). Even still, he trusts his Father. In challenging moments, sin says, "Fear it," when God says, "Faith it." Jesus chooses faith because he knows that his Father will go before him, leading him to victory over sin and death. You can bring all your fears to this God who rescues you.

Our God goes before us, fights our battles, and leads us to victory (Judges 4:16). My mom knew this. Deborah and Barak knew this. Jesus knew this as he endured the cross and shed his innocent blood for our sins. He defeated sin and death so we can trust him in the midst of our fears.

Prayer: Lord, help me trust you, even when I feel afraid or uncertain. Comfort me as I lean on the truth that you give me the victory because Jesus has overcome the cross and the grave.

Reflection Question: Think about a recent challenge or fear. How did you try to handle it? Could things have been different if you had fully trusted God?

God's Patience with Our Doubts

MAC HARRIS

On the surface, I looked like a model Christian. I was a youth group regular, a student leader in church, and I read my Bible (almost) every day. But I was also ashamed and paralyzed by my secret doubts about God. Worse, I felt like I couldn't tell anyone. No one would see me the same if they knew.

I find a fellow doubter in Gideon. Granted, he's one of the messiest characters from one of the messiest books in the Bible, but during a time when Israel is surrounded by enemies, God calls Gideon—a no-name guy from an unimportant family in a backwater town—to rise up and deliver Israel (Judges 6:15).

Repeatedly, God promises to be with Gideon (vv. 12, 16), who struggles to believe. He *knows* that God has promised to save Israel (v. 36), but his doubts haunt him, and he tests God. Gideon can't escape one burning question: *If you really are God, can I trust you?* So he asks God to defy the laws of physics, not once, but twice. Gideon is trying to understand *who God is* and *whether he can be trusted.*

I love Gideon's story because I so badly needed—and still need—to be reminded that it is okay for me to have doubts and questions, to ask God (and others) if I can really trust him. While we are quick to judge ourselves for our doubts, God leans in with patience, tenderness, and assurance. Your doubts, your questions, and the hidden weaknesses you're most ashamed of—those are *precious* to God. More than that, when we ask God questions, he points us directly to his Son, crucified for you and me, and says, *This is how I feel about you, even and especially when you doubt me.*

Prayer: Father, thank you for being gentle with me when I doubt. Help me bring my questions, fears, and doubts to you, and be gracious to me. Amen.

Reflection Question: Do you have doubts or questions about God? Is there someone who loves God you could talk to about it?

Disoriented

CHARLOTTE GETZ

Pilots who are not instrument-trained rely on their instincts and their ability to see the horizon when they fly. But in rough weather, a pilot's senses can get scrambled. If they are not able to use instruments, a pilot might be 100 percent convinced they are pulling their plane higher, when in fact they are plummeting toward the earth and their eventual death—a phenomenon known as spatial disorientation.

This is what happens to us when we choose to trust our own best judgments instead of looking to Jesus. As much as we like to think we know where we're headed, we don't always have the ability to accurately read the horizon. Left to our own devices, we will often believe we've saved ourselves, while in reality we're nosediving toward certain destruction.

This is what's happening in the book of Judges. Sin and disaster in the lives of the Israelites and their leaders (judges) are rooted in their determination to do things their own way. Rather than following the Lord, they do whatever they think is right in their own eyes.

This is often my temptation too. I can be so sure my salvation lies in things like a fit body, the right group of friends, or success in achieving my goals. For you, it may look like getting into a certain college or being invited to a particular party. Our culture (the "horizon") and all our human instincts tell us these things will finally make us feel better.

Our misguided wisdom actually disorients us and leads us into sin. Thank God, there *is* a King in Israel and in our world today—and his name is Jesus. Jesus reorients us to the truth—to wisdom and abundant life. When all our instincts are screaming at us that we're failing, that we're not enough—we can look to the cross, where King Jesus died for our sin to bring us back to him. Like instruments in a cockpit, Jesus restores us with these lifesaving words: "I have loved you with an everlasting love" (Jeremiah 31:3); "My yoke is easy and my burden is light" (Matthew 11:30); "Neither death nor life . . . nor anything else in all creation, will be able to separate us from the love of God that is in Christ Jesus our Lord" (Romans 8:38–39).

Prayer: Lord, remind me that with King Jesus and your Holy Spirit to look to, I am instrument-trained. No matter what my instincts are, your way is better.

Reflection Question: Where have I been trusting my own best judgments instead of looking to Jesus?

Faithful in the Hard Things

SYLER THOMAS

Early in my dating relationship with my wife, Heidi, her mom died in an ice skating accident. There was no warning, no chance to say goodbye. We were devastated and confused. *Why did this happen? Where was God in all of this?* We got engaged a few months later, and instead of a joyous time, the engagement was filled with the heaviness of grief. Despite her overwhelming sadness, Heidi stayed committed to God, and her faith has never stopped inspiring me.

We're moved by people who show faithfulness, despite the challenging circumstances they face. That's what we see in the book of Ruth. We meet here a Jewish woman named Naomi. She escapes a famine in Bethlehem with her family by going to Moab, where her two sons marry Moabite women. After her husband and sons die, she decides to return home.

Naomi urges her daughters-in-law to stay behind, saying that her life has become bitter and the Lord's hand has turned against her (1:13). The hopelessness in Naomi's words encourages me because it's honest and relatable. When life doesn't go the way I want it to, it's easy to wonder where God is.

Despite Naomi's blessing Ruth with encouragement to stay with her own people, Ruth chooses to go with Naomi and to follow Naomi's God. She has no idea what will happen but still entrusts her life to the God of Israel.

The rest of the story is one of God's faithfulness to Naomi and Ruth, as Ruth *just so happens* to meet a man named Boaz, who is her guardian-redeemer, a biblical term for a person obligated to care for a relative in need. Boaz feeds Ruth and Naomi with grain from his fields, buys back all of Naomi's land, and gladly marries Ruth.

Matthew's genealogy lists both Boaz and Ruth in Jesus' family line (Matthew 1:5). When Jesus comes, he redeems not just our tough situations but redeems our souls—once and for all on the cross. When you wonder if God is with you in a difficult time, as Heidi and I did, and as Naomi did too, the cross is the reminder that he was faithful to Naomi and to Ruth . . . and he is faithful to you.

Prayer: Lord, when life gets hard, I wonder where you are. Help me to be honest in my disappointment yet confident in your perfect faithfulness to redeem every difficult thing through the work of Jesus. Amen.

Reflection Question: What are you dealing with today that you know God wants you to entrust to his loyal character?

Waiting on an Answer

KATHERINE PRECHT STINE

Have you ever felt like your grief would never end? I've been there. A few years ago, after surviving cancer and going through chemo as a young mom, we tried to have another baby. After years of waiting, disappointments, and doctor appointments, we finally got pregnant, then quickly miscarried our baby. It felt like the grief would consume me—like I'd never be happy-go-lucky again. My prayers at that time were made up of mostly bitter tears and wordless groans.

This is where we find Hannah in 1 Samuel 1. For years, she has longed for a child and continually prayed, with no baby to show for it. It's not just that she longs to cuddle a precious newborn; in Hannah's time, having a child meant financial stability, a retirement plan, social status, and perceived favor from the Lord. Hannah is desperate, filled with grief. And she takes it all to God.

Rather than trying to pray the "right" prayer or attempting to earn God's favor with good deeds, Hannah is "pouring out her soul to the Lord" (v. 15). She does not hold back any emotion or worry about what others will think. She sounds so distraught that Eli the priest assumes she is drunk.

Jesus also prays in great distress to the Father right before he goes to the cross. He is crying so hard that he actually sweats blood (Luke 22:44). But the key difference in Jesus' prayer is that he willingly endured the punishment meant to be ours because of our sin so we can be with him forever. Jesus "endured the cross, scorning its shame, and sat down at the right hand of the throne of God" (Hebrews 12:2), where he now "lives to intercede for [us]" (7:25).

When God answers our prayers with a yes—as he did Hannah's prayers (and eventually mine as well)—we rejoice, knowing his gifts are just a hint of the joy to come. When we are still waiting, or when we hear a no to our prayers, we fix our eyes on Jesus. We can take comfort in knowing that because Jesus suffered in our place, God is with us and Jesus is praying for us. In the end, God will wipe away all our tears and fill us with joy forever.

Prayer: God, I give you all my anxieties and burdens, because you care for me. Thank you for your loving presence on my hardest days.

Reflection Question: What longing, doubt, struggle with sin, or experience of suffering do you need to pour out to Jesus? Give it all to him, and let him fill you with the hope found only in Jesus.

God Speaks!

ANNA MEADE HARRIS

Whenever I pray, what I really want is for God to respond on a billboard, in large and unmistakable letters. But I would happily settle for a simple, spoken word that I can hear: "Do *this*, Anna, and all will be well."

I envy Samuel in this story from 1 Samuel 3 because he hears God actually speaking out loud. Samuel is a young boy living at the temple, learning to serve God. The priest Eli and his undisciplined sons have abused the priesthood for their own gain, and Israel suffers under their poor leadership. God literally calls Samuel awake in the middle of the night to deliver a message of judgment for Eli and establish Samuel as his prophet. Samuel will faithfully share the word of the Lord with Israel.

Notice three things from this story: (1) After the chaotic guidance of judges and corrupt priests, God mercifully intervenes to give Israel a new leader who will proclaim his word. (2) Samuel is a kid when God gives him important work to do. God doesn't wait until you're a card-carrying adult; he works through people who obediently listen to him (1 Timothy 4:12). Which brings us to number three. (3) As much as we might want to hear his voice, it's hard sometimes to know how to listen to God. He doesn't sit down next to us; he's not on Snapchat. But he still speaks: "In the past God spoke to our ancestors through the prophets . . . but in these last days he has spoken to us by his Son" (Hebrews 1:1–2).

If you want to know what God is saying, look at Jesus. Jesus represents God to us exactly as God is. He sustains communication with us through his Word (Hebrews 1:3) and Spirit (John 16:13). When we read our Bible, God is telling us who he is. Through the life, death, and resurrection of Jesus, God tells us how much we mean to him. The Holy Spirit helps us understand what we are reading, and through the Scriptures, he guides us into all truth.

I tell myself that if God did put up a billboard, I would gladly do whatever he told me to do. In reality, I'd still find ways to justify doing what I want. Remember, God *has* spoken to us clearly, in a sign written larger than any other. Jesus on the cross, giving his life to reconcile us to himself, tells us everything we need to know.

Prayer: Father, help me trust that you say all I need to know in your Word.

Reflection Question: How does thinking about the ways God speaks to you through Scripture impact how you think about reading it?

How Did We Get Here?

JOEY TURNER

Pow! The sound of one student punching the other in the face was louder than you would think. Before the red-faced attacker could continue, I jumped in to break it up. The entire school watched as I hauled both students to the principal's office.

When we enter a story during a traumatic scene, we have to wonder, *What caused this?* In 1 Samuel 4–6, thirty thousand Israelites soldiers have been slaughtered; the Philistines have captured the ark of the covenant (the place of God's presence); and God's priests are dead. What caused this traumatic scene?

To put it simply, bad priests—Phinehas and Hophni. Their dad, Eli, has not disciplined them as he should have. They are sleeping with women who serve at the tabernacle, and they disregard God in their priestly duties. These wicked priests think they can use God to fulfill their desires. As a result, God allows the Philistines to defeat Israel's army and carry off the place of his presence, the ark of the covenant (4:22).

In the ancient Near Eastern culture, one nation's victory over another suggests who has the stronger god. So it appears the Philistines' god is stronger. But 1 Samuel 4–6 proves the opposite. Wherever the Philistines take the ark of the covenant, their people suffer and their gods fall over (chapter 5). God's presence makes them so sick they send the ark back (chapter 6). Even when the ark returns to Israel, God's people need a good servant. The faithful prophet, priest, and judge God raises up in Eli's day is Samuel.

Like the Israelites, we know we are not good enough to represent ourselves or others before a holy God. The good news is we have a greater high priest than any who filled that role (Hebrews 4:14–16), and his name is Jesus—the Savior. The deaths of Phinehas and Hophni were a sign to the Israelites that God was establishing Samuel as faithful prophet and priest. Jesus' death and resurrection is our sign that God has raised up our final faithful priest. We look at the traumatic event of the cross and Jesus' miraculous resurrection and think, *God caused this for my salvation.*

Prayer: God, thank you for Jesus, our good, eternal, and perfect priest. Amen.

Reflection Question: When you are tempted to think you can earn your way to God, how can you look to Jesus as your high priest instead?

Looking like Everyone Else

CHELSEA KINGSTON ERICKSON

As a freshman in high school, I desperately wanted a boyfriend. I had discovered the thrill of boys' attention, and I wanted more of it. Even my prayers became directed toward this goal. The Lord eventually allowed me to have what my heart craved, but it wasn't what I had expected. Along with a rotating cast of boyfriends came anxieties about holding on to relationships—and heartache when they ended. I had allowed something (or someone) else to be king of my heart.

In a similar way, the Israelites approach Samuel, demanding a king like the surrounding nations have. When Samuel asks God for wisdom, God explains that Israel is not rejecting Samuel, but God. You see, from the beginning of creation, God had planned to be his people's only King. Instead of appreciating this unique relationship, Israel wants to be like everyone else. They want a leader they can see with their eyes.

God warns that a human ruler won't ultimately satisfy Israel. Instead, a king will demand the people's labor, requiring the service of their sons and daughters and the use of their livestock (1 Samuel 8:11–18). Yet the people still cry out for a king. So God says he will give them what they want. Even the best kings of Israel's monarchy will bring the people pain; yet even in this, God will use them as part of his plan to rescue the Israelites—and us.

Many generations later, God will send his own Son through the human line of Israel's most faithful monarch, King David. Jesus will be born in David's hometown of Bethlehem. Jesus is the "KING OF KINGS AND LORD OF LORDS" (Revelation 19:16), who comes to bring God's kingdom to earth once more, just as God intended in Eden. Unlike even the best kings in Israel's history, Jesus will sacrifice himself on behalf of the people, dying to pay for all the ways we rebel against his good rule and then rising again to secure his forever kingdom. He is the true King we long for.

Prayer: Lord God, I often look to human relationships to give me security instead of finding my identity and rest in you. Forgive me, and help me look to you as my only King.

Reflection Question: Whom or what are you tempted to put first in your heart above the Lord? What might need to change to help you shift this priority? Ask God for his help.

Looks Can Be Deceiving

MIKE MCGARRY

Have you ever wanted to blend in with the crowd? Blending in is why, after five hundred years of existing without a king, Israel asks God for one (1 Samuel 8:19–20). Israel wanted to be just like every other nation around them.

Saul doesn't want to become king. He has been searching for his father's lost donkeys and has given up. One of the family servants convinces him to consult Samuel the prophet for help finding the herd. What Saul doesn't realize is that the people have been pleading with Samuel to appoint a king. God chooses Saul and tells Samuel to anoint him as the new king.

Saul appears to have the qualities that make him the perfect king for Israel. We read that he is handsome, highly regarded, comes from the elite warrior tribe of Benjamin, and stands "a head taller than anyone else" (9:2).

While these chapters describe Saul as a man who *appears* royal, chapters 9–10 foreshadow trouble ahead. Israel wants to be like everyone else instead of embracing their identity as God's chosen people. And Saul repeatedly pursues his own interests instead of the LORD's. Saul will later even seek to kill God's servant David. He will prove to be a poor leader. God's people will learn that conforming to those around them may feel comfortable in the moment but can leave us disappointed in the long run.

It can be hard to stand apart from the crowd, especially if you don't have other Christians standing with you. It's tempting to blend in with others and to believe that Jesus isn't enough. But conforming to those around you rarely turns out to be the blessing you hoped it would be.

When you're tempted to conform, take comfort in the presence of God, who is with you. Standing with King Jesus means you're standing with the Good Shepherd (John 10:11–18), and he is very good company.

Prayer: Father, help me trust you when I feel insecure about being different from those around me. May I look to Jesus as my faithful Shepherd instead of accepting substitutes that will only disappoint. Amen.

Reflection Question: In which areas do you feel pressured to blend in instead of living by faith? What is difficult about being different from your nonbelieving peers?

The Lord Looks at Your Heart

MIKE MCGARRY

Comparison leads us to remember other people's highlights and our own bloopers or to boost our own egos while looking down on other people. Instead of comparing based on what can be seen and measured, the Lord weighs our hearts.

In 1 Samuel 16, we meet God's choice for a king who will one day replace Saul—the shepherd boy David. The contrast between David and Saul is undeniable. Saul quits searching for his father's lost donkeys; David keeps busy tending the sheep. Saul is taller than everyone else; David is overlooked because he's young. God tells Saul, "Your kingdom will not endure; the LORD has sought out a man after his own heart and appointed him ruler of his people, because you have not kept the LORD's command" (13:14). And David, not Saul, is from the promised royal line of Judah (Genesis 49:10).

God doesn't compare their appearances; he knows their hearts. Both men sin. Saul is rejected as Israel's king because he refuses to repent of his sin. But David confesses and repents, which shows us what it means to be after God's own heart. Although Saul is outwardly impressive, David's heart belongs to God. God sees differently than we do.

Being a person after God's heart doesn't mean you're sinless; it means you repent, or turn away from sin, to pursue godliness. Saul makes excuses for his sin (1 Samuel 13:10–12), but David confesses his sin and pleads with the Lord for mercy and forgiveness (Psalm 51).

If you have trusted in Jesus Christ, your heart is the temple of the Holy Spirit. God has united you with Christ through faith (1 Corinthians 6:19). God's acceptance of you isn't dependent on your ability to keep all of his commands, but on the new heart you've received from him. He has given you a heart that leads you into obedience as you grow to love him more. It also leads you into repentance when you sin, because you know that God is rich in mercy and deals gently with those who love him.

Prayer: Gracious Father, teach me the gift of repentance. Strengthen me to love you and others in a way that honors Jesus. Amen.

Reflection Question: Are you more concerned about being impressive, or are you learning to love God with your whole self?

The Only Way to Happiness

KRISTEN HATTON

Follow your heart. Do what you want, what feels good and makes you happy. This is the key to life, the world says. As a culture, we've embraced this philosophy. Our own personal happiness is our highest aim. Yet studies show as many as four out of every ten teenagers experience persistent sadness or hopelessness.[1] If we're doing what's supposed to make us happy, why are we so *unhappy*?

Psalm 1 tells us why. We see here two types of people, two things to delight in, and two ultimate destinies—life and death. The righteous delight in God's Word and are blessed. The wicked don't and are cursed. According to the psalmist, the wicked are those who reject God's Word and ways. They conform to the world by accepting its advice, acting according to its ways, and adopting its values. They delight in their own ways, believing their choices will bring happiness and life. But in their pursuits, they "are like chaff" (v. 4), which is weightless, empty, and worthless, used only for kindling a fire and then blown away.

On the other hand, the righteous aren't striving. They are at peace, like a tree planted by streams of water. Their contentment, strength, nourishment, and growth are dependent on the living water, which is God's Word. Deep roots securely anchor the tree. Adversity will not knock it over. It will not perish.

While we see a clear contrast between these two types of people, the temptation to follow the way of the world is real. It looks so appealing, and we fear missing out. So what will lead us to delight more in God's Word?

Look to Jesus—the only truly righteous one who was without sin. He not only delighted perfectly in God's Word—he *is* God's Word (John 1:1). By taking our sin upon himself, he walked in the counsel of the wicked and stood in the way of sinners for us. He hung on a tree in front of scoffers so you could sit in his assembly as righteous. If you want to be happy, to experience true contentment and lasting joy, delight in him and receive life.

Prayer: Lord, help me believe that only you bring life. Give me a hunger for your Word so I will delight in you alone.

Reflection Question: How can God's Word sustain you what you thought would make you happy leaves you empty?

---

1. "Adolescent Mental Health Continues to Worsen," Adolescent and School Health, CDC, November 29, 2024, www.cdc.gov/healthy-youth/mental-health/index.html.

The Bully and the Boy

LUKE PAIVA

In a Greek myth, a man named Sisyphus spends eternity rolling a giant boulder up a hill, only to have it roll back down. Day after day, he struggles to do an impossible task he has no hope of ever finishing.

Have you ever tried to do it all by yourself? To do enough to feel you are worthy of being loved? That is as impossible as shedding the curse of Sisyphus. Praise God, he gives us good news in the account of David and Goliath.

The Philistine army sends a giant named Goliath to bully Israel. He calls for any of God's people to face him in combat. If Goliath wins, God's people will be killed or enslaved, showing everyone that the God of Israel can't save his people. The Israelites look at Goliath and feel paralyzed with fear. Meanwhile, David, filled with the Holy Spirit (1 Samuel 16:13), sees that his hope is not in himself or in earthly tools, but in God alone. David is so young and small in stature that he cannot even wear a soldier's armor. He stands before an enemy no one dared to face. Yet he trusts that the Lord is with him and kills Goliath with his simple shepherd's sling. David delivers God's people as he trusts in God's rescue. This is our hope too.

In Jesus, God has saved his people from our greatest enemy—sin, death, and separation from God. Jesus did not come with earthly fame or power to conquer the Roman Empire; instead, he was born in a lowly manger. He spoke God's truth and offered salvation as a gift. Jesus turned what looked to the world like defeat into victory on the cross.

When we try to overcome fear or perform for the approval of others, our focus is on our own strength. Jesus doesn't ask us to perform. He already loves us. As we trust Jesus, he renews us and restores the loving relationship between us and the Father. You can rest. Your place is secure in Christ.

Prayer: Father, give me eyes to see that you are with me in every circumstance. Help me believe that my strength to stand and fight comes from you alone.

Reflection Question: What boulders are you pushing up a hill that you can surrender to God in trust?

Safe and Secure

KATHERINE PRECHT STINE

When you feel insecure, where do you look for reassurance? When I was in high school, I thought security would come from getting a college scholarship, a boyfriend, and the "ideal" body size. For you, it may be something different—like getting the lead part in the play, the baseball championship ring, or entry into a friend group. But do any of those things actually make you feel secure?

Whenever I've tried to find my security in something or someone other than Jesus, it inevitably failed to meet all my expectations. Psalm 16:4 says those who run after other gods (or idols) will suffer. Isn't that the truth? When I've tried to make good things God has given me (like achievements or relationships) into ultimate things, I'm robbed of the joy of that gift and still feel insecure.

This psalm reminds us of the one who is all we need—the Lord, our living hope. All good things come from him. The only way to be completely secure and eternally filled with joy is in the presence of God (v. 11) made possible for us through Jesus. While we were trapped in sin and unable to save ourselves, Jesus died to bring us into relationship with him.

Romans 8:38–39 says that nothing can keep us from God's love: "I am convinced that neither death nor life . . . nor anything else in all creation, will be able to separate us from the love of God." Even when our idols fail, even when we mess up big-time, even when we face scary situations, we can be completely secure in God's love for us: "With [the Lord] at my right hand, I will not be shaken" (Psalm 16:8).

Remembering that the Lord is with us fills us with joy. Remembering that God gave us everything we need in Jesus helps us trust him to continually provide for us. When we feel alone or in danger, we can remember his promise to "not abandon" our souls (v. 10). This is the humble submission of making the Lord "my portion and my cup" (v. 5). When we find our security in the finished work of Jesus and walk daily with him, we can say with the psalmist, "My heart is glad and my tongue rejoices; my body also will rest secure" (v. 9).

Prayer: Father, you are my refuge, my portion, and my cup. Thank you for reminding me that in you, I am always secure.

Reflection Question: Recall a time when you realized that Jesus is better than any earthly thing you might be tempted to seek for security.

No Need to Do Great Things for God

DANNY KWON

Before an elected politician takes office, the government often holds a swearing-in ceremony. The politician takes an oath or makes a pledge to serve their constituents faithfully and do their best for them.

In 2 Samuel 7, we find David anointed as Israel's new king in a kind of spiritual swearing-in ceremony. But instead of David making a pledge to the people, God makes a sacred oath to David and his family. This oath is called the "Davidic covenant"—God's promise to establish David and his offspring on the throne of Israel.

At the beginning of the chapter, we read that David wants to build God a house. While David is living in a palace, God's presence dwells in a tent—the same tabernacle from Moses's days (vv. 1–2). But surprisingly, God commands David *not* to build him a house. Instead God promises to build *David's* house, meaning he will establish David's royal family line forever. God explains that one of David's descendants will build a permanent dwelling place for the Lord. Once again, God is faithful. History depends on God's faithfulness in keeping his promises, not on the ability of human beings to keep ours.

Eventually, David's throne passes to his son Solomon, who builds the temple in Jerusalem that replaces the tabernacle. But God's ultimate throne is established in Jesus, our Savior who reigns eternally and refers to himself as the true temple of God. Luke writes, "The Lord God will give [Jesus] the throne of his father David, and . . . his kingdom will never end" (1:32–33). Luke echoes what 2 Samuel 7 establishes—that God fulfills his promises through Jesus.

Maybe, like David, you think you need to do something for God. But our relationship with God is not about our promises or what we do for him; it's all about what *God* has done for us in Christ. Rather than looking to your own strength, you can put your hope in Jesus. If your faith feels shaky or you feel the need to prove yourself, remember how God kept his covenant promises to David. He will keep his promises to you, through Jesus, our eternal King.

Prayer: Lord, help me believe your Word and know that salvation doesn't come by my strength. I rest in the certainty of your promises in Jesus.

Reflection Question: When are you tempted to trust in what you can do for God rather than what he has done for you in Christ?

One Sin Leads to Many More

SYLER THOMAS

I was talking with some student leaders about sad reality that many marriages end when one of the spouses is unfaithful, when Brandon spoke up. "I'm never gonna cheat on my wife, Syler. She's gonna be so hot, man. I'll never *need* to cheat." Many people think what Brandon thought—that the only thing needed for a successful marriage is finding the "perfect" spouse. Sadly, King David seemed to think his happiness was always just one more wife away.

In 2 Samuel 11, David, who already has multiple wives, notices a beautiful married woman named Bathsheba and has an affair with her, which results in a pregnancy. David goes to great lengths to hide his sin by bringing her husband, Uriah, back from war, hoping that he'll sleep with Bathsheba. Instead, Uriah refuses, declaring that it would be dishonoring to his fellow soldiers who are still in battle. So David sends Uriah to the front lines, where he's killed. David then takes Bathsheba as his (additional) wife.

This "displeased the Lord" (v. 27). So where did David go wrong? He was handpicked by God. He was known as a "man after his [God's] own heart" (1 Samuel 13:14). But here he is, lying, committing adultery, and guilty of murder. David had everything he could have asked for—wealth, women, and the favor of God—but instead of responding to God with gratefulness and obedience, he responded with greed. He wanted *another* beautiful woman.

God has provided everything we can possibly need. He promises to give us "daily bread" for our physical needs, and the Bible says that in Jesus, we have everything we need from a spiritual standpoint. Second Peter 1:3 gives this assurance: "His divine power has given us everything we need for a godly life through our knowledge of him who called us by his own glory and goodness." His gifts begin with the cross, where Jesus purchased our salvation, but they extend to every aspect of our lives. He. Is. Enough.

Today, no matter what tugs at your heart, no matter what the world offers that promises to satisfy, remember that only God delivers on his promise. He is enough.

Prayer: Lord, help me remember that no matter what temptation may promise me, only you satisfy me completely.

Reflection Question: Despite David's sin, God shows him mercy. Do you believe God's mercy extends to the *worst* of sinners?

Lying to Ourselves

CONNIE LEUNG NELSON

There are many ways to rationalize our sins. We can compare our own sin to a "more serious" one so that we feel better about ourselves: "It's just porn. I'm not having sex." Or minimize the sin by painting it in a more flattering light: "I'm sleeping with my girlfriend, but we're going to get married anyway."

Perhaps David rationalizes summoning Bathsheba in the same way. *I am the king, and I have the right to choose any woman to be my wife.*

In 2 Samuel 12, the prophet Nathan tells King David a story of a rich man who, despite having many sheep of his own, steals the only (much beloved) lamb of a poor man to feed the rich man's guest. Angered by the rich man's arrogance, David declares that the rich man should die for his crime. Then Nathan speaks directly to David: "You are the man!" (v. 7). Nathan lists all of David's wrongs, which, of course, God has not failed to see. David's eyes are immediately opened. He is devastated to realize that the person who deserves the justice he is so eager to pronounce is *himself*. In Psalm 51, David acknowledges his sin without excuse and turns to God.

When we rationalize our sin, we are attempting to rebrand it as something less offensive than it really is. We shift the blame because we don't want to admit our responsibility. But here's the problem with trying to make sin reasonable or excusable: We are only lying to ourselves because, try as we might, we can't erase the reality of sin or its effects. Sin is never hidden from God.

In the same way God's words through Nathan opens David's eyes, the Holy Spirit uses God's Word to open the eyes of our hearts too. We can experience God's forgiveness if we turn to him and confess sin as *sin* (1 John 1:9). Don't run away from the Holy Spirit's work by dismissing, denying, or hiding your sin, trying to deal with it on your own. Our sin is no surprise to our heavenly Father, who loves us with a love that's unfazed by any sin we can commit. His love paid the penalty for our every sin at great cost to himself. Surely, our Father waits for us to bring our sin before him so he can both heal and forgive us.

Prayer: Lord, show me my sins so I can lay them before you. Forgive me. Thank you for Jesus, who died so you will always welcome me when I confess my sins to you. Amen.

Reflection Question: What sins do you rationalize or make excuses for? Ask for God's forgiveness and help today.

We Confess; God Forgives

CHRISTINA FOX

I broke my arm showing my sons how to roller-skate. My skates flew out from underneath me, and I ended up flat on my back. When I stood up, my arm hurt really bad. I drove one-handed to the urgent care center. Needless to say, I haven't taught anyone to roller-skate since!

In Psalm 51, David compares the pain of a broken bone to feeling God's displeasure for his sin. David's first instinct was to cover up his sin, but now he offers a prayer of confession to God.

Like David, sometimes we try to ignore or hide our sin. When God shows us our sin, it truly is an act of grace. It may not feel gracious at the time. He invites us to see our need for rescue and cleansing, a conviction that is painful. We may feel guilt, shame, and sorrow. The apostle Paul called this feeling "godly sorrow" (2 Corinthians 7:10). Sometimes we experience painful consequences because of our sin, which makes David's comparison to a broken bone appropriate. But David's psalm also shows us that God cleanses, heals, and makes things right. God shows us our sin, helps us grieve it, and then cleanses us so that we are restored to relationship with him. David confesses his sin to God, and God forgives him. What grace!

We live on the other side of the cross, where Jesus paid for our sins with his own blood. By trusting in him, we receive forgiveness for all of our sins—past, present, and future. "If we confess our sins, he is faithful and just and will forgive us our sins and purify us from all unrighteousness" (1 John 1:9).

If you feel convicted by sin today, rest assured that God loves you. Seek his forgiveness and know that because of Jesus' perfect sacrifice on the cross, you are forgiven. You are cleansed and made new. You can use Psalm 51 as your prayer, thanking God for his grace.

Prayer: Gracious Father, I know I have sinned against you. Forgive me and make me new. Help me rejoice in my relationship with you because of what Jesus has done for me. Amen.

Reflection Question: What do you feel when you have sinned? Where do you see God's grace at work?

Rituals Don't Impress God

KATIE POLSKI

I used to teach high school writing, and each week, I gave a vocabulary quiz. One student consistently took off her shoes before she started the test. When I asked about this, the student said, "Mrs. Polski, that's my ritual. I pray, then take off my shoes. I think my prayers work better that way." My student imagined she could ensure a better end result by taking off her shoes, but that's not how God works.

Second Samuel 15 describes the cunning plot of Absalom to overthrow his father, King David. Absalom's strategy causes David and his officials to flee the city. They take with them the ark of the covenant, where God's presence dwells. David's men pass through the Kidron Valley, where Zadok and the priests set down the ark of the covenant and begin making sacrifices. They are trying to manipulate God into hearing their plea for safety. I imagine they think, *Prayer plus the ark—maybe God will hear us better this way*. David knows the men are putting their hope in the ark to protect them, so he sends it back to Jerusalem and declares that the Lord will do what he will do, whether or not the ark is with them.

Absalom seeks power through deceit, and David's officials seek safety through the ark. We also can fall into believing that certain actions or rituals will guarantee God's favor or a desired outcome instead of completely trusting in God's sovereignty.

As much as we want better outcomes, we cannot manifest an end goal through our own words or meditations, like my student tried to do with her shoes. Instead, God wants us to put our trust in him. God's plan for us is perfect, whether we understand it or not. We can fully and completely trust him. Ultimately, our assurance does not come through rituals but through the finished work of Jesus, who invites us into a relationship with him. He will lead us through every challenge, just as he did for David.

Prayer: Lord, teach me true faith—beyond rituals—as I trust your perfect plan with unwavering confidence in your sovereign love.

Reflection Question: How can you tell the difference between genuine trust in God's sovereignty and using religious practices or objects to manipulate outcomes?

A Father Grieves for His Rebellious Son

LIZ EDRINGTON

Have you ever picked a fight for no good reason with someone who loves you? I'm embarrassed to say I did fairly often when I was a teenager. My mom might use a particular tone of voice or throw out a cliché, and I'd find myself seething with irritation. I'd lob sassy comments or passive-aggressive remarks in her direction. Time after time, she met me with undeserved, patient love. Her heart for me was never deterred by my rebellion.

In 2 Samuel, we read the story of Absalom, a son who rebels mightily against his father, King David. He goes behind his father's back. He gains influence through flattery and deceit. He raises his own army and even declares himself king. His betrayal is massive. He is out for power.

In chapter 18, David prepares for war with his son. As he does, he issues a strong and clear command to the leaders of his troops: "Be gentle with [my son] for my sake" (v. 5). He does not want to see his son killed. His love for his boy is unshakable. So when David's disobedient men kill Absalom (vv. 14–15), David is heartbroken. He weeps in deep grief. His persistent love for his son never stops. He mourns over the consequences of Absalom's sin—over the loss of one he loved. Even though his relationship with Absalom is muddy and complicated, his love is clear. We see David's heart in his statement, "If only I had died instead of you."

God goes one step further by sending his Son to die for us. Jesus sacrifices his life for us in the ultimate act of love. God's determined, fatherly love extends to us when we're at our worst. He isn't put off by our moody apathy, irritated reactions, or outright rebellion.

In our sin, we rebel over and over, telling God we don't need him. We want to be in charge of our own lives. Yet God's love never stops coming for us—no matter how far we run, no matter how terribly we treat God. There is no place his love cannot find us. Jesus' death on our behalf means that his love has the final say over our lives.

Prayer: Lord, it can be hard to believe you love me at my worst. Help me receive your love, and let it transform how I relate to those around me.

Reflection Question: Can you think of a time you did or said something you'd be embarrassed to tell someone about? This is the very place the Lord sees, knows, and comes to you with love.

God Hears Our Cry for Help

LIZ EDRINGTON

Imagine if the adults in Harry Potter's life had actually listened to him. When his cousin bullies him, he has no support from his aunt and uncle. When his life is endangered because someone enters him in the Triwizard Tournament, few believe he didn't enter himself. When he tries to warn people that Voldemort is up to something (over and over again), he seems to receive a resounding "Nah, it's all good." It's exhausting and infuriating to see Harry's struggles ignored and downplayed.

In Psalm 18, we see that God never ignores our cries for help. When David calls to God in distress, he is not met with passivity, deaf ears, or disbelief. Instead, he is *heard* by his God. His suffering at the hands of his enemies is *seen* by the One with the power over all things. What's more, not only is his struggle acknowledged, but the Lord is truly *moved* by his pain. God becomes angry, causing the earth to shiver and the mountains to shake. Then he takes action, scattering David's enemies with arrows and bolts of lightning.

What a passionate, relational God we have! How different would this story have been if David had written down a list of good things he'd done and a list of complaints against his enemy, and then submitted both lists to a judge, who weighed everything out impartially? This would be impersonal and transactional. It would not be reflective of our God, who is both loving and just.

Jesus is the most vivid picture we have of who our God is. In his life, we see a Psalm 18 pattern of heart-level responsiveness time and again. His heart is moved by the horrific grief of a widow who has lost her son (Luke 7:13), by a crowd of starving people (Matthew 15:32), by the death of his friend Lazarus (John 11:33), by the injustice of money changers in the temple (Mark 11:15). Ultimately, Jesus' compassionate heart leads him to the cross, where he gives his own life to bring his people back to him. He is anything but a distant, passive, unfeeling God. He is love embodied as a Person. He is ready to listen and act on behalf of his people.

Prayer: Lord, thank you for seeing and hearing my suffering. Help me believe that your plans for me are good, even when you don't answer my prayers in the way I hope for.

Reflection Question: What makes it hard to bring your struggles to God?

God's Mercy Is Greater

CONNIE LEUNG NELSON

Have you ever read a Bible passage and wondered, *What on earth is going on here?* We might feel that way about David and the census recorded in 1 Chronicles 21. At first glance, David's census (counting the number of men eligible for battle) seems harmless. But in Moses's time, God mandated the census as a way to signify *his* ownership of each Israelite life. Every person counted was to pay a tax—money used toward God's place of meeting (Exodus 30:11–16).

It's unclear why David initiates the census, but in any case, he disregards God and misuses the census, as though Israel's power is for his own personal use. Rightfully displeased, God sends a plague and an angel to destroy Israel.

It can be hard to connect with this historical narrative. The consequences of our sins are rarely matters of life and death, and they're not always played out visibly. Some sins—like cheating on a test or lying to our parents—don't seem so bad if we're not caught. We're tempted to think our sins have no effect. But don't be fooled. God is deeply offended by sin, and the magnitude of the consequence for David's presumption reminds us of this truth. Because we belong to God, we must fight sin, and never mistake the absence of immediate consequences to mean that God isn't bothered by our sins.

Thankfully, there's more to the story. Though God will not tolerate sin, *his mercy runs deep*. God allows the plague to kill only a fraction of the people numbered in the census, and he quickly calls the angel of destruction to a halt (1 Chronicles 21:15). When David cries out to God over the suffering he himself caused, God makes a way for David to offer a sacrifice of temporary atonement for his sin. Because God accepts it, the destruction stops well before it reaches the agreed-on level of damage (vv. 12, 14–16, 27).

Our sins are great, but God's mercy is greater. In his greatest act of undeserved mercy, God gives us his Son Jesus as the perfect sacrifice to atone for all our sin, once for all time (Hebrews 10:11–14). So we can be confident, like David (1 Chronicles 21:13), that God's mercy will always meet us when we've sinned.

Prayer: Father, help me see how destructive my sins are. Forgive me. Thank you for your mercy. Amen.

Reflection Question: Consequences exist to help us learn wisdom. What are some consequences you've experienced as a result of sin?

God Remembers We Are Dust

EMILY MENENDEZ

My friend Grace had the kind of dad I was jealous of—someone who was genuinely interested in us exactly as we were, with no agenda. I remember marveling at how Grace plopped down on the sofa close to her dad, acting as naturally with him as she did with me. With my dad, I felt like I needed to have my stuff together. I was afraid my dad wouldn't love me much if I showed all my cards like Grace did.

As great as Grace's dad was, he was but a dim reflection of the Father we see in Psalm 103. Throughout the psalm, David reflects on God's forgiveness and compassionate pursuit of us, just as we are.

Compassion is a powerful word in Scripture that means much more than God simply feeling sorry for us. The compassion of the Lord is deep empathy compelled to action—empathy with wheels. Throughout the Bible, compassion is most often tied to God's rescue and deliverance of his people in need.

In Luke 15, Jesus tells the story of a reckless son who has made a mess of his life and dejectedly heads home to ask for mercy. "While he was still a long way off, his father saw him and was filled with *compassion* for him; he ran to his son, threw his arms around him and kissed him" (v. 20, emphasis added). This is a picture of radical love that runs toward us in our brokenness.

Jesus is compassion in human form. He took action in the ultimate rescue. Your sin does not surprise God. Jesus lived perfectly for you in every way and has rescued you through his death and resurrection. While you were still a sinner, Christ died for you (Romans 5:8). God knows your frame. He loves the whole, real, messy you! This true Father invites you to respond by trusting him with your life. He "remembers that we are dust" (Psalm 103:14). God knows you are prone to wander away like the reckless son did. He knows you are unable to choose good apart from him; that's why he came. Our compassionate God longs for you to turn to him, and he will draw out the beautiful, unique ways he made you to reflect his image.

Prayer: Lord, thank you for being my perfect Father who runs after me with compassion. Thank you for loving me as I am. Help me trust you.

Reflection Question: In which part(s) of your life do you feel like you need to have it all together? How does God's compassion help you stop trying to measure up?

The Master Artist

MAC HARRIS

I want you to close your eyes for a moment. No, really—close your eyes, take a deep breath, and imagine your *favorite* place in the whole world. What do you see? Hear? Smell? Maybe it's summer camp, a beach, or the spot of a treasured memory. I'm envisioning a stream nestled deep in the Idaho mountains. Wherever you are, breathe it in, soak it up, and turn to Psalm 19.

Psalm 19 highlights the two ways God speaks and shows us who he is—creation and his Word. In verses 1–6, David marvels at how all creation, at all times, proclaims the glory of God. All creation radiates and reflects the immensity, majesty, and creativity of God. Meditating on this reality, the apostle Paul writes that God's "eternal power and divine nature" are on full display in all creation (Romans 1:20). It's often easiest to feel closer to God when we're in the presence of his breathtaking creation. God is a master artist, and he loves to reveal himself to us through his handiwork.

But crucially, the psalm doesn't end there. In Psalm 19:7–11, David pivots and starts talking about God's *law*, about his truth given to us in the Bible. God's Word, according to David, makes us wiser (v. 7), teaches us what is good (v. 9) and warns us of what is bad (v. 11). But surprisingly, God's Word actually *does something to us*. It is a treat that refreshes us (v. 7), brings joy to our hearts (v. 8), and draws back in for more (v. 10).

Throughout the Bible, God clearly reveals truths about himself and ourselves that we wouldn't otherwise know. In the first half of Psalm 19, David uses the generic, impersonal term for God, but from verse 7 onward, he uses the personal covenant name *Yahweh*. David encourages us to look for beauty in the world, to be captivated by God's awesome creative power. But if we want to know God personally—if we want a relationship with the triune God (Father, Son, and Holy Spirit)—we must seek and find him in his Word.

Prayer: Father, I'm grateful you are not a God who hides from me, but rather a God who wants me to know you. Help me want to know you more.

Reflection Question: According to David, why is reading the Bible so necessary? Do you have an adult in your life who could help you grow in reading it for yourself?

Jesus Knows Our Loneliness

DAVIS LACEY

I've always been friends with people who are older than me. This tendency proved to be a double-edged sword in high school. As a freshman, I became close with juniors and seniors. By the time I was a senior, my friends had moved away. For the first time in my life (though not the last), I dealt with inner anguish as I battled feelings of abandonment and loneliness.

Perhaps you are struggling with similar experiences. Maybe you feel deserted because you've never really known your mom or dad. Or perhaps you feel these things because your commitment to follow Jesus has placed you at the margins socially. If so, you may resonate with the words of Psalm 22:7–8: "All who see me mock me; they hurl insults, shaking their heads. 'He trusts in the LORD,' they say, 'let the LORD rescue him. Let him deliver him, since he delights in him.'" As he prays this anguished prayer, King David is facing a danger so intense that he feels as though God has abandoned him.

Loneliness, social isolation, and the accompanying emotions came into the world when Adam and Eve rebelled against God. As soon as sin crept into God's creation, they hid from one another (Genesis 3:7). Humanity has experienced broken interpersonal relationships ever since.

The good news of the gospel is that Jesus lived, died, and rose again to conquer this symptom of sin. In his life, he took our loneliness upon himself as he was betrayed and abandoned by those whom he called friends. He died bearing the weight of our sin, echoing the words of Psalm 22:1. "My God, my God, why have you forsaken me?" (Mark 15:34).

Jesus experienced the loneliness you feel so that you would never be fully alone. Because Jesus died for you, we can trust he will *never* leave you nor forsake you (Hebrews 13:5). He has given you the Holy Spirit to live in you forever (John 14:6). He calls you friend rather than servant (John 15:15). He has made you a member of his family, the church. You are reconciled to God in Christ and given new hope for your relationships with other people. When others forsake you, trust that God does not—because Jesus was forsaken in your place.

Prayer: Jesus, thank you for sharing my loneliness. Give me grace to grasp your fellowship with me and enjoy you in tangible ways.

Reflection Question: Do you know someone who suffers social isolation? How can you share the good news of Psalm 22:1 with them?

The Lord Is My Shepherd

MICHAEL GOLDSTEIN

I was sitting on the balcony of my house when I saw something unexpected—a sheep sprinting through my front yard, followed closely by my roommate yelling, "No! No! No!" My friend had been keeping a sheep in our backyard (long story . . .), and it somehow managed to escape and run into oncoming traffic on one of the busiest highways in Denver. I watched, laughing anxiously, as my friend stopped traffic and brought the sheep back to safety.

In Psalm 23, David compares himself to a sheep when he declares, "The Lord is my shepherd." *Shepherd* is a common metaphor used for God in the Bible. David, the shepherd boy, knew firsthand the qualities of a shepherd that reflect God. Shepherds are caring authorities who guide, provide for, and protect their sheep.

We read in this psalm how the shepherd leads the sheep to green pastures and quiet waters—places of nourishment and rest in stressful, busy lives. Shepherds also defend their sheep from danger. When David lived in the wilderness, he risked his life to fight off lions and bears to protect his flock (1 Samuel 17:33–37). Like my friend, David wouldn't have hesitated to sprint onto a highway to chase a wayward sheep.

Having the Lord as our Shepherd is good news because, like sheep, we often stray from what is best for us (Isaiah 53:6). We are ruled by sin, a power that urges us to resist God's good guidance and run from him to pursue our own destructive decisions. When we rebel and run away, our Shepherd doesn't abandon us to our bad choices. He leads us back to safety and the fullness of his blessing. Jesus says in John 10:11, "I am the good shepherd. The good shepherd lays down his life for the sheep."

When Jesus gave his life for us on the cross, he provided eternal security from sin and death. His sacrificial love assures us that he will stop at nothing to bring us back into his fold. If you have trusted Jesus as your Good Shepherd, you are being led into "right paths for his name's sake" (Psalm 23:3).

Prayer: Lord, you are my Shepherd. I confess I often act like a wayward sheep. I praise you for chasing me down. Jesus, thank you for laying down your life to deliver me from sin and death.

Reflection Question: What is one area of your life where you need to trust God as your loving Shepherd to guide you along the right path?

Waiting with Hope

KATIE POLSKI

I don't like waiting. Whether it's a never-ending red light, a long line at the drive-through, or a delayed text response, I can easily become impatient. In our fast-paced society, instant gratification is the norm.

Because I struggle with patience, I find Psalm 40 so helpful. In this psalm, David waits, but not for something trivial like fast food. Rather, David waits on God to step in and deliver him from deep spiritual and physical troubles. Can you imagine waiting to be delivered from enemies who desire to take your life (v. 14)? Of course, this causes David great emotional turmoil. While it's easy to assume he is waiting in frustration for God to fix his situation immediately, the verse says David waits *patiently*. He expresses a deep longing for God to save him from his troubles, and then he waits, knowing that God is actively present in his hardship. David knows that God will deliver him in his perfect timing.

Our lives are full of difficult seasons of waiting. We ask God to mend a relationship with a friend, and we wait. We ask God to heal us from a disease, and we wait. We ask God to help us overcome a sin, and we wait. So how do we wait for these things patiently?

Patient waiting is waiting longer than expected or desired. In Hebrew, this verse reads, "Waiting, I waited." It asks us to let go of the expectation that what we pray for will be immediately resolved. It certainly might be, but it also might be a longer time of "waiting in the wait." What we can know for sure is that as we wait, God is not indifferent to our worry and pain. He is present, responsive, and attentive to our cries. While we wait on God, he gives us patience.

In Romans 8, Paul describes how we are ultimately waiting for God's redemption through the work of Christ to be complete: "If we hope for what we do not yet have, we wait for it patiently" (v. 25). If we plant a seed in the ground, we can't see it grow at first. We don't give up on what's planted, but we water it and care for it because we are hopeful that growth will come. In the same way, although we can't always see God's answers right away, we trust in hope that he is working. In our patient waiting, Jesus draws near with his love.

Prayer: Jesus, teach me to wait on you with patience. Give me hope in the unseen and draw my heart closer to you as I wait.

Reflection Question: How do you experience waiting? How can you use this time of waiting to grow in your love for Jesus?

You Are Fearfully and Wonderfully Made

REBECCA LANKFORD

Just before I sat down to write this devotion, I caught myself criticizing my reflection in the mirror. I focused on the dark bags under my eyes and the pesky blemishes. But I wonder what God saw? According to Psalm 139, he saw his fearfully and wonderfully created daughter—the one he personally formed and knows with an intimacy beyond comprehension (v. 15).

Male or female, I bet you can relate. You know what it's like to feel unlovable or insignificant. You're positive that people would recoil if they knew what you were *really* like, so you do your best to cover up your messiest parts.

Psalm 139 offers a better way. It shows a God who is acquainted with "all our ways" (v. 3) and yet still calls us his beloved creation. Perhaps it's a little unnerving to consider that God knows *every* single part of you—the hairs on your head, the number of times you've lied, the thoughts you would never consider voicing out loud. And he still loves you. God knows every detail—good and bad—about you, and still, out of his great love, Jesus willingly went to the cross for you. Why? Because you are his. His care for you is intimate and tender right now, as it has been since before you took your first breath.

Even better, because Jesus' death on your behalf has granted you unhindered access to God, there is now no place you can go where God won't be too. You may try to run as far as you can, fearing that God will be disgusted by your real self, but God will still be there (vv. 9–10). Not even the ugliest sin or flaw can separate you from God's love for you (Romans 8:38–39), because he willingly died for the parts of you that make you feel ashamed.

God's Word combats your deepest insecurities with the truth: The most important thing about you is that you are created and loved by God. You need not fear a God who is acquainted with all your ways, for "the things about you that make you cringe most, make [God] hug hardest."[1]

Prayer: Jesus, help me bring my true self to you, knowing how deeply and personally you love me.

Reflection Question: How does it feel to know that God is acquainted with all your ways? What things about yourself that make you cringe can you talk to God about, knowing he loves you in spite of them?

---

1. Dane Ortlund, *Gentle and Lowly: The Heart of Christ for Sinners and Sufferers* (Crossway, 2020), 173.

If You Could Ask God for Anything . . .

CONNIE LEUNG NELSON

What draws you to follow an influencer? Do you seek advice? Want product recommendations? Letting YouTubers direct us to the prettiest lip glosses, show us how to level up in a video game, or teach us how to solve a linear equation is one thing. But what about when we need insightful advice? Sometimes we have questions about navigating relationships between people. Or we may wonder how best to handle confusing, not-black-and-white situations.

Distinguishing between right and wrong (1 Kings 3:9), smart and foolish, is what the Bible calls *wisdom*. Shortly after receiving the throne from his father David, Solomon meets the Lord in a dream. God offers to give him whatever he needs to rule the kingdom, and Solomon's answer is astonishing. Rather than asking for riches or military glory, Solomon asks for *wisdom*. Solomon's request demonstrates a proper understanding of himself. Although he is the honored son inheriting the kingdom of great King David, Solomon reminds God that he is "only a little child" (v. 7). To lay hold of wisdom, we must humbly acknowledge that we always need God, no matter how successful we may be. We are like little children perpetually in need of our heavenly Father's guidance.

Solomon's request also shows that he recognizes wisdom's origin. True wisdom comes from an all-wise God (Proverbs 2:6; Romans 11:33–34), and all other truth must be measured against it. True wisdom reflects God's way of thinking and doing things.

God's wisdom, his way of doing things, is most clearly displayed in the life, death, and resurrection of Jesus Christ to save sinners. The apostle Paul calls Jesus the "power and wisdom of God" (1 Corinthians 1:24, 30). God's way of saving rebellious people through Jesus—a plan that seems foolish and nonsensical to some (1:18)—is actually the ultimate demonstration of God's wisdom. True wisdom begins with believing that you need Jesus' sacrifice on the cross to save you from your sins.

We grow in wisdom as we walk in relationship with Jesus. So we engage with God's Word, trusting that it gives the best direction for our lives. Those who honestly seek God's true wisdom will always find it (James 1:5).

Prayer: Father, give me wisdom in confusing areas of my life. Help me seek out and listen to godly, wise people.

Reflection Question: Whose ideas most frequently influence your choices?

What Is the Fear of the Lord?

STEVE EATMON

When I was a teenager, caps and T-shirts imprinted with the phrase "No Fear" were popular. Fear was (and still is) considered weakness, but fearlessness was cool. Projecting an air that you weren't afraid of anything or anyone garnered respect and popularity among the cool crowd in high school. Despite the popularity of "No Fear" apparel, though, we need healthy fears in order to survive. If we had no fear at all, we wouldn't respect any power or authority. We fear our teachers because they can flunk us; we fear police officers because they can arrest us. How much greater should we revere the power and majesty of the Lord!

Pairing the words *fear* and *knowledge* in Proverbs 1:7 may seem strange, but when it comes to the Lord, they fit. The idea of fearing God may conjure up images of a threatening deity who wants to destroy us or make us miserable. But that's not true of our God; *fear* here is more like awe and adoration. Because we know he saved us when we were still sinners, we gladly worship him (Romans 5:8).

In fact, the foundation of a spiritual life is the knowledge that we are frail and weak beings in the loving hands of an all-powerful Creator. When we're young, we often live like we're invincible, sleeping a few hours a night and surviving on energy drinks. But knowing we are weak and powerless leads us to the gospel. If you feel no need to revere God or fear his wrath for your sin, you'll have no compelling reason to need a Savior. Acts 4:12 reads, "Salvation is found in no one else, for there is no other name under heaven given to mankind by which we must be saved." "No one else" includes you and me. We cannot save ourselves, but Jesus can.

Those who fear God in this way are wise. Fools despise this wisdom and reject instruction, which comes from the Lord. The world bombards teenagers with the message that they can do anything they want, but wise teenagers understand there is a God who made them, loves them, and died for them—and that God deserves their trust. He deserves the reverent fear, wholehearted worship, and adoring love of all of us.

Prayer: Father, teach me to fear you, not as one who may harm me, but as one I revere for giving me life and salvation through Christ.

Reflection Question: What is the difference between the fear of people and the fear of God?

Trusting the Wisdom of God

SKYLER R. FLOWERS

In a song from the movie *Moana*, Moana's grandmother tells Moana that her father doesn't always know best, and while she should pay attention to what he says, she must remember that her "voice inside" is who she is. Echoing the wisdom of this world, Moana's grandmother wants her to believe that wisdom, purpose, and happiness can only be found by listening to her own heart.

Proverbs 3:5 declares that the wisdom of God is the opposite of the world's wisdom. The "voice inside" does not speak the wisdom of God. Biblical wisdom is the art of living faithfully by God's Word in God's world. Biblical wisdom says that in a world created by God, *he alone* shows us the way to live that leads to our flourishing.

The way to live wisely in this world is not always obvious to us. Sin has infected our minds and hardened our hearts (Ephesians 4:18). Our own understanding convinces us that we know the best path, but it leads us instead to pursue fleeting pleasures with no power to guide us into a life of flourishing. Thinking we are wise, we become fools (Romans 1:21–22). According to the Bible, we do not merely need better wisdom; we need freedom from the sin that enslaves our hearts and darkens our understanding. And this can only happen when we give our hearts to the Lord in faith.

At the cross, Jesus paid for our sins and triumphed over the sin in our hearts. When we place our trust in him, our hearts are freed from captivity to the world's wisdom so we may live as God intended us to live. God gives us a new heart and a new understanding (2 Corinthians 4:4–6).

We keep being tempted to think our wisdom is better than the wisdom of the Lord. But when we look at all that Jesus has done for us, we can have confidence that God understands this world better than we do and has our best interest at heart. We can trust and obey the Lord's wisdom, even when it's hard or contradicts our own understanding. We can give him our whole heart because we have seen him give Jesus for us.

Prayer: Lord, I confess that I often think I know best, but I need your wisdom to live in this world. Help me trust you with my whole heart and lean on your understanding, even when I cannot understand it. Amen.

Reflection Question: Why is the voice inside unreliable? Why is trusting the Lord the solution to our lack of wisdom?

The Difference Between Wisdom and Foolishness

JOEY TURNER

What do you get when you mix a fresh Sharpie, a poster board, a cleverly worded question, flowers, and a high school boy and girl? "Promposals," the modern tradition in which a young man comes up with a creative way to ask a young woman to accompany him to prom. It's cute. It's thoughtful. It shows intentionality and, dare I say, some courage.

In Proverbs 9, two women are trying to persuade the "simple" to come to their house. A simple person is naive, inexperienced, possibly foolish or easily deceived. The first woman is named Wisdom, and she sounds amazing. She builds a beautiful house, prepares delicious food and drink, and sets her table in a way that would put Grandma's Thanksgiving decorating to shame. She invites in those who "have no sense" to eat, to leave their simple ways and walk in wisdom instead. This woman represents the practical godliness of living wisely, according to God's Word. The second woman is named Folly (vv. 13–18). She is loud, seductive, and ignorant. She has prepared nothing. She has simply stolen someone else's hard work and pawned it off as her own. Folly represents the foolishness of sinful choices.

The reader is left wondering, *If the invitations sound the same, what hope do I have of avoiding Folly and following Wisdom?* That's just what the text wants you to ask. Proverbs 9 puts us in a hopeless situation so you'll focus your hope on God. Knowing Jesus gives you the hope of growing in wisdom, because Christ is the wisdom of God (1 Corinthians 1:24). In Christ, you have the hope of learning to avoid foolish choices and make wise ones.

Jesus came for those who have chosen Folly's invitation and who know they are foolish. He perfectly chose Wisdom's invitation, and he offers us the greatest invitation of all—himself. Jesus suffered death on the cross, taking on the consequences of sin for a simple person who chooses Folly and promising them a feast prepared by his Father at a better table. The simple person's hope is the Christ who invites us to come and dine with him (John 21:12).

Prayer: God, thank you for sending Jesus, your power and wisdom, to a simpleton like me. Thank you for not leaving me in my folly.

Reflection Question: Jesus himself invites you to follow him. What encouragement does that invitation bring you today?

God's Plans Are Greater

ANNE SANFORD

I had a plan. It made perfect sense to me. As a freshman in high school, I had my next four years perfectly laid out. I would take all the right classes and make the best grades. I would make the varsity volleyball team. I would serve in the most prestigious school leadership roles. And, of course, I would be a leader in my church youth group. Then I would apply for early admission to my dream school, be accepted, and live happily ever after. Imagine my surprise when God had something else (ultimately better) in store for my life!

Solomon wrote today's proverb to the Israelites, a group of people who also seemed to have a plan. They got impatient in the wilderness and thought that heading back toward Egypt would be a good plan (Numbers 14:2–4). They got nervous that God wouldn't provide enough manna, so they thought that storing up more than God dictated would be a good plan (Exodus 16:13–30). They were jealous of the surrounding nations so they thought having a king rule over them would be a good plan (1 Samuel 8:4–22). But in each of these instances (and many more), God reminded them that his plan is always the best plan.

God will always order our steps, and when he does, he directs them toward himself. In my case, I did not attend my dream college, but made godly, fun, lifelong friends at the school I did attend. I have zero regrets that my plan didn't go my way, because God used my disappointment to teach me to trust him in a much deeper way.

We may never see God's full plan until we see Jesus face-to-face. But as we read our Bible and learn to walk with God, we realize our heavenly Father is the perfect planner. He's had a plan and has been executing it since before the beginning of time. There was never a backup plan. His plan has always been to sacrifice his Son to save us from sin and death. We can trust him with our earthly plans. The God who gave everything on our behalf can certainly be trusted to order our steps for our eternal good and for his glory (Ephesians 2:10).

Prayer: Dear Lord, thank you that I can entrust to you my hopes, fears, and dreams. You are good. You are sovereign. You are holy. In your perfect plan, you sent Jesus to bring me to yourself. Increase my trust in you every day. Amen.

Reflection Question: In which areas do you find it most difficult to trust God with your plans?

The Pitfall of Pride

HUEY LEE

I grew up going to church. I was the youth group president, played my guitar for worship, and led Vacation Bible School for several years in a row. Everyone saw me as the "model" Christian. *I loved it.* On the outside, it looked like I had the perfect spiritual résumé. But in reality, it was one of the darkest seasons of my life. I was struggling with serious doubts about the Christian faith and gravely insecure about being a Korean American in a majority white culture. I developed a habit of shoplifting, and I was plagued with an overwhelming sense of shame and guilt that I was too scared to admit to. I felt like I had to keep up my appearance. Then one day—*by God's grace*—I got caught shoplifting, which exposed what I was trying desperately to hide. The fall was hard because I'd built my life on the pride of performance, not on God's grace.

Pride leaves very little room to be honest about the reality of living in a fallen world. Pride preaches a false (and exhausting) gospel of self-reliance. Pride makes it difficult to admit our own weaknesses, to be vulnerable about our shortcomings, and to be needy with God and other people. Pride distorts the way we view ourselves; we prefer to present ourselves as flawless and competent. Ultimately, pride prevents our flourishing because we are designed to be dependent on God and to find our identity in him alone. The good confession of the Bible is that we've been created *by* God and *for* him (Colossians 1:16).

The Bible is refreshingly honest about the trials and temptations that plague our lives, yet one of God's most often repeated invitations to us is, "Do not fear." Therefore, it's okay to not be okay. There's no need to pretend, to hold it in, to suffer alone. The sin of pride has been nailed to the cross, and pride's power has been disarmed by Jesus' life, death, and resurrection. Believers are forgiven and granted access to the throne of grace, where we find mercy and help in our times of need (Hebrews 4:16). The only sufficient antidote to pride is the gospel that sets us free from self-reliance and moves us into lives anchored in all that God promises to be for us in Jesus.

Prayer: Jesus, thank you for being the God of the broken, the weak, and the weary. You draw near to the vulnerable and the needy. Help me not to live as an imposter in this world.

Reflection Question: In which area of your life do you feel the need to be self-reliant? How can you practice healthy dependence before God and others?

Sex Is a Good Gift

SYLER THOMAS

Christians often get accused of a lot of things—being hypocritical, judgmental, anti . . . [fill in the blank]. Sometimes the critique is deserved; other times, it's misguided. Take the issue of sex. Many assume that Christians have too many rules about sex and are afraid of it. That critique could be true of some Christians, but it might surprise you to know there's a whole book of the Bible devoted to celebrating married sex as a good gift from God. Song of Songs is an erotic poem—Can I say this in a devotional for teenagers? I think I just did!—a romantic conversation between a man and a woman who are engaged and then married.

So why aren't we ashamed to include this poem in our *holy* Bible? In his perfect design, God made sex. Sex is holy—that is, it is uniquely set apart for God's purposes. It's a miracle that sex creates human beings *and* that it's a gift God provides for married couples as a celebration of their covenantal union. But the poet also gives a proper warning about sex. In three places, he says, "Do not arouse or awaken love until it so desires" (2:7; 3:5; 8:4). There's a time to embrace physical love, while boundaries for the proper expression of that love are to be heeded. Waiting for the "right time"—marriage—can seem like an eternity, but living according to God's plan will always be worth it in the end.

All Christian marriages point to a bigger story—that of Christ and his bride. In Ephesians 5 and Revelation 19, Christians are referred to as the bride of Christ, being prepared for an eternal union, whether or not we ourselves get married. God wants to have a close, intimate relationship with us, one where we are single-heartedly devoted to him, the kind of commitment that marks a healthy Christian marriage. Singleness points to this same spiritual reality from a different perspective. Single people can be even more fully devoted to our bridegroom, Jesus, and to his kingdom (1 Corinthians 7:6–8).

We were bought with a price through Christ's blood on the cross, which paved the way for us as the church to one day be ready for "the wedding supper of the Lamb" (Revelation 19:9), where we'll enjoy the most perfect union imaginable with Jesus.

Prayer: Lord, thank you for creating me for relationship with you. Help each of my relationships bring glory to you.

Reflection Question: How does the fact that God designed sex for good and holy purposes affect how you think about it?

Boss Woman

ALEXIS ANDRE

The day my parents dropped me off for my freshman year of college, I could not fathom making a home somewhere far from them. I felt afraid, insecure, emotional, and unsure of who I was. Thinking about the days ahead filled me with anxiety. I did not feel much like the "Proverbs 31 woman" I learned about as I was growing up.

In Proverbs 31, a mother advises her son about the "wife of noble character" (v. 10) we presume she wants him to have. This woman that the mother speaks about is undeniably a "boss woman." She is her family's own fashion designer, a real estate guru, a generous giver, a businesswoman, and a mother who is admired by both her children and husband.

The Proverbs 31 woman has all of her affairs in order, so she can "laugh at the days to come." The most noteworthy thing about her, however, is not her "bossness"; it's that she "fears the LORD" (v. 30). The book of Proverbs repeatedly teaches that wisdom and understanding begin with fearing God. This doesn't mean she's afraid of the Lord, but rather that she reveres God enough to order her life after his commands. The wife spoken about here is the woman she is because she has chosen to serve God. She does not worry about the future because she intimately knows the Author who writes her story.

Thankfully, Christ's sacrifice is already written into our own stories. Therefore, even when we do not feel as faithful as the Proverbs 31 woman, we can trust that God's grace will continue to cover us. I had to remember this truth as I sat in my freshman dorm room. My anxieties were valid; I had to get used to a whole new world. However, college life could not be my greatest fear. I had to remember that if I feared the Lord and trusted him when I felt inadequate, he would do the rest.

As God's people, we don't flourish and accomplish what we hope to by accident. The Proverbs 31 woman was intentional about her daily activities, but she was most intentional about honoring God. We have the choice to live in community with God because of Christ. Even when we mess up, Jesus has made it possible for us to run back to God without hesitation (Hebrews 4:16).

Prayer: Although this world gives me many reasons to fear, let my greatest reverence be for you. Amen.

Reflection Question: In what ways do I allow my fear of God to govern my life?

Solomon (Finally) Builds the Temple

MARK HOWARD

It's nice when someone does something thoughtful for you, like sharing their hoodie or unexpectedly paying for your boba tea. But what really makes a relationship special are the intangibles like time spent together, trust, and shared memories. This is the sort of close, intimate relationship God wants with us.

King David wanted to do something for God because of everything God had done for him. So David comes up with the idea of building God a magnificent temple in Jerusalem. But God says no to David, informing him that David's son, Solomon, is the one who will build the temple. What God really wants from David is a deep, covenant relationship, not a building.

Solomon does eventually construct an extravagant temple to replace the tabernacle from Israel's era of wilderness wanderings. The new place of worship symbolizes God's fulfillment of his promise to give the promised land to his people and dwell in their midst. Yet God is still more interested in the relationship than the temple building. What God wants is his people's love and trust. Tragically, Solomon and the people slowly neglect their relationship with God.

In time, God's people begin to care more about the temple itself than God. Still, God doesn't give up on his people. In an effort to shift their priorities, God eventually lets the Babylonians destroy Solomon's temple. It was never really about the building for God; it was always about the relationship.

Centuries later, when Jesus comes to rescue creation, he lets himself be destroyed for the sake of our relationship with God. Jesus dies not only so we can live, but also so we can be adopted into God's family as deeply loved children (Galatians 4:6). One day when Jesus comes again to make all things new, the relationship that Solomon's temple was pointing to will finally be our eternal reality. The whole earth will be filled with God's presence (Revelation 21:3).

While we wait, God has made us mini-temples by sending his Spirit to live within us (1 Corinthians 3:16; 6:19). So wherever you are and whatever you're feeling today, know that you can draw near to God. After all, what he wants most is to be close to you.

Prayer: God, thank you for loving me. Fill me with your Spirit that I may know you are near. Help me draw close to you all my days. Amen.

Reflection Question: What places or practices help you feel God's continual closeness?

A Party and a Warning

KENDAL CONNER

Every time we went on a road trip, my parents warned, "Behave yourself, or we'll turn this car around." I remember thinking it seemed strange: *Were my parents really willing to cancel a trip they had planned and saved for because I misbehaved?*

Second Chronicles 7 describes a grand celebration, followed by a strange warning. The dedication of the temple in Jerusalem marks one of the most spectacular celebrations in Israel's history. After years of prayer, planning, and work, the people have finally completed the temple. Israel gathers to watch God's Spirit fill that place. God is finally living among his people again!

But after the celebration, the Lord warns King Solomon. God promises to answer all those who call on him. But if Solomon falls into sin, God will destroy the temple. After all the planning and work on the temple, will he really destroy it?

The answer is yes. Roughly four hundred years later, God's people have repeatedly turned away from him in sin. So God allows a foreign ruler to destroy his house (2 Kings 24:13) and remove his people from their homes (2 Kings 25).

God gives this warning not because he doesn't care, but because he cares so much for his glory and his people. In the same way my parents were more concerned about the person I was becoming than our vacation, God was more concerned for his people than he was for a place. His temple mattered deeply. Yet the purpose of the temple was always to create a way for God to draw near to his people. This warning shows us that God is willing to make all the necessary sacrifices to bring his people near—even to the point of sacrificing his own Son.

God's people would fall back into sin. But God would send his only Son to fulfill the goal of the temple. He is Immanuel—*God with us*. In Jesus, God's presence dwells fully (Colossians 1:19; 2:9). Jesus taught that he himself is the true temple that, although destroyed on the cross, was rebuilt, or raised from the dead, in three days (John 2:19–21).

Jesus came to restore us to God's presence. When we come to Jesus in faith, our sin no longer has power to destroy. Thanks to Jesus' death and resurrection, God hears our prayers and offers complete forgiveness for all of our sins (1 John 1:9).

Prayer: Father, thank you for sending your Son to bring me into your presence. Help me look to Jesus as my rescuer. Amen.

Reflection Question: How does seeing Jesus as the new temple help you draw near to God in prayer?

What's the Point?

JENNIFER M. KVAMME

So much of life can feel pointless. You finished your homework yesterday; today you have even more. You cleaned your room over the weekend, but it's already a mess. You trained for months for a spot on the soccer team, only to tear your ACL. You've prayed the same prayer every day for years and haven't yet seen an answer. It's easy to wonder, *What's the point?*

If you've felt this, you'll appreciate the book of Ecclesiastes. It's the journal of a teacher (many think it was King Solomon) who spends his life searching for meaning and happiness in lots of places—work, wisdom, wine, women, wealth. But he grows discouraged by the futility he experiences. Sometimes the foolish are rich, the wicked are happy, and the righteous face trouble. Pleasures don't last. In the end, death comes for all.

While Ecclesiastes can feel depressing, I'm glad it's included in the Bible. God knows that life can feel frustrating, unfair, or mundane. Scripture doesn't sugarcoat or ignore the uncomfortable realities of life on earth. Centuries later, Paul writes to the Romans, "We know that the whole creation has been groaning as in the pains of childbirth right up to the present time. Not only so, but we ourselves, who have the firstfruits of the Spirit, groan inwardly as we wait eagerly for our adoption to sonship, the redemption of our bodies" (Romans 8:22–23). As long as sin and its curse infect this world, we face meaningless suffering, frustrating work, and wearying monotony.

But that's not the end of the story. The writer of Ecclesiastes closes his observations on the meaninglessness of life with this: "Fear God and keep his commandments, for this is the duty of all mankind" (Ecclesiastes 12:13). Paul finishes his reflection on the groaning of creation with the call to patient hope, trusting God to complete the redemption that Christ purchased on the cross.

God included Ecclesiastes in his Word to remind us that he gets it. He knows the brokenness of the world and the pain and frustration it brings. But our call remains firm—to fear and follow God, who assures us that in Christ, none of our work is meaningless (1 Corinthians 15:58). The gospel infuses our present, imperfect lives with meaning and offers hope for a better life to come.

Prayer: It's a great comfort to know you understand the frustrations I face. Help me wait patiently for the perfect eternity you're preparing for us.

Reflection Question: What parts of life feel most meaningless, and how does Jesus give them meaning?

Longing for Forever

CONNIE LEUNG NELSON

Making a living through work is a necessity for most people. But money aside, people work for many different reasons. Work helps others, utilizes God-given skills, and can even be enjoyable. King Solomon comments on the purpose of human work: "What do workers gain from their toil?" (Ecclesiastes 3:9). He answers his own question: "He has made everything beautiful in its time."

While human beings work for survival, productivity, or pleasure, God works too. Solomon says that not only is God at work; he also works *to make all things beautiful* in the time God determines. The word *beautiful* here means more than aesthetic beauty; it means complete, whole, and without flaw. Think of *beautiful* in the way that the best stories come full circle—for example, the oppressed, underdog hero grows strong through adversity and later returns to rescue others from the suffering he once endured. The broken being made whole is *beautiful.*

Solomon goes on to say, "He has also set eternity in the human heart" (v. 11). He is rightly observing that human longing—for peace, for good to overcome evil, for perfection, for all things *to be beautiful*—is actually a God-given longing for *eternity.* Human toil aims to fill this longing, but God has achieved, and is achieving, what human beings deeply long for.

"Yet no one can fathom what God has done from beginning to end." Solomon doesn't know when, how, or what exactly God will do to make all things beautiful, to bring eternity about. He doesn't even know what eternity will be like. But he knows that God will do it.

Hundreds of years later, "the mystery that has been kept hidden for ages and generations is now disclosed to the Lord's people" (Colossians 1:26). As God's people, we participate in God's work of the ongoing restoration of the world through our work. One day, eternity will arrive in full, when Jesus returns to eradicate all evil, make the world new, and dwell with us (Revelation 21:1–4). Then all things will be beautiful forever and ever.

Prayer: Thank you, Jesus, for going to the cross so that one day, the whole world will be made right again.

Reflection Question: What aspects of eternity does your heart most long for?

Trusting God with Your Future

STEVE EATMON

Several years ago, my family ate at a restaurant with my older brother, his wife, and their teenagers. My wife and I had to leave early because our kids got cranky and tired, as preschoolers do. Slightly embarrassed about having to leave, I remarked to my brother and sister-in-law, "Aren't you glad you left these years behind?" They encouraged me to enjoy the "little kid years" because they go by so quickly.

As a teenager, you may feel constantly preoccupied with the future: *Where will I go to college? Will I get married? What will I do for my career?* We assume that tomorrow is inevitable and whatever we want is in our control, but Ecclesiastes teaches that no one is immune to the surprises or trials of life. The writer wants us to savor the moments God has given us in the present because only God knows the future.

Knowing how good God has been to us in Jesus Christ means we are free to enjoy each moment in deeper ways. We don't need to fear future hard times or disappointments, because we know that "our light and momentary troubles are achieving for us an eternal glory that far outweighs them all" (2 Corinthians 4:17). Whatever the trial you are facing today—college rejection letters, the loss of friends, your parents' divorce—you can rely on the fact that the God who sent his Son to die for you has promised you a beautiful future with him. We may never end up with what we think we want in this life, but with Christ guiding our lives, we can have confidence in a God who will work in all things, good and bad, for our good and his glory.

Take time to thank God for the blessings he has given you today. If your future is uncertain, pray that God will help you trust him in the waiting. Maybe you're waiting for an SAT result, a decision from your top school, or your crush to accept an invitation for a date. Though we may feel anxiety while we wait and trust, remember this: Even if you don't get what you are looking for, God will use it to make you like Christ.

Prayer: Lord, help me believe that no matter what comes my way, you hold my future. Teach me to seek you, even in trials, because you hold all things together by your power.

Reflection Question: What parts of your present or your future cause you to worry? How can you turn those areas over to God?

Life's True Purpose

ISAIAH A. MARSHALL

In high school, my teammate and I would often strategize before a race. I had a habit of making it all feel more complicated than it needed to be. Running is already hard, but my overthinking only made it harder. Sometimes you just have to get on the line and run when the gun goes off.

In a similar way, life can overwhelm us when we overcomplicate our search for meaning: "For with much wisdom comes much sorrow; the more knowledge, the more grief" (Ecclesiastes 1:18). Reflecting on all his pursuits, the author, King Solomon, concludes that life's true purpose is simple: "Fear God and keep his commandments" (12:13).

To fear God is to revere him, to show respect and awe for who he is. God is our holy, just, and righteous Creator. Reverence for him leads us to pursue him and surrender our lives to him. Yet we often complicate life by chasing temporary things to make ourselves feel valuable and meaningful.

Maybe you pursue popularity or good grades to give you meaning. Maybe it's something else. Jesus warns us that whatever we value most will have a hold on our hearts (Matthew 6:21). When we take good things, like musical talent or a knack for making people laugh, and turn them into the most important thing about us, we make that good thing an idol. An idol is a false god, and it can never give us the meaning we crave.

The author of Ecclesiastes declares that fearing the Lord is the answer to our meaningless pursuits. True meaning and satisfaction are only found in worshiping and honoring the God who created us. The fear of the Lord offers freedom from the dissatisfaction of idolatry.

Who can understand our hearts? Our Savior, who made them to beat for him. Jesus calls you his workmanship (Ephesians 2:10) and invites you to abide in, to live inside, his love (John 15:9). God loves you enough to send his perfect Son to die on the cross for your sins. The pursuit of satisfaction is the pursuit of Jesus himself because he is life (John 14:6) and he alone satisfies (Matthew 5:6). Christ is the solid rock on which we stand; all other pursuits are sinking sand.

Prayer: Lord, help me abide in you and find true satisfaction in your love, not in worldly pursuits. Amen.

Reflection Question: Where have you been searching for meaning in your life? How can you worship and honor God with your life?

Bad Decisions

REBECCA LANKFORD

When was the last time you made a bad decision? Maybe you chose to sleep in too long, making you late to first period. Maybe you decided to accept a drink at a party or to peek at a classmate's paper during a test.

In 1 Kings 12, we read about a *really* bad decision, ultimately leading to the division of the nation of Israel. Years later, this split will domino into the more serious consequence of *exile*, or removal from the land, for God's people.

When King Solomon's son Rehoboam takes the throne, the people of Israel ask him to go easier on them than his father had. Solomon's former advisers tell Rehoboam to *serve* God's people, not place heavy burdens on them (v. 7). Unsatisfied with this answer, Rehoboam consults his peers. Their advice? Bring the hammer down even harder. Rehoboam takes their foolish advice.

A military official named Jeroboam rebels against Rehoboam, igniting a civil war. Rehoboam, the rightful king, rules over what becomes known as Judah (the Southern Kingdom), and the false king Jeroboam rules Israel (the Northern Kingdom). The division of Israel's monarchy weakens the people's allegiance to Yahweh, as both kingdoms pursue idol worship for generations to come until other nations conquer them. Imagine what might have happened if Rehoboam had listened to the wise older men instead of to his peers.

When we make poor decisions, we may wonder if we have thwarted God's good plan for our lives. But verse 15 reminds us that even Rehoboam's poor choice was a "turn of events" from the Lord. Because of God's *sovereignty*, or ultimate authority over the world, he can use even our worst decisions for good. We simply are not powerful enough to get in the way of God's plan.

We see this truth profoundly displayed in the cross of Jesus. In the worst decision ever made, Roman officials sentenced Jesus to a death he didn't deserve. Yet God used Jesus' crucifixion to put an end to sin and death. Jesus is a direct descendant of the line of Judah (Rehoboam's family). He is the culmination of all of God's plans for the redemption of his people (2 Corinthians 1:20). No poor decision or consequence is beyond the scope of God's redemption.

Prayer: Lord, nothing can stand in the way of your good plans and purposes. Thank you that one day, all of my sins and bad decisions will be redeemed.

Reflection Question: Have you made a choice recently that you long to see God redeem? How might he be teaching you through that mistake?

Showdown

DAWSON COOPER

You do you. Live your truth. YOLO. Our culture tells us this is the life of freedom and happiness, and our self-centered selves readily agree. Who doesn't like to call the shots? But what we do and how we do it reflects who and what we worship.

In 1 Kings 18, the Israelites are caught waffling between worshiping the true God of Israel and the culturally cool pagan god Baal as they search for meaning and satisfaction. Yet there is only one God who has the power to change hearts.

God sends Elijah to speak to Israel's wicked king Ahab and to call God's disobedient people back to himself. Elijah calls for a dramatic sacrifice showdown, in which 450 prophets of Baal prepare a bull to sacrifice, while Elijah prepares a bull for Yahweh's sacrifice. Baal's prophets try to coerce Baal to set fire to their sacrifice, but he does not answer. Then Elijah douses his sacrifice with water and prays to God to send fire to consume the sacrifice. God does just that, demonstrating his physical and spiritual power. The people fall to their faces and proclaim how great God is.

Our hearts were made to worship the one true God. But we are prone to follow other gods that claim to bring meaning to life (Colossians 2:8). Like Baal, these are not deserving of our worship and obedience, nor can they deliver what God alone can. The miracle is not just the fire that consumes a water-soaked sacrifice; the greater miracle is that God did not consume the idol-worshiping people but instead changed their hearts.

Only when God changes our hearts are we able to worship and obey him. This should take the pressure off of us. In his goodness and kindness, God pursues and changes us through Jesus' life and death, as well as through the Holy Spirit and Scripture. We see the ultimate demonstration of God's power in the work of Jesus, who turns our stubborn hearts away from sin and toward him—all because he loves us (Colossians 2:13–14).

Prayer: Lord, I confess that I am often like the Israelites, turning to false gods that will never satisfy. Thank you for turning my heart to you. Help me to worship you alone. Amen.

Reflection Question: Where have you seen the Lord pursue you in order to turn your heart back to worship him?

When You Don't Know What to Do

DANNY KWON

Many things in life can make you feel anxious and even helpless. A huge exam or the SATs. A tryout for a team. A band or orchestra performance. Whatever it is, anxiety before a big event is part of life, and there is nothing unnatural about it. Big challenges can make you feel powerless.

Second Chronicles 20 describes a time when the surrounding nations are ready to attack the southern kingdom of Judah. With this impending doom about to befall his land, King Jehoshaphat is afraid—a natural feeling when a huge army is approaching his country. However, the Chronicler says that Jehoshaphat "resolved to inquire of the LORD" (v. 3). Likewise, the people of Judah come to seek the Lord's help.

King Jehoshaphat stands before the people and prays. He acknowledges God as the ruler of all kingdoms and recalls all that God has done for Israel in giving them the land he promised to Abraham. Speaking of the potential disaster about to come on him and his people, Jehoshaphat prays, "We do not know what to do, but our eyes are on you" (v. 12).

What do you do when you feel fearful? How do you handle situations that seem threatening or dark? Jehoshaphat shows how to find hope in the midst of fear when we turn to God in prayer.

The apostle Peter instructs, "Cast all your anxiety on him, because he cares for you" (1 Peter 5:7). Instead of living in worry or fear, we can place our trust in Jesus and give him our anxieties. When we worry, we carry the weight of anxiety. God, who cares for us, wants to lift that burden. In fact, he cared for us so much that he sent Jesus to die on the cross to free us from the penalty and power of sin. Through Jesus, we can relate to God as our good Father and trust him in all things.

When worry paralyzes you, you can borrow Jehoshaphat's prayer: "Lord, I do not know what to do, but my eyes are on you."

Prayer: Lord, help me trust you with my anxieties, even when life is hard. Let me know you are good and that you care for me.

Reflection Question: How can you let your anxiety take second place to trusting the goodness and faithfulness of God?

God Whispers

MARK HOWARD

I used to think that if I tried hard to be good, my life would be easier. But this hasn't been my experience. I've been anxious and depressed; I've faced deep rejection and loss. I expected some suffering in life, but not as much as I've had to endure.

Stories like Elijah's have been a source of comfort for me. Even after God powerfully uses Elijah to raise someone from the dead and to call fire down from heaven, Elijah struggles to trust when life doesn't go as planned. He flees to the wilderness (fear) and asks God to take his life (depression). When God refuses, Elijah complains bitterly about God's apparent lack of power. Still, God doesn't give up on Elijah. After giving Elijah some food and rest, God reminds him that God's true power isn't always found in flashy displays of destruction like a terrible wind, an earthquake, or a fire. Rather, God's presence comes to Elijah in a gentle whisper.

Generations later, Elijah will appear and talk with Jesus on a mountain at the transfiguration, a rare moment when the lines between heaven and earth blur (Matthew 17). I'm sure they had a lot to talk about, like the struggle of preaching to stubborn people and Satan's power to kill and destroy. But most importantly, Elijah could testify to how God's true power is shown in what might look like weakness, and the truth that suffering is *not* the end of the story. Jesus would cling to both truths as he faced crucifixion. And both truths would be on display when Jesus rose from the dead. On that day, God again revealed himself with a whisper as he rolled away the stone from the tomb (Luke 24:1–3).

I wish following Jesus meant that life would be easier—that we would never experience pain or disappointment. But that's not the witness of Elijah, and it's certainly not the witness of Jesus. Instead, they teach us that even in our darkest hour, we can trust that God is with us. He is powerfully at work to bring about new life, even in our weakness. That's a hope we can cling to, especially when life isn't going as we planned.

Prayer: God of the gentle whisper, speak your life and love over me today. Refresh me by your Spirit to follow you, and renew me in the hope of your salvation. Amen.

Reflection Question: If Jesus were standing before you today, what would you want to say to him? How do you think he would respond?

Elisha Gets a Second Helping

MARK HOWARD

If your hero offered to grant you any request, what would you ask for?

Elisha has been traveling with Elijah for years now, and he knows that Elijah is about to die. When Elijah offers to meet one final request, Elisha asks to "inherit a double portion of your spirit." Elisha isn't asking to be twice as powerful as Elijah. Rather, he is requesting to be treated as Elijah's firstborn son, who would get a double portion of the inheritance in that culture. Elisha asks to inherit Elijah's ministry.

"You have asked a difficult thing," Elijah responds (v. 10), for this is something only God can give. Elijah tells Elisha that if he can see Elijah departing, then God has granted his request. By God's grace, Elisha sees the heavenly chariots as Elijah is taken up in a whirlwind. As if to confirm what happened, after Elisha stands by the Jordan River and asks, "Where now is the Lord, the God of Elijah?" (v. 14), God parts the river, just as he did for Elijah. God is now with Elisha just like God was with Elijah. The narrative goes on to show how Elisha receives a double portion in more ways than one. Twice as many miracles are recorded for Elisha as Elijah. Elijah raised one person from the dead, while Elisha raises two.

Some nine hundred years later, John the Baptist became known as another prophet who went "in the spirit and power of Elijah," just like Elisha (Luke 1:17). John would travel to the Jordan River, where he would lead many to repentance, just as Elijah and Elisha did. But Elijah, Elisha, and John the Baptist each point to a greater prophet—Jesus, "the straps of whose sandals I [John] am not worthy to untie" (John 1:27).

When Jesus enters the Jordan at his baptism, the heavens part and a voice declares, "You are my Son, whom I love," and the Spirit descends on him (Luke 3:22). Jesus also calls people to repentance, and through his death and resurrection, he fulfills the hope of every nation by securing our salvation.

Those baptized into Jesus' death and resurrection join in his mission to call people to repentance and faithful obedience to the true God. When we trust in Jesus, we receive the same Spirit to strengthen us as we seek to follow him.

Prayer: God of Elijah, Elisha, and John, help me join your mission in the power of your Spirit.

Reflection Question: What might it look like to point others to Jesus in your home, school, and community?

Happy Ending Guaranteed

ANNA MEADE HARRIS

Confession: As much as I love to read, I do *not* enjoy the suspense of wondering how a novel will end. Sooner or later, I flip to the end of the book so I don't have to worry about how things will turn out.

In our passage today, Elisha's servant anticipates an unhappy ending to his own story. The king of Syria has sent his army to capture the prophet Elisha, and Elisha's servant is terrified to see that they are literally surrounded by hostile forces. But Elisha prays for his eyes to be opened. When they are, the servant sees angel armies filling the hills and knows their victory is secure.

We can trace this theme throughout the Bible: In all things, God is always working for our good, even when we cannot see what he is doing. Think of Joseph, sold into slavery by his brothers, who becomes a ruler of Egypt with the power to save those brothers' lives. Remember Ruth, a widow and foreigner, who remarries and becomes the great-grandmother of King David.

We read of Jesus' road to the cross. Though he had often warned his disciples of his coming death, they could not see that God's plan of salvation was unfolding exactly as he said it would. Because he was both fully God and fully human, even Jesus struggled with the Father's plan. He pleaded, "My Father, if it is possible, may this cup be taken from me," before he prayed, "Yet not as I will, but as you will" (Matthew 26:39). At the darkest moment in history, when all hope seemed dead and buried, God was actively working for our good, even though no one could see it.

Sometimes facing our problems feels like standing defenseless against an enemy army. When you are worried about how things will turn out, don't hesitate to flip to the back of your Bible, where you'll find that God has planned the happiest ending for all those in Christ (Revelation 21–22).

Prayer: Father, in Hebrews 11, your Word says that faith is confidence in what we hope for and assurance about what we do not see. When life is hard, give me faith to believe you are still at work.

Reflection Question: What circumstances in your life seem hopeless today? Ask God to open your eyes to see all that Jesus has done for you.

Unqualified? No Problem

DANNY KWON

Most of us struggle at times with feelings of inadequacy. Maybe you got a bad score on a test. Or you didn't make the starting lineup on your team. Maybe you don't have a boyfriend or girlfriend, and you feel like a loser. Or perhaps someone in your life has made you feel that you are not good enough.

In Isaiah 6, we read about a prophet's personal encounter with God. As Isaiah stands in God's presence, he is having the biggest feelings of not being good enough, and rightly so, because he knows he is a sinner. He proclaims, "Woe is me" (v. 5), because for a sinner (in Isaiah's words, an "unclean" person) to see God surely meant death.

Instead, something wonderful happens. Isaiah describes the Lord on his throne, with robe filling the temple, and seraphim, winged heavenly beings, calling out, "Holy, holy, holy is the LORD Almighty; the whole earth is full of his glory" (v. 3). One of the seraphim flies over to Isaiah with a burning coal from the altar, touching Isaiah's lips, and taking away his guilt.

This scene seems pretty strange. But the angel tells Isaiah that his sins are atoned for. Atonement involves both paying for sin and cleansing impurity so that human beings can come back into relationship with a holy God.

We all share Isaiah's predicament. Because of our sin, we really aren't good enough to be with God. But just as God made a way for Isaiah to be cleansed, he has taken away our sin through the sacrifice of Jesus on the cross. First John 4:10 reads, "This is love: not that we loved God, but that he loved us and sent his Son as an atoning sacrifice for our sins." This atonement came about through the life and death of Christ, which resulted in a restored relationship between God and human beings.

Because of Jesus, we are no longer less than or not good enough before God. Today we can stand before God confidently and boldly through the atonement of Jesus Christ on our behalf.

Prayer: Lord, give me confidence to stand before you without feeling I am not good enough. Thank you for the atonement of Jesus Christ that makes me right with you.

Reflection Question: When you feel you don't measure up, what truth can you remember about Jesus and his atonement?

What's a Plumb Line?

JALYN PORTER MIKELL

A plumb line is an ancient tool still used today. It's a long string with a weight on the end used to determine whether a structure is perfectly vertical, or "plumb." The Lord uses the imagery of this tool as a representation of the standard for righteousness—utter perfection. Through the prophet Amos, God tells the people of Israel that he will no longer tolerate the widespread oppression of the poor among them. God's people are not plumb.

Amos writes to God's people in the northern kingdom of Israel, where idolatry and injustice have become widespread. In Amos and throughout the Bible, we see that God loves justice and hates injustice. The real challenge we face, though, is when *our own sin* is the source of injustice.

Many generations later, Jesus addresses this problem of sin and injustice with the teachers of the law and Pharisees. These religious rulers of his day "do not practice what they preach" (Matthew 23:3). Jesus calls them out for their injustices: "Woe to you, teachers of the law and Pharisees, you hypocrites! You give a tenth of your spices—mint, dill and cumin. But you have neglected the more important matters of the law—justice, mercy and faithfulness. You should have practiced the latter, without neglecting the former" (v. 23).

Jesus is addressing the same challenge Amos faced so many years earlier. God's people are still living in rebellion far from God. Now fast-forward to today. According to God's Word, we are not so different. Romans 3:23 reads, "For all have sinned and fall short of the glory of God." How can we be made right in view of God's perfect justice?

The law of Moses, like the plumb line, shows we're out of line with God's character, but it can't make us right with him. Only Jesus can do that. We can reconcile God's justice with God's grace only when we realize what Jesus did for us: "God made him who had no sin to be sin for us, so that in him we might become the righteousness of God" (2 Corinthians 5:21). Because Jesus is plumb, so are we.

Prayer: Father, thank you for sending Jesus to pass the test that I never could. Lead me to hunger and thirst for your Word and draw near to you all my days.

Reflection Question: Do you have trouble reconciling the concept of God's love of justice with his gift of grace? Why?

Running from God

CAMERON COLE

When I was in high school, a couple in my friend group started dating, which was a fun item of hot gossip. We all thought it was so exciting, and we enjoyed teasing them. Then the girlfriend did the boyfriend wrong. When she broke up with him, she insisted that she just needed a break. However, two days later, she started dating another guy she'd been flirting with leading up to the break. An unsurprising thing happened. The girl who broke our buddy's heart started to avoid our group of friends. In fact, when we saw her at the movies with her new boyfriend, she scurried away. She stayed away from all of us in every way possible.

In Jonah 1, the prophet Jonah plays a similar game, not with a group of people, but instead with God. The Lord calls Jonah to preach repentance to Israel's mortal enemy, the Assyrians. Jonah wants nothing to do with ministering to the Assyrians, so, like our friend, he goes into avoid mode.

Jonah takes the avoidance to the next level. He goes to the port city of Joppa and boards a ship for Tarshish, the farthest known point from Israel in Bible times. One thing to notice is the use of the word *down* in this passage. Jonah travels "down to Joppa," which was south of his home and down below Nineveh on the map. When he boards the ship, he goes down underneath the deck. When Jonah travels down, he goes spiritually downward too. As he resists God and tries to avoid his call, distance grows between Jonah and the Lord.

As sinners, by nature we avoid obeying the Lord. In his law, he calls us to do things that our flesh, or our natural inclination, simply does not want to do. When we resist him, life will spiral downward. We will feel distant from God, our hearts as dark as the cabin of a boat. But in dying on the cross, Christ descended to the depths for us to call us up to God. His grace meets us when we run away. His Spirit has the power to pull us back.

Prayer: Lord, convict me when I am running away and draw me back by your Spirit.

Reflection Question: Where may you be running away from the Lord? How does it feel spiritually in your heart when you run from God?

Praying in the Belly of the Fish

JOEY TURNER

When my grandmother died, she was surrounded by her family just as the sun was setting. She was a great and godly woman, beloved by all of us. We sang hymns, told stories, and offered prayers as she passed from this life into the next—a sacred event. Our hearts were grieving and rejoicing at the same time. The truth is, death visits us all. The only comfort we have in life and death is that salvation belongs to the Lord.

In Jonah 2, we find Jonah in the belly of the fish, crying out to the Lord as if he is as good as dead. The image we get is that he is going deeper and deeper into the depths of the sea, seaweed strangling him, water overcoming him. He is about to enter "the land whose bars closed upon me forever" (v. 6 ESV).

Jonah personifies the Israelites, who would rather run from God's clear commands than see their enemies, the Ninevites, forgiven. In response, God swallows up Jonah, who petitions the Lord from inside the fish. Jonah's prayer from inside the fish is poetic. He cries out to God and affirms what he knows to be true: Salvation belongs to the Lord. These three days in the belly of the fish are a sign to God's people that only God can save the hopeless.

In the New Testament, these three days point to Christ as well. When Jesus speaks of "the sign of the prophet Jonah" to the Pharisees in Matthew 12:38–41, he reveals that Jonah is a type of Christ. This means Jonah prefigures Christ by pointing forward to him. Jonah's three days inside the fish point to the three days Jesus will spend in the grave.

Because we live in the days after Christ has come, we can read Jonah's prayer and see Christ as the fulfillment of that prayer. Like Jonah, we deserve death for rejecting God's word to us, but Christ gets swallowed up instead of us. God uses the story of Jonah to show us himself. We see that our death is swallowed up in the death of Christ (1 Corinthians 15:54), and our salvation is assured in the resurrection of Christ. When death visits us, we can know with confidence that salvation belongs to our Lord.

Prayer: Lord, why do I still fear death so much if death is dead in Christ? Change my heart to say with Paul, "Where, O death, is your victory? Where, O death, is your sting?" Thank you for saving me.

Reflection Question: How would your life be different if you could overcome the fear of death?

No One Is Beyond God's Reach

SKYLER R. FLOWERS

Have you ever known someone so horrible that you think there's no way God can change their life? They are too far gone—too mean, too wild—and they've done too much to turn around now. It's just who they are, and nothing will change that. Have you ever felt that way about yourself?

Nineveh was the capital of Assyria, the great enemy of Israel. They had hurt Israel, mocked Israel's God, and brought many of the people into slavery. There was no way a city like Nineveh would turn from their wicked ways and suddenly trust Israel's God. But God sends Jonah to preach to the city: "Forty more days and Nineveh will be overthrown" (v. 4). Now all that is left is to watch these wicked people reject him and receive their punishment.

But that's not how things go down. A miracle happens: "The Ninevites believed God" (v. 5). Once the message reaches the king's ears, he sets out to ensure that the whole city, top to bottom, from child to adult—even the animals—participate in the repentance. This wicked city turns from "their evil ways and their violence" and seeks the Lord's compassion (vv. 8–9).

While getting swallowed by a fish gets a lot of attention in the book of Jonah, the greater story is that God can change the heart and rescue even those who seem beyond redemption. Later in the New Testament, Paul unveils a stark reality about ourselves. In our sin, we are like the Ninevites. We deserve wrath. We are prone to following the lures of this world, and we are dead in our trespasses and sins (Ephesians 2:1–3). In other words, we have no hope of changing ourselves. But God, who is rich in mercy and full of love, sent Jesus Christ to die for our sins and give us new life (Ephesians 2:4). He calls us from death to life, frees us from our worldly passions, and rescues us from the judgment we deserve.

The story of Nineveh is our story as well. It is the story of the gospel. God's free gift of salvation is extended to all who believe. You are never too far gone to receive God's grace when you call on him in faith.

Prayer: Lord, I often doubt you can forgive someone like me. Thank you for Jesus, who gives me the assurance of your forgiveness. Lead me to embrace the experience of your grace. Amen.

Reflection Question: Is there someone in your life you think could never change? How do we know that God can change even their lives?

Jonah Wants Justice

CLARK FOBES IV

Our modern society puts a high value on justice—the quality of being morally right and fair. It's hard to imagine showing mercy to someone who has committed injustice, so society cancels them instead.

Our own experience mirrors the Israelites' view of justice in Jonah's day. As God's chosen people, they believe they are the rightful recipients of God's mercy, but that Israel's enemies deserve God's wrath. The hometown of some of Israel's worst enemies, Nineveh, is the capital city of Assyria—a kingdom that laid siege to Jerusalem and committed unspeakable atrocities against the Israelites.

Because of this history, Jonah is angry that God has allowed the Ninevites to repent. Jonah testifies to God's mercy and steadfast love, but he doesn't want God to give grace to his enemies. God graciously provides Jonah with a plant for shade in the oppressive heat (v. 6), but quickly takes away the source of comfort through a hungry worm (v. 7), then adds to Jonah's suffering through a scorching wind (v. 8). God uses these experiences to teach Jonah that he gives mercy to all who repent, including the Ninevites and Jonah himself.

Jonah wants a God of justice when it comes to his enemies, but a God of only mercy and compassion when it comes to himself. Just like Jonah, we want to decide who gets God's justice and who gets his mercy. But God is at work to draw to himself all the nations of the world by showing mercy.

In Christ, all of our cries for justice and mercy are fulfilled. Jesus was the recipient of the greatest injustice in human history, bearing the punishment reserved for God's enemies (Romans 5:10). Yet in Christ, we also receive the greatest compassion in human history, as God extends his offer of mercy to all peoples. We should, of course, desire and pursue justice in our world, as we also recognize that we deserve God's justice to fall on *us*. Just as Christ shielded us from God's wrath and covered us with his mercy, so we, too, can give our enemies the same compassion we received from God.

Prayer: God, thank you for being a God of justice and mercy. Help me see how Jesus extended mercy to me for the injustice of my sin. Lead me to identify with those who are suffering and show them my compassion.

Reflection Question: How does Jesus' mercy to you compel you to extend compassion to others?

Why Does a Prophet Marry a Prostitute?

DANNY KWON

In the game Truth or Dare, the group asks one person a question they must answer truthfully, no matter how humiliating the answer may be. The person can choose instead to complete a dare, which can also be something embarrassing, but perhaps less so than the truth. Either way, they may be made to say or do something they may not want to say or do.

God calls the prophet Hosea to do something he would not choose to do—marry a prostitute. At first glance, this may seem like a horrible thing that God has called his holy prophet Hosea to do. It certainly seems scandalous to those who know Hosea.

Yet during the time of Hosea, the people of God are living in sin and unfaithfulness to the Lord. God explains how the people themselves have been acting like prostitutes, worshiping other gods besides Yahweh (v. 2). God calls Hosea to act out God's love for his people, despite their history of forsaking the Lord. Hosea's assignment is specifically commanded for him and designed to compare the people's betrayal of God to promiscuity and unfaithfulness in marriage. The people may be shocked by a holy prophet's choice to marry a prostitute, but how much more shocking is it for them to realize that God loves them despite their unfaithfulness to him!

On the cross, Jesus shows us he loves us, despite the ways we have forsaken him. He makes us righteous (gives us right standing with God) by his blood, even though we have worshiped idols just as the Israelites did. Second Corinthians 5:21 reads, "God made him who had no sin to be sin for us, so that in him we might become the righteousness of God." Christ, who was without sin, made us—unrighteous people who have forsaken God—the very righteousness of God.

Prayer: Lord, help me see that it is by the love demonstrated by Jesus on the cross that I am loved by you—even when I have forsaken you.

Reflection Question: How does knowing the work of Christ help you understand God's love for you?

Mighty God, Prince of Peace

MARK HOWARD

Have you ever been in a hole so deep you're not sure how to get out? Maybe you got fired from your after-school job. Maybe you messed up so badly you worry your parents will never forgive you. Some circumstances feel hopeless.

By the time of the prophet Isaiah, God's people are in a deep pit of their own making. Their sin and betrayal of God, coupled with their selfishness and neglect of one another, have caught up with them. Assyria, the biggest and baddest empire in the area, has Israel in its sights. No wonder Isaiah describes the people as "walking in darkness" and "living in the land of deep darkness" (Isaiah 9:2). But even in the darkness, Isaiah finds hope in God's character. God will not stand by forever and watch his people suffer. He loves them too much. Isaiah clings to a promise that God gives many times in Israel's history—that God himself will provide a Deliverer, a Messiah, who will rescue Israel from its enemies . . . and from themselves.

Isaiah's hope is so certain that the promise is written in the past tense, as if it has already happened. The promise is that a child will be born, a son in the lineage of King David, who in wisdom and power will assume the rule of God's kingdom, bringing a rightness to our relationships with God and one another. Shockingly, this child will also be Mighty God, the One who has an everlasting reign. To Isaiah's first readers, this must have felt like a riddle: *How can this be?*

Centuries later, a child is born in a manger. Jesus is fully human and yet also fully divine. He becomes the light that "shines in the darkness," the light that will never be overcome by the darkness (John 1:5). He conquers the enemy without and within—sin and its effects on our relationships with God, ourselves, others, and the world.

Through his life, death, and resurrection, Jesus secures our peace. One day, when Jesus returns, night will be no more (Revelation 22:5). Even now, in the midst of the darkness, his light can shine in us and through us. So don't let whatever hole you're in overwhelm you. As hard as it is, it will not last forever. Cling to the One who rescues.

Prayer: Wonderful Counselor, Mighty God, Everlasting Father, Prince of Peace, shine your light into the dark places in my heart.

Reflection Question: What might it look like for God's light to shine into a particularly dark part of your life or community?

No Matter How Bad Things Get

LUKE PAIVA

A leveled forest is a heartbreaking sight. Imagine looking out on all the shades of green and brown and the woodland creatures one day. Then the next day, all you see are dead stumps. This is how God's people feel about themselves in Isaiah 11.

We learn from Isaiah that God's people have wandered far from his love and his ways. Leaders are cruel and corrupt; neighbors don't care for one another; and people pursue power and pleasure more than God. As a result, God has let them suffer the consequences of their choices. God has promised his people that a Savior will come from the line of King David, but things have gotten so bad that the prophet doesn't even mention David here. The people feel as though the dead stump of David's father, Jesse, is all that's left. It seems their hopes of peace and redemption are gone forever, but lost hope is never the case with God.

We are not so different from the people of Israel and Judah. We sin against others and are hurt by their sin. We drift from God and lose hope. We are suffering, just like they were suffering. And we have the exact same hope. God has always promised his people that he will be their God and will redeem them, no matter how bad things get.

It looked hopeless, but the Savior came—through the line of David, just as God promised. God is always working in love to save his people. His love cannot be stopped. We must remember that our God "stretches out the heavens like a canopy" (Isaiah 40:22) and keeps our tears in a bottle (Psalm 56:8). He is the same God who came to earth as a helpless infant, who took on human flesh and died for us while we were still sinners (Romans 5:8). He has promised to finish what he has begun and to bring us home (Philippians 1:6). We are never hopeless in Christ.

Do you ever look in the mirror or read the news headlines and feel like things are so bad that all hope is gone? Here is the truth: God never abandons his people, and Jesus' death on the cross proves God's love. He promises in Revelation 21 that he will wipe away every tear and draw us to him, bringing what once was dead back to glorious life.

Prayer: Lord, when I am overwhelmed by my sin and the brokenness of the world, help me trust in your finished work.

Reflection Question: Where do you think you may have lost sight of God's love and promises? Ask him to help you look to Jesus as your living hope.

You Are What You Eat

MAC HARRIS

During my freshman year of college, my mom called to tell me she was concerned about my dietary choices. We both knew I wasn't eating very many vegetables, but she grew worried when she saw my bank statement. "Let me read something to you," she began, silencing my protests. "Bojangles, Chick-fil-A, Chick-fil-A, Bojangles, Tenders, Chick-fil-A . . ."

"Okay, okay, I understand," I mumbled.

"I'm not done! That's just the first few. If you keep eating like this, you'll turn into a chicken!"

Setting aside my fried chicken addiction, my mom's earnest concern that "you are what you eat" echoes a biblical principle, found here in the darkness of 2 Kings 17.

Two hundred years after Solomon's kingdom was split in two, both kingdoms are still rebelling against Yahweh—but the northern kingdom of Israel is particularly sinful. God has repeatedly warned his people that destruction and devastation will overwhelm them if they break his covenant (Deuteronomy 28; 30). Here we find the heartbreaking fulfillment of that warning as Assyria takes Israel into exile, removing them from the land.

In verses 7–23, God explains why he allows such devastation to occur. Israel has repeatedly turned from God's commandments, worshiped other gods, and practiced idolatry of all stripes. Like a stubborn puppy that refuses to listen, the Israelites are "stiff-necked." They aren't just following worthless idols; they have actually become like the idols they worship (Psalm 115)—worthless themselves.

Sound harsh? Instead of "you are what you eat," this chilling warning cautions us that *we become what we worship*. The idols we worship don't really look like carved golden images; they look more like appearance, success, popularity, or something else in which we seek identity. Still, they are just as real, just as dangerous, and just as worthless as Israel's idols. But when our worship is rightly directed toward our Savior, Jesus, we find that we "are being transformed into his image with ever-increasing glory" (2 Corinthians 3:18).

Prayer: Father, help me recognize and repent of the things I prioritize and worship over you, and help me worship you alone. Amen.

Reflection Question: What one thing are you looking to for comfort, security, or significance? Ask God to help you identify and repent of an idol.

Looking for a Leader

KEVIN YI

I had five different youth pastors from sixth to twelfth grade. Even though I had other great youth workers, it was pretty confusing trying to understand what it means to be led spiritually when our pastors were so inconsistent. I felt spiritually lost throughout my teens. The shifts left me questioning, *Who's leading me? What do I make of this chaos?*

At the time of today's passage, the Israelites are experiencing a lack of leadership. Their kings are supposed to reflect God's heart, but many utterly fail to do so. Instead of pointing people back to God, they lead them further away. Spiritually, both the Northern and Southern Kingdoms are wandering. So God sends prophets like Micah to confront the people's sin and call them to repentance. Micah 5 comes right in the middle of all this tension—judgment for their disobedience, but also a promise of hope.

God promises a future King who will be born in Bethlehem, the city of David. Unlike the flawed leaders before him, this King will be different. He won't rule with selfish ambition but with compassion and justice. Micah says this future King will "stand and shepherd his flock in the strength of the LORD" (v. 4). He will bring security, peace, and identity to his people. This King is the long-awaited Messiah, Jesus Christ.

Jesus is our Shepherd King. When life feels unstable or we don't know where to turn, we can rest in the assurance that Jesus sees us, knows us, and leads us. In John 10:27, Jesus says, "My sheep listen to my voice; I know them, and they follow me." He isn't a distant or passive leader. He is close. He knows you deeply. When everything around you feels chaotic or directionless, he invites you to listen—to hear his voice through Scripture, prayer, and the wisdom of the community.

Prayer: Lord, when I'm feeling stuck or lost, remind me of your grace and love. Be my protection, my strength, and my source of belonging in this world. Reassure me that you're with me, and give me wisdom and discernment through your Word. Amen.

Reflection Question: In which area of your life do you feel lost? How can you ask Jesus to shepherd and guide you?

Requirements Fulfilled

PETER ONG

"He has shown you, O mortal, what is good. And what does the Lord require of you? To act justly and to love mercy and to walk humbly with your God." The word *require* can feel like a proving ground, an audition, or a test for a grade. You begin to wonder, *Am I enough?*

The prophet Micah tells the people of Judah about God's requirements for them, which they have repeatedly failed to keep. Instead, the people have acted unjustly toward one another and have worshiped other gods.

Micah 6:8 is a short verse, but it unveils a fullness of God's heart and, dare I say, the deepest desire of his heart for *you*. The verse starts with, "He has shown you . . ." It is God who is showing us "what is good." God's definition of *good* transcends worldly achievements. It's about reflecting his heart.

Act justly means treating others fairly and with dignity, advocating for the oppressed. It means letting what is right guide our interactions, and standing for the unfairly treated. *Love mercy*—oh, this is so important. The world can be a harsh, broken place that uses power to minimize those created in God's image. But in the gospel, God reaches out in mercy to show his abundance of kindness, which he gives to us because of Christ. God fiercely defends the oppressed and also extends mercy to the oppressor. Loving mercy means offering forgiveness, showing compassion, and extending grace, just as God extends it to us. *Walk humbly with your God*—this may be the most challenging of all. Humility isn't weakness; it's strength—putting yourself in a lowly posture to serve out of an overflow of who you are in Christ. No one could ever show more humble strength than Christ as he experienced humiliation on the cross.

God shares these requirements as a heartfelt plea because he loves you and wants you to know his heart, which beats with justice, mercy, and humility. But here is the central anchor for this invitation to follow him: Jesus fulfilled these requirements on your behalf.

A life of faith in Christ is filled with action and love. Act in love, and you will find yourself walking in the footsteps of the One who loves you more than you can imagine. You will know the heart of your heavenly Father.

Prayer: Gracious Father, guide me to act justly and love mercy, reflecting your heart. Teach me to walk humbly with you.

Reflection Question: What do God's commands reveal about him?

Bargaining with God

ISAIAH A. MARSHALL

I was sitting in anatomy class about to take a test I hadn't studied for. I prayed, "Lord, if you help me pass this test, I promise I'll study for the next one." Let's just say, I struggled to keep my promise. Have you ever prayed this type of prayer?

Hezekiah is one of the better kings of the Southern Kingdom of Judah, who trusts God and restores proper worship in the temple. In a moment of crisis, he prays to the Lord for deliverance, which leads to victory over the Assyrian king, Sennacherib (2 Kings 19; 2 Chronicles 32:1–23). The Assyrians are notoriously wicked, torturing their enemies and engaging in the despicable practice of child sacrifice. I imagine Hezekiah is thankful for God's rescue from this enemy.

Fast-forward to today's passage, and Hezekiah is in another crisis. He is at death's door. He prays, and the Lord heals him. But instead of celebrating what God has done, Hezekiah's heart becomes prideful. (It seems that the king and I are not very different.) As a result, God places his wrath—his righteous punishment against sin—on Hezekiah. Overcome by God's wrath, Hezekiah repents and turns away from sin and toward God in humility.

Pride will have us believe we are entitled to God's favor, but in reality we don't deserve it because of our rebellion against him. Yet God gives us the gift of his grace—favor we haven't earned.

The fullness of God's grace was on display on the cross, where God poured out his wrath on his own Son on our behalf. Instead of letting us face the judgment our sin deserves, God sent Jesus to take away the sins of the world (John 1:29).

Hezekiah calls on his deliverer for victory and healing, and God brings victory and healing. You can call on God's name with confidence because of what Jesus has done. Whether or not God answers our prayers the way we hope, Jesus' death and resurrection assure us that he is with us and for us.

Prayer: Lord, you are my deliverer. Forgive me for the times I have sinned against you. Keep me from taking your work in my life for granted, but guide me to humbly accept your grace as a gift. Amen.

Reflection Question: How can you practice humility and thanksgiving in your daily life, recognizing God's hand in all things?

Learning to Love Your Bible

SKYLER R. FLOWERS

I once boasted to some friends in my senior English class, "I just don't think I need to read the Bible anymore. There's not much more for me to understand." Though I projected arrogance, I felt spiritually dry. Am I alone in that feeling?

In 2 Kings 22–23, God's Law was literally lost. Under the wicked king Manasseh, the temple has gone to ruin and the people don't have access to the early books of the Bible. God's people are living without God's Word. The next king, Josiah, begins to repair the temple (22:3–8). Then a remarkable thing happens—a priest finds the book of the law! You know what it's like to find your phone when you lose it, but imagine if your church had lost the Bible for decades. That's what happens here. The people renew covenant (23:1–3), restore worship (23:21–23), and tear down their idols (23:4–7), committing themselves to God's Word (23:3, 25).

Maybe you feel like God has gone silent in your life. But 2 Kings 22–23 reminds us that God still speaks. Nowhere is this more powerfully seen than Jesus Christ, the Word of God, who comes to us in our spiritual dryness and ruin. By his work on the cross, he restores our relationship with God. As we trust in him, the apostle Paul says that together we become the new temple (1 Corinthians 3:16; Ephesians 2:20–22).

God continues to speak through his Word today, even if it is only a faint whisper under the rubble of a stony heart. The Bible once felt dry and distant to me. But over time, through friends and pastors who cherished God's Word and taught it with depth and clarity, his Word came alive to me—even exhilarated me.

You may feel lost and alone, but God's Word is within arm's reach (maybe already on your bedside table). Reach out for God's Word—for the living Word, Jesus Christ—and he will renew you.

Prayer: Lord, thank you for sending Jesus into this world so that I might know you. I confess I have distanced myself from your Word and ignored it. I ask you to bring new life to my heart through the work of Christ. Amen.

Reflection Question: Do you struggle to prioritize reading God's Word? What causes you to set it aside? Think of an adult or peer whom you could ask to hold you accountable.

Wrath and Rescue

CONNIE LEUNG NELSON

If I asked twenty people, "What's going to put an end to the world?" responses might range from climate change to AI. Answers would vary, but everyone would agree that the world is threatened by *something.*

The prophet Zephaniah agrees. He prophesies God's pending judgment over the kingdom of Judah and other nations because of corruption, disobedience, and unrepentance—a refusal to trust in God (vv. 2–3). In justice, God will pour out his wrath and decimate the land (vv. 5, 8).

The same corruption and injustices in Zephaniah's day are present all over the world now. But God has not turned a blind eye to the atrocities that people are committing. He has heard the cries of those who suffer at the hands of evil. With relief, we read that all heinous evil is held under the threat of the day when God's righteous wrath will be poured out in justice (1:14–18; 3:8). But we his people live in the same world where God plans to unleash his wrath. That's like learning a wild tornado is headed to your home address. Read on. God's tone changes in verse 9, when he speaks of how he will treat his people. God's people know they need the Lord to save them (v. 12). God says they will no longer suffer punishment but will be restored to him (v. 20).

We who belong to God do not need to fear the day of judgment. If we are joined to Jesus by faith, God has saved us completely from his wrath (1 Thessalonians 5:9–10). In love, Jesus bore God's wrath on the cross that was due to us for our sins. We are now and forever restored to a right and peaceful relationship with God. Our ultimate destiny is to be brought back *home.*

This home is both now and not yet. It is here now because we are safely hidden with Christ (Colossians 3:3). No wrath threatens us. Instead God sings over us with delight (Zephaniah 3:17). And home is yet to come, when there is no more suffering but only rejoicing, praise, and honor (vv. 19–20).

The hope of the world is not space exploration or green energy; the true hope of the world is that Jesus will return one day to live with us in a new home of his making—the new heavens and the new earth (Revelation 21:1–7)—where everything will be right again.

Prayer: Father, thank you for saving me and for your promise of the best future ever.

Reflection Question: Knowing that Jesus will come again to make everything right, how can use what God gave you to care for others?

Guilt Meets Goodness

KEVIN YI

When I was a freshman in high school, I was bullied by an old acquaintance, who mistakenly thought I had made fun of him. He would intimidate me during our mid-morning breaks, threatening to fight me. Mercifully, after I endured two weeks of nonstop bullying, a friend stepped in on my behalf.

If you've been bullied or hurt, did something inside you cry out for things to be made right? That cry for justice is something God shares. He is not indifferent to evil, and we see this in the book of Nahum. Although the people of Nineveh repented in Jonah's day, their change of heart didn't last. The Assyrian Empire (of which Nineveh was the capital) resumed oppressing God's people. Nahum's message is God's final word: Judgment is coming.

In Nahum 1:2–3, we see the beauty of God's character. He is "slow to anger," which means he gives people time to repent. But he is also *just*. He does not ignore sin that goes on and on. God's goodness resides not only in his mercy; it's also in his refusal to let evil reign unchecked. This is important for us to understand. God's wrath isn't a contradiction of his love; it's an expression of it. Because he is holy, he *must* deal with sin. Because he loves his people, he *must* stand against those who harm them.

We see the intersection of this most clearly when Jesus dies on the cross for us. He absorbs God's wrath and judgment. He clears the way for God's mercy to be fully available when we put our faith in him. This is how we become fully clean and acceptable to God. The cross is God's ultimate expression of both of these aspects of God's character—justice and mercy. God is both a righteous judge and a refuge for those who trust in him. He will not ignore evil forever. And that is what makes him *good*. He is our defender and protector—the one who purifies us so we can walk in freedom.

Prayer: Father, thank you for being just and good. When evil seems overwhelming, help me remember that you see, you care, and you will act. Amen.

Reflection Question: How does knowing that God stands against evil bring you comfort? Where do you need God to purify your life in alignment with his character?

Not Too Young

MAC HARRIS

Relief and exhaustion swept over me as I finished preaching my second sermon ever. As a baby-faced twenty-four-year-old preaching to adults, I felt woefully unworthy and out of place. With sweaty palms and a racing heartbeat, I packed my things and prepared to leave. An older woman stopped me and asked, "Did you forget to shave this morning so you would look older up there?" We both laughed, knowing she saw right through me. My scraggly attempts at facial hair were sadly comical. I couldn't deny the truth. I had intentionally not shaved because I felt *far* too young to be taken seriously.

Despite a direct calling from God, Jeremiah felt too young to be God's prophet. He was likely around your age right now, and God was calling him to bring warnings of God's judgment to his own people in Judah and to foreign nations. Jeremiah must have been terrified.

God hasn't called you and me to be prophets, but he offers us the same comfort he gave to Jeremiah: *Before you were even born, I knew and loved you. You are not too young, for I have called you. You do not need to fear, for I am with you.*

When people tried to shoo away kids gathering around Jesus, he said, "Let the little children come to me, and do not hinder them, for the kingdom of heaven belongs to such as these" (Matthew 19:14). In a letter encouraging his young protégé, Timothy, Paul writes, "Don't let anyone look down on you because you are young, but set an example for the believers in speech, in conduct, in love, in faith and in purity" (1 Timothy 4:12).

There is much wisdom we can and should learn from older Christians. But no matter how old you are, your heavenly Father knows you, loves you, and calls you to himself. There is no age restriction in God's kingdom.

Prayer: Father, I come to you as your beloved child. Give me humility to realize I don't know everything, and confidence to know I am wanted and welcomed. Amen.

Reflection Question: Can you point to a time when you learned something from someone younger than you? Ask an adult or two, "Have you ever learned anything from me?"

Yet I Will Rejoice

CAMERON COLE

Have you ever had a day—or a whole season—where it seems like everything that can go wrong has gone wrong? You got a bad grade on your math test. Your girlfriend broke up with you. You saw a post with all of your friends out to dinner and you weren't invited. Or maybe things were even worse. You found out that your grandmother has cancer. Your parents fought yet again. Your family is tight on cash already, and now one of your parents lost a job. In these times, a massive, dark cloud and a sad, depressed mood hover over your life.

The book of Habakkuk outlines a conversation between the prophet and the Lord. One piece of bad news after another comes to Habakkuk's ears until he feels utterly distraught. The Lord reveals that Israel's worst nightmare will come true. God will respond to Israel's unfaithfulness by sending the terrifying Babylonians to conquer his people.

In the face of extreme misfortune and sadness, Habakkuk laments to the Lord. He does not pretend everything is fine. He compares his people's current circumstance to a time when the fig trees won't bear fruit, the fields can't grow food, and the stables are empty of livestock.

In other words, Habakkuk is saying that things in Israel are as bad as they can possibly get. But despite these deeply disappointing circumstances, he declares, "I will rejoice in the Lord; I will take joy in the God of my salvation" (3:18). In choosing to focus on the Lord and his salvation even in the midst of disaster, Habakkuk finds joy. He remembers, "God, the Lord, is my strength; he makes my feet like the deer's; he makes me tread on my high places" (v. 19). A choice to praise God on his worst of bad days leads to a restoration of hope in his heart.

When you encounter terrible days, both of the normal variety and those that are tragic, I encourage you to be honest with God. Tell him how sad and disappointed you feel. Remember, though, that in that sorrow, the God of your salvation can restore hope in your heart as you praise him.

Prayer: Lord, I'm frustrated and sad about these things in my life. Yet I praise you as the God of all hope who can refresh my sorrowful heart.

Reflection Question: What are the attributes of Jesus' character that can enable you to praise God in times of disappointment?

Our Good King Is Coming

MARK HOWARD

Disappointment never feels good, but its sting is particularly painful when the person letting you down is someone who should take care of you, like a parent, teacher, or pastor.

The prophet Jeremiah knows this pain well. He is living under the reign of some of Israel's worst kings and religious leaders. Despite his faithfulness to God's call on his life, Jeremiah spends his life hated, maligned, and persecuted by those who should be seeking his good. The failure of Jeremiah's leaders (the kings in David's line) results first in the destruction of his home and Judah's exile to Babylon. It doesn't seem fair, but in this world, the sin of those in power can have devastating consequences on others. But in God's grace, the worst parts of the story are never the last part of the story. Through Jeremiah, God gives a promise for a future king who would rule with wisdom, goodness, and justice. This king will be a righteous Branch (v. 5).

Being called a "branch" may seem weird, but we often encounter trees at key moments in the Bible. Trees are in Eden. Noah's ark is built from trees. Moses's staff is crafted from a tree, and trees feature in the descriptions of both the tabernacle and temple structures. Trees become a reminder of God's persistent and gracious desire to give us eternal life with him in heaven, first declared for Adam and Eve (and humanity) through the tree of life in Eden.

So maybe it's not surprising that God gives Jeremiah the hope of a Branch King who will become a source of new life. What *is* surprising is that the righteous Branch is ultimately nailed to a tree and killed by the religious leaders, the bad shepherds of his day. Yet in his death and resurrection, Jesus becomes not just a Branch, but the true Vine in which life is found (John 15:1–5).

Parents, teachers, and pastors have an important role to play, but they are not the source of true life. Only Jesus, the true Vine, is the source of true life, which we graciously receive when we are connected to him by faith. So cling to him. As you receive new life from the righteous Branch, you can bear the fruit of goodness and justice in this world.

Prayer: God of life, help me cling to you that I may receive your life and love and bear fruit for your kingdom.

Reflection Question: What in your life needs healing as you draw new life from the righteous Branch?

God Has Plans for You

ANNA MEADE HARRIS

"'I know the plans I have for you,' declares the LORD, 'plans to prosper you and not to harm you, plans to give you hope and a future. Then you will call on me and come and pray to me, and I will listen to you. You will seek me and find me when you seek me with all your heart.'" As you read these wonderful words, don't separate the first sentence from the next two. It's easy to believe that God is promising a kind of "good luck in this life," so we miss the greater good he has planned for us.

In Jeremiah 29, some of God's people have been carried off from Jerusalem and are being held captive in pagan Babylon. They are wondering how God's promises for them will ever come true. Prompted by God to send them an encouraging letter, Jeremiah tells the first of the exiles that in seventy years, God will bring them home to the land of promise (vv. 1–10). But the even greater good is found in verses 12 and 13: God promises his people that when their troubles lead them to call on him in prayer, he will listen.

Almighty God listens to what *you* have to say. He cares deeply about your thoughts, needs, worries, hopes, and confessions. What's more, if you seek him—talk to him, read his Word, sing his praises, spend time with Christian mentors and friends—you will find him. You need this reassurance sometimes. Maybe your family moved to another state and you can't find a single friend to eat lunch with at your new school. Or your parents are divorcing and you wonder if your family will ever be happy again. Perhaps you pour out your heart to God or read your Bible into the wee hours of the night and you still question whether God is listening. You may feel like God is playing hide-and-go-seek instead of making himself known.

Take heart! Although we are encouraged to seek God, Jesus has already come looking for us. In Luke 15, Jesus compares himself to a shepherd who loves one lost lamb so much that he leaves ninety-nine other sheep to look for the lost one (vv. 3–7). Jesus took on human flesh to seek and find *you*, to give *you* hope and a future—glorious fellowship in eternity with him.

Prayer: Father, thank you for seeking me, even when I feel lost and discouraged.

Reflection Question: What makes it hard for you to seek God?

Everything Changes but God

SKYLER R. FLOWERS

In many ways, change defines the teenage years. Your classes change each semester, and with them, your homework load, friend group, and sports team or other extracurricular activities also shift. Change happens so often and so fast that it may feel like you're sailing a wide ocean in a tiny boat. One day the waves are calm and life feels stable, but then the wind picks up and everything you know is out of balance.

The prophet Ezekiel knows the feeling, as he is among the exiles being taken into captivity in Babylon. They have been taken from their homes, from their city, and, most importantly, from their place of worship. The exiles must have wondered, *With everything changing, will God stay with us?*

God answers Ezekiel through stunning visions. But for the modern reader, the visions are more than a little confusing. How do all these odd images answer the exiles' question? Consider the imagery. The whirlwind, clouds, and lightning symbolize the arrival of God's whole presence (vv. 4, 24). The multifaced creatures speak of God's rule over all creatures (v. 10)—humans (human face), wild animals (lion face), domesticated animals (ox face), flying animals (eagle face), and heavenly beings (cherubim). God speaks from above as they move over the face of the earth like an army (v. 24). Ezekiel sees God, riding on a chariot across the earth, symbolizing his power and authority over all things.

When storms rock your boat, it will be easy to wonder if God has left you. Ezekiel's vision shows that God remains powerfully with us. Nothing can defeat him, change his plans, or stop him. God will remain committed to his people. Here's what is even more stunning: This powerful, awe-inspiring God remains so committed to his people that he took on human flesh. Jesus is the ultimate answer to the question, *Will God stay with me?* Amid change, Jesus is God with us (Matthew 1:23). He remains committed to us through all the chaos and change that life brings. He gives us peace in the midst of fear, anxiety, expectations, and the unknown through his stable, powerful, loving presence.

Prayer: Lord, I praise you for your power and majesty. Thank you that in your power, you draw near to me and are always with me, even when everything else is changing. Amen.

Reflection Question: What changes are you facing right now? How can God's presence bring comfort?

Eat My Words

KENDAL CONNER

Anyone who posts on social media knows the threat of rejection that comes with putting yourself out there. One "thumbs-down" or mean comment can overshadow a hundred likes.

Imagine what Ezekiel feels when God calls him to be his messenger to Israel (Ezekiel 2–3). Israel has already rejected God's warnings, which has led to their current exile. Yet even though they rejected God, God has not abandoned them. Instead, God has a new message, and he asks Ezekiel to deliver it—even knowing that many will reject it (2:5, 7; 3:11). God hands Ezekiel this message in a scroll and tells him to fill himself with the words by eating it (3:1–3). Wait, *what*? This symbolism suggests that God wants Ezekiel to receive the message as much as he wants him to share it with Israel. Knowing the message is one of warning to Israel, Ezekiel assumes the words will be bitter. When Ezekiel obeys and eats, however, he finds the words taste "as sweet as honey" (3:3).

God's words are more than a warning. They are a promise of redemption. God is making a way of salvation for Israel—and for Ezekiel—not because they are worthy, but because God is. This is why God tells Ezekiel not to be afraid of the people's response (2:6). Most will reject his words, but he is to speak anyway, because some will hear (2:5, 7; 3:11). Proclaiming God's message of redemption is worth Ezekiel's feeling the temporary sting of rejection.

Centuries later, God sends his own Son, Jesus, to Israel, knowing many will reject him (Mark 6:4). Counting the cost of the suffering he would face, Jesus laid down his life so that we might be redeemed.

Now God calls us to deliver his salvation message (Matthew 28:18–20), knowing that proclaiming his redemption is far greater than feeling the world's rejection.

Prayer: Father, thank you for redeeming your people. Give me courage to speak your words, no matter the cost.

Reflection Question: How does this story in Ezekiel 2–3 encourage you to speak God's words in faith?

Carrying the Team

VINCE GREENWALD

Have you ever seen an athlete put the team on their back? Only the best players can do it, like Michael Jordan, Caitlin Clark, and Patrick Mahomes. The player thinks, *I guess I'll just have to do this myself*, then isn't a sentimental pity but a profound emotional response single-handedly brings the team back into the game, doing everything necessary to ensure victory.

In Jeremiah 31, the armies of Babylon are bearing down on Jerusalem, yet no star player emerges to deliver Israel. Defeat is all but certain for the Southern Kingdom. Rather than giving Israel victory on the battlefield, God speaks through his prophet Jeremiah, promising eternal victory through the new covenant.

A covenant is a sacred agreement between two parties, a personal and permanent promise. But this new covenant in Jeremiah's prophecy is unique among others in the Old Testament. It includes three promises: (1) God will write his law on the hearts of his people; (2) his people will *know* him; and (3) their sins will be forgiven and remembered no more. God had not messed up in his previous covenants with his people, but his people had failed to stay faithful. They had gotten themselves into this mess, and they were being punished for it. Who would put these people on their back and accomplish the new covenant promises?

At the Last Supper, Jesus explains to his disciples, "This cup is the new covenant in my blood, which is poured out for you" (Luke 22:20). In the life, death, and resurrection of Jesus Christ, our sins are forgiven; our hearts are made new and stamped with his law; and we truly know God as Savior and friend.

The great news of the new covenant is that God puts us on his back to accomplish it. God doesn't just give instructions; he writes them on our hearts. God doesn't ask us to climb a ladder in order to know him; instead, he sent his Son to earth for us. God doesn't ask us to pay our own way; he paid the price for our redemption himself.

Prayer: Thank you, Lord, for forgiving my sins, for writing your law on my heart, and for helping me to know you—not because of my half-hearted efforts, but because of your loving-kindness.

Reflection Question: How can these new covenant promises give you hope?

God Is Never Surprised

CHELSEA KINGSTON ERICKSON

At the end of 2023, the United Nations' agency for refugees estimated there were nearly *120 million* displaced people worldwide.[1] The displacement of so many people made in God's image is one of the most significant crises of our time.

Second Kings 25 reveals one of the saddest moments in Israel's history, when God's people are forcibly removed from the land he has given them. The Babylonians burn Solomon's temple, destroy the city walls, and carry the people into exile. The Southern Kingdom of Judah falls, and with it the pride and joy of Israel—the city of Jerusalem and its temple.

It's difficult to grasp the national and spiritual significance of this event, but it is monumental in the ancient world. The Babylonian victory represents defeat and disgrace for Israel. But God is not surprised. He has warned of a coming exile if Israel continues to worship other gods (Jeremiah 25), and he has a plan for what he knew was coming. He has pledged to send a Savior who will rescue his people despite their sin and rebellion. That Rescuer is none other than Jesus Christ.

Many years later, the apostle Peter would speak to the early Christians, referring to them as "foreigners and exiles" (1 Peter 2:11) because they trust in Jesus in a crooked world. Peter explains that as Christians suffer for following Jesus, we can look to his sacrifice for our sins on the cross: "When they hurled their insults at him, he did not retaliate" (v. 23).

The Bible is not naive about the suffering we face—whether others mock our faith in Jesus, or brothers and sisters become refugees. God understands our condition and theirs. Jesus, too, was a refugee, who fled from Israel to Egypt (Matthew 2:13–18). He was mocked, spit on, and treated like an outsider. Jesus endured these things in order to save us from sin. And one day he will rescue all who trust in him, bringing us to our true home with him.

Prayer: Lord, you have drawn near to my suffering by sending your Son to die and rise again for me. Help me trust in you when I face persecution and when I see others suffering.

Reflection Question: Take a few moments to lament (express grief and sorrow) about the world's suffering to the Lord, knowing he will one day make it right.

---

1. "Refugee Data Finder," UN Refugee Agency, accessed December 22, 2025, www.unhcr.org/refugee-statistics/.

Be Honest with God

SYLER THOMAS

Do you and your friends like to watch postapocalyptic movies? Think *A Quiet Place*, *Maze Runner*, or even *Wall-E*. Some kind of apocalypse has left the world decimated, and not many people are left.

That sense of picking up the pieces after a time of destruction is the background for the book of Lamentations. It was written by an anonymous author (many believe it was the prophet Jeremiah) after the Babylonian siege of Jerusalem and subsequent exile of God's people to Babylon. Lamentations opens with the depressing line, "How deserted lies the city, once so full of people!"

The first four (of five) chapters are written as an acrostic poem—the first letter of each line begins with succeeding letters of the Hebrew alphabet. The highly organized acrostic structure stands in contrast to the disarray of Jerusalem, and the book is a lament (it's right there in the name), which is a particular kind of song/poem expressing sadness about a situation.

Amid the desolation, faith is side by side with sadness. So we see honest questions like, "Why do you always forget us?" (5:20) directly next to "You, Lord, reign forever; your throne endures from generation to generation" (5:19).

This kind of honesty in sorrow accompanying a desire that God will move in power brings me comfort. Our world is full of tragedy, disappointment, and defeat. It would be confusing if God's Word ignored that? It'd be hard to trust a Bible that pretended life was painless and easy, when our experience is often the opposite. God's Word shows us he knows what it is to live in this world.

We are reminded here that God's faithfulness never runs out, but rather is brand-new every morning. Jesus demonstrates this hope in God amid his sadness. On the night before he would go to the cross for our salvation, he pleaded with God to provide another way. His anguish caused him to sweat *blood*. Yet he trusted in God, praying, "Not my will, but yours be done" (Luke 22:42).

No matter what you're going through today, Scripture assures you that (1) God wants you to be honest with him, no edits, and (2) he wants you to trust him. Each and every morning, his mercies are new. He is with you and for you.

Prayer: Lord, help me remember in the midst of whatever difficulty I face today that your faithfulness is great and your mercies are always new.

Reflection Question: Are you encouraged when you see expressions of sadness in the Bible next to those of God's faithfulness?

When You're Worn-Out

ASHLEY KIM

We often think rest is right around the corner. When we sit in class, we watch the clock. We wait for the weekend, summer break, or graduation, telling ourselves that once that day comes, so will our rest. And that day of rest does come—but so does Monday. The work begins again. Are you tired of the cycle? You're not alone.

In Isaiah 40, God speaks to his people in exile through the prophet Isaiah, who lived nearly two hundred years earlier. The people of Judah have been captured, plundered, and carried off to unfamiliar territory. They have lost so much and don't know when, or if, it will end. *Will the royal line of Judah see the promised land again? Is Israel lost forever? Has God given up on us?* Day by day, it becomes harder to find hope.

It is to these exiles—powerless, poor, weak—that Isaiah writes. Weariness will not have the last word. God promises strength to endure, but not by vanquishing their captors nor by numbing them to their pain. Rather, he promises strength to those who hope in him. Isaiah calls his readers to direct their hope toward the promise of a future Messiah. Our hope is also fixed on Christ. The writer of Hebrews encourages his audience, "Let us run with perseverance the race marked out for us, fixing our eyes on Jesus, the pioneer and perfecter of faith" (12:1–2). It can be challenging to know how to persevere. How do we find the strength to continue praying when we don't see an answer? To share the gospel with friends who don't want to listen? To pursue a deeper relationship with the Lord when we feel apathetic?

We fix our eyes on Jesus. We remember that he is the pioneer and perfecter—the one who begins and completes every good work in us and for us. Just as the exiles didn't know if they would ever see Jerusalem again, we often don't know when seasons of weariness and suffering will end. But we do know this: The Lord promises, in his faithfulness, to grant us strength for today and bright hope for tomorrow.

Prayer: Father, thank you for your faithfulness. You have promised to make all things right and to be with me as I wait. Help me to hope in you today, that my strength may come from you and not from myself. Amen.

Reflection Question: What feels most wearying in your life, and what would it look like to hope in the Lord?

God Sticks with Us in the Hard Times

ISAIAH A. MARSHALL

When I mention water, what comes to mind? Maybe lying on the beach and watching peaceful waves lapping the shore. Fire? Maybe sitting by a crackling fire on a winter night. The warmth of the fire brings calm, and the sound of the waves gently rising and falling brings peace. But water and fire can also be dangerous.

In Isaiah 43:1–2, the prophet warns that water consumes and fire burns, but he also reminds us that God is Lord over both. God says to the rebellious people of Judah, "You are mine." He is a holy God, perfect in all his ways, and yet he offers peace and protection for imperfect human beings. He communicates his commitment to them, saying, "I will be with you." God comforts a defeated people who live under foreign domination, telling them, "Do not fear." Why? Because the God who created them is *with them*, bringing them peace and protection.

When they pass through the waters—in other words, the chaos of life—it won't sweep over them because he is the same God who parted the sea (Exodus 14). When they go through the fire of judgment and trials, they won't be burned because he is the same God who protected Shadrach, Meshach, and Abednego in the fiery furnace (Daniel 3). But here's the problem: When we walk through challenges, we're prone to lose hope because we forget where our help comes from.

Our God is an all-consuming fire (Hebrews 12:29), but to those who trust in him, he brings life, calmness, and protection. His commitment is crucial as we live as exiles in a world that does not worship him. The same God who formed us in his image, redeemed us through his Son, and called us to himself is *with us*. When we put our trust in him, we find peace, even in life's storms. So will you trust him today?

Prayer: Lord, thank you for your presence and protection. Help me remember that no matter the challenges I face, you are with me, guiding me through the waters and the fire of life. Amen.

Reflection Question: What challenges are you facing, and how can you trust God's presence and protection?

Wounded for Our Healing

LIZ EDRINGTON

When I was six months old, I had surgery on my left foot for a club foot deformity that would have made it nearly impossible to walk. My parents entrusted my tiny body to the hands of a surgeon. He had to cut into my skin and to saw into my bones to make things better for me. He actually had to wound me to bring about a better reality. We don't often consider how surgery wounds before it heals. We generally just imagine what it will be like after we've recovered and simply forget about the process.

God often uses methods that seem backward to us to bring healing. We see this with God's people in Judah. They have been exiled for not following God's ways. Obedience would have allowed them to thrive. Instead, they have worshiped false gods (idols) that they've become enslaved to. Their hearts are entangled and in need of rescue.

Why couldn't God blaze onto the scene and blow up all the idols? Then he could grab his people and bring them back to the land and they'd finally be free! Or would they? In God's wisdom, he knew his people were made for more than physical rescue. They needed a total overhaul of their hearts to be able to experience real freedom, which could only come through a perfect sacrifice for their sins.

God's way of healing his relationship with his people was counterintuitive. Strange, even. Jesus' crucifixion would have looked like weakness and defeat to his followers. It would have felt like the Enemy, Satan, had finally won. Yet by allowing himself to die—to become the perfect sacrifice for our sin—Jesus truly turned death on its head. He opened the way for love to heal not only our relationship with God but with ourselves and one another as well. Not by his triumphant military might nor by his gifts for teaching and leading, but *by his wounds* we are healed. His *vulnerability* invites us into life-giving, identity-securing, love-filled relationship with the One who made us. Just as with the surgery I had as a baby, wounding was the process used to bring about a better reality.

Prayer: Jesus, thank you for giving up your life for me. Help me to trust you with my wounds.

Reflection Question: What wound in your life might God use to bring healing?

Too Good to Be True?

ANNA MEADE HARRIS

On the first day of school, your chemistry teacher says that everyone in the class will master lab reports by the end of the year. If you're like me—bad at science—you'll think the teacher is slightly delusional. That promise sounds way too good to be true.

When Jesus stands to read Scripture in his hometown of Nazareth at the beginning of his ministry, he reads this passage from Isaiah (see Luke 4:16–30). He then sits down to teach (as teachers did in his day) and declares to the worshipers, "Today this scripture is fulfilled in your hearing" (v. 21). In other words, Jesus says, when Isaiah wrote those prophetic words, he was talking about *me*.

The crowd gets excited and then angry. After all, they argue, Jesus is just Joseph's boy who has been making some pretty strong accusations about their unwillingness to believe. Of all people, how can *Jesus* be the Anointed One, the promised Messiah who fulfills all these glorious promises? His claims seem too good to be true. Yet Jesus can do absolutely everything he says he can do.

Because Jesus begins his ministry with these promises, we can consider Isaiah's words as Jesus' mission statement. *This is what Jesus came to do for us*:

Jesus is Messiah, the Anointed One, who will save his people (Matthew 16:16).
Jesus heals the brokenhearted (Psalm 147:3).
Jesus frees sin's captives (all of us) to walk in the light of obedience (1 John 5:7).
Jesus comforts those who mourn and blesses them with joy (Matthew 5:4).
Jesus offers us his beauty, taking the ashes of death and destruction in our lives. (Matthew 5:3–10)
Jesus stirs our hearts to praise, replacing our despair (Acts 16:25).

If all these things seem too good to be true, look at the empty tomb. Jesus has the power to defeat death and live again forever. He can fulfill every one of these promises in your life. This is "his incomparably great power for us who believe" (Ephesians 1:19).

Prayer: Jesus, I believe you can do what you say you can do; help me overcome my unbelief.

Reflection Question: Which of God's promises in our verses above do you most long to see fulfilled?

A New Heart

DAWSON COOPER

We all love getting something new—new Nikes, a new dress for homecoming, the latest *Madden NFL* video game. We enjoy the thrill of using our purchases—that is, until the next best thing comes along.

God's people who are exiled in Babylon while Jerusalem lies in ruin are in need of something new too. Beyond an improved living situation, the Israelites need a renewed relationship with the Lord their God. They are not only physically separated from the land God has promised, but they are spiritually distant from the life of worship their holy God requires.

God's people have begun to look, act, think, and worship like the culture surrounding them. They no longer look "set apart" as God has designed. This new look is not one that God can abide. God graciously says he will first cleanse his people from their uncleanness (sin), and then he can address their hearts. The natural state of their (and our) hearts is so dire that it calls for a full transplant of a new heart that leads to a new life. This new life should look like worship in all facets of life—work, play, and home—and set them apart once again from the surrounding culture.

New things often have a high price because they are just that—new. A new heart and life that is reconciled to God cost God his only Son. God's promise in Ezekiel to cleanse, regenerate, and send his Spirit foreshadows Jesus' life and death. Despite our uncleanness and because of his great love for us, God sent Jesus to die on the cross for our sins—past, present, future.

In Jesus Christ, we are made new (2 Corinthians 5:17). Our old heart and life do not have the final victory. Our new life in Christ is our secure reality. Its newness will never fade away. When we are in Christ, we are promised that which Ezekiel speaks of—God's Spirit. By giving us a new heart and the Holy Spirit, God equips us to live in the power and hope of Christ.

Prayer: Lord, thank you for sending Jesus to die for me while I was still a sinner, cleansing me fully so that your Spirit might dwell in me. May the joy of a new heart in Christ eclipse all other new things in my life and satisfy me deeply.

Reflection Question: How does a new heart in Christ provide a foundation amid life's changes and trends?

The Valley of Dry Bones

REBECCA LANKFORD

In the spring, the buds on the large cherry tree outside my apartment window transform into a glorious shade of pink. In the winter, though, the tree is dark, barren, and lifeless. It's hard to comprehend that any bright buds could emerge, but there they are.

Ezekiel addresses exiles living in Babylon—those who are hopeless, homeless, and far away from the presence of God and the temple in Jerusalem. Their situation is bleak and barren, much like a dead tree in winter. These exiles desperately need the reminder that even in the hopelessness of their exile, God is working to bring forth new life.

Imagine how Ezekiel feels looking out at the valley of dry bones. Can you imagine anything more lifeless? And yet these deaf bones hear the life-giving word of the Lord, and through his Spirit, they come to life! The Lord's resurrecting power transforms the dead bones into "a vast army" (v. 10). God uses this vision to show that the people of Israel will one day rise from their graves and return to their homeland. For God's people, all hope was not lost.

We all have valleys of "dry bones" in our lives—an ongoing conflict with a parent, a chronic illness, or a sin struggle you can't seem to win. Yet Jesus offers the hope that nothing is beyond his redemption. This sure hope is tethered to the historical reality of his own resurrection from the dead.

The dry bones are a mere shadow of Jesus' resurrection. God displayed his power over the forces of sin, death, and evil when he raised Jesus from the grave after his death on the cross. God's Word promises that when we place our trust in him, we, too, will be resurrected and brought to new life with Jesus. We can be sure that "if the Spirit of him who raised Jesus from the dead is living in [us], he who raised Christ from the dead will also give life to [our] mortal bodies" (Romans 8:11). We may not see all of our hopeless situations fully restored in this lifetime, but the day will come when we will enjoy the fullness of resurrection life with him forever.

Prayer: Jesus, thank you for the miracle of bringing life out of death. You alone are able to redeem even the bleakest circumstances. Help me wait on your resurrecting power to work in my life.

Reflection Question: What "dry valley" are you experiencing in your life right now? What does Jesus' resurrection and victory over death mean for you?

The Day Justice Wins

CAMERON COLE

In 1963, four Ku Klux Klan members planted an estimated nineteen sticks of dynamite in the basement of the Sixteenth Street Baptist Church in Birmingham, Alabama. It was youth Sunday at the church, and at 10:22 a.m. children were attending Sunday school or preparing for the worship service. A massive explosion killed four young girls and left a fifth blinded. In the face of this atrocity, the victims' families had to wait twenty years for the murderers to be brought to justice.

Coping with outrageous injustice and evil in the world is profoundly challenging. Stories like this church bombing rightly make us angry. Will justice and goodness ultimately prevail?

The Jews experience these feelings toward the Edomites during the Babylonian exile. The Edomites, who are essentially cousins of Israel, have stood by and watched as the Babylonians carried the Israelites away. Verse 11 says they "stood aloof" while the Babylonians committed injustice. Some even believe they assisted the Babylonians in conquering the vulnerable Jews.

The Israelites feel wronged by the Babylonians and betrayed by the Edomites, and there is nothing they can do about it. They desire justice—a good, godly desire that they cannot satisfy. But through the prophet Obadiah, the Lord promises his people a day of vindication. At Christ's second coming—the day of the Lord—Jesus will right all wrong (Revelation 19). He will bring justice for all the evil that seems to have slipped through the cracks.

I'm sure you desire justice for wickedness you've seen on the news or learned about in history. I'm also sure you've been wounded by the sins and wrongs of others that feel as though they've gone overlooked. Know that God sees all of the injustice in the world. You may not witness justice accomplished in this life, but you can trust that the Lord sees all evil and will bring it under judgment in the end. Goodness will prevail.

Prayer: Lord, the evil in the world breaks my heart. I am often tempted to live with bitterness. Jesus, fill me with your Spirit so that I can trust in your justice and live with hope.

Reflection Question: What wrong do you see in the world that breaks your heart? How does the promise of justice at the second coming give you a sense of peace and hope?

God Wants to Live with You

CHELSEA KINGSTON ERICKSON

Is there someone who makes your home feel safer and more complete? Maybe it's your grandmother standing at the kitchen stove. Or a parent saying good night at bedtime. Or a sibling who looks out for you.

Just as our homes are shaped by the presence of people we love, Israel was marked by God's presence in their midst. The whole point of God's forming them as a nation was so that he could dwell with them personally. This is why he had instructed Moses to build a moveable tent (called the tabernacle), which Solomon's temple later replaced. But Israel's ongoing idolatry results in God's glory leaving the temple (Ezekiel 10), shattering Israel's sense of security and identity—just as the loss of a family member can shatter our sense of home.

Still, God does not abandon his rebellious people. He gives Ezekiel a vision of the new temple (Ezekiel 40–43) and of God's glory coming to fill it once again. While the temple is rebuilt when the exiles return to Jerusalem (recorded in Ezra and Nehemiah), there is, sadly, no indication that the Lord's glory has returned. That is, not until God comes as a person—Jesus, who comes to dwell with us.

The apostle John beautifully expresses this when he uses a Greek word (*skenoo*, meaning "to tabernacle," or "to dwell") that evokes the tabernacle in Exodus. "The Word became flesh and *made his dwelling* [*tabernacled*] among us. We have seen his glory, the glory of the one and only Son, who came from the Father, full of grace and truth" (John 1:14, emphasis added). In spite of our sin, we encounter God's glory personally through Christ.

Jesus refers to his own body as the new temple (John 2:21). Not only that, but Jesus gives the gift of the Holy Spirit, God's presence with us (15:26; Acts 2). We who follow Jesus are being built into "a spiritual house" (1 Peter 2:5), the true and lasting temple in which God's presence will dwell forever.

In whatever you are facing, take heart. God has promised you his eternal, glorious presence. He is with you, now and forever your truest home (John 14:23).

Prayer: Heavenly, Father, thank you for sending Jesus and giving the Holy Spirit to dwell in me. Help me find my comfort and security in you.

Reflection Question: Is it hard to believe that God is with you now and forever? Talk and pray with a godly adult this week to help you in your struggle.

God's Goodness Guaranteed

JOEY TURNER

It was evening when the youth group arrived back at the hotel from their day of volunteering. Suddenly someone said, "Where's Johnny?" Looking around in panic, the leaders realized they had left a student behind. They found him back at the facility, waiting quietly. When the leader apologized, Johnny said, "I knew you'd come back. I wasn't worried." Johnny had assurance. He trusted his leaders would come back and get him.

In Daniel 2, God gives Daniel and all the exiles assurance of the future victory of his kingdom. Daniel lives confidently among Babylonians, who worship other gods and eat foods that are forbidden to Israelites, because Daniel has the assurance of his leader, God himself. Daniel trusts in God's faithfulness, and he lives faithfully for him in Babylon, a spiritually dark and lonely place. Daniel shows us a life lived with confidence in God.

The context of Daniel 2 reveals the Babylonian king Nebuchadnezzar has a dream that none of the wise men of Babylon can interpret. What they cannot do, Daniel, the man of God, can do, because God reveals the dream to Daniel. God shows Daniel that God will establish a kingdom that will reign over all nations forever.

Just as Johnny trusted that his leaders would return for him on that dark night, Daniel follows God joyfully in dark Babylon because he trusts that God will keep the promise he has made to his people through Nebuchadnezzar's dream. You can look back at the birth, life, death, resurrection, and ascension of Christ as your assurance that no matter how dark life seems to be, God's kingdom has come. You can *know* he will come again to make all things new. Just as confidence in God's faithfulness enabled his people to live faithfully in exile, we have the assurance of our victory in Christ to live faithfully in the present.

Prayer: Father, sometimes I feel so alone and out of place in this world. Even though you have given me the greatest assurance of all, I still get afraid. Forgive me and help me embrace a right understanding of my life in this world and the confidence I have in Christ. Amen.

Reflection Question: In which part of your life (family, school, friends) do you need to be reminded of Christ's current reign and his promised return?

The Chain Breaker in the Fiery Furnace

ANNA MEADE HARRIS

When you get right down to it, no movie, comic book, or video game can deliver a storyline more thrilling than that of the Bible. And God's stories are *true*.

In Daniel 3, we see the struggle between an epic ego and a humble faith. King Nebuchadnezzar builds a ninety-foot statue of himself and commands everyone to worship it. Shadrach, Meshach, and Abednego refuse. Even though the penalty for defying the king means they will be roasted alive, these men assert that either God will save them from the fire or they will die. Either way, they will not break the first commandment: "You shall have no other gods before me" (Exodus 20:3).

Enraged, Nebuchadnezzar orders soldiers to bind these men and throw them in the furnace, which burns so hot it kills the soldiers. Gazing into the flames, the king exclaims, "Look! I see four men walking around in the fire, unbound and unharmed, and the fourth looks like a son of the gods" (v. 25).

Unbound, unharmed, and . . . someone has willingly joined them in the fire. Bible teachers call this a *Christophany*, meaning that Jesus himself, before he was born, visibly appears in order to help or instruct God's people. We know this is going on because Nebuchadnezzar calls it: The fourth man looks like "a son of the gods." The fourth man is *the* Son of *the* God—Jesus.

We also know it's Jesus because he is doing what Jesus does throughout Scripture. He is with them—and us—in the fire, just as he promised he would be (Isaiah 43:2). He breaks the chains of sin and oppression and sets these men—and us!—free to walk with him, even in the fieriest circumstances (Psalm 107:14; John 8:36; Acts 12:7). When he was born as a baby, Jesus willingly joined the human race in the furnace of this world, and when he laid down his life on the cross, he shattered the chains of death for us forever.

Like me, you may look at the three men and think, *I would never have the courage to obey God like that.* While their obedience is remarkable, it's not the reason God helps them. He helps them because they need the help that only he is powerful enough to give. He will gladly do the same for you.

Prayer: Jesus, thank you for walking with me, even in the fiery trials I face.

Reflection Question: What chains do you need Jesus to break for you?

The Peril of Pride

KATIE POLSKI

Elizabeth Holmes was nineteen when she founded the company, Theranos, a healthcare corporation that claimed to have developed life-altering blood-testing technology. As her wealth grew, so did her pride. She dismissed influential people who warned her to investigate some of her unreliable products. Ignoring their advice, Holmes deceived investors to hold on to her wealth. It didn't take long for her failures to result in criminal fraud charges. She allowed power and money to distort her judgment, resulting in personal devastation.

In Daniel 5, King Belshazzar's wealth and power blind him to his arrogance toward God. He throws a huge party that uses special cups stolen from the Jerusalem temple. Suddenly, a mysterious hand appears and writes a message on the wall. Belshazzar panics. He calls in his advisers, but no one knows what the message means. Finally, the queen suggests that he call Daniel, knowing his ability to interpret dreams.

Daniel interprets the message with God's help, but it's not a good one for the king. "Mene, Mene, Tekel, Parsin" means God is about to take Belshazzar's kingdom from him. Blinded by his arrogance and disbelief in God, Belshazzar ignores the message and continues with his party. Later that evening, he is killed, and his kingdom is quickly divided.

Pride is dangerous. It can cause us to think too highly of ourselves, damage relationships with others, and make us justify our sin. Desire for success is good, but allowing pride to guide our ambition will hurt us and others. As we seek success, whether in school, sports, dance, or another pursuit, we must remain open to wisdom from godly people. People who've walked with God for years are often the tools God uses to help us focus on his glory more than our own.

When we confess we've been blinded by pride, God graciously forgives us. Jesus shows us what humility looks like. Though he is the Son of God, he did not boast in himself. He humbled himself and became obedient to death on the cross (Philippians 2:5–8). Honor God by living for him and giving him all the glory in your success today.

Prayer: Lord, help me recognize my pride and seek humility. Guide me to honor you and listen to godly counsel. Amen.

Reflection Question: How can you identify moments when pride influences your decisions? How can you remain open to godly counsel?

The Better Way

CHARLOTTE GETZ

My son has become obsessed with the song "Your Way's Better." The singer is searching for the world's treasures until his head hurts, only to discover there is a better way.[1] The point? No matter what "the world" offers—popularity, a starring role, a college acceptance letter—God's way is better. That's a hard pill for me to swallow. Maybe for you too.

Daniel knows God's way is better. "An excellent spirit was in [Daniel]. . . . He was faithful, and no error or fault was found in him. . . . He had trusted in his God" (vv. 3–4, 23 ESV). His ability to interpret dreams has elevated him to second-in-command, which angers the other officials. They convince the king to sign a law punishing those who pray to any god or person except the king, hoping Daniel will break the law. He does and is thrown into a den of lions. The next day, when the king rolls away the stone, he finds Daniel unharmed.

Why didn't Daniel just skip his prayers that week? He could have prayed in private. But no. In broad daylight, right in front of his window, Daniel kneels and prays. He doesn't care about his position in the court or even whether or not he lives.

It would be easy to walk away from this story with the message that God rescued Daniel because of how faithful he was—be more like Daniel!—or that God's "way" is a set of rules to follow. But Daniel is not responsible for his own rescue. He says so himself. "My God sent his angel and shut the lions' mouths" (v. 22).

This is a story about the God who delivers. It points to another stone that was rolled away, another person who should have been dead found improbably alive. Unlike Daniel, Jesus was abused and torn apart so that you and I—prone to be *un*faithful, filled with fault, constantly doubting whether God's way or ours is better, searching the world until our heads hurt—might be saved.

While we were still sinners, Jesus closed the mouths of our lions—our hurts, our addictions, our unmet dreams and longings—*for us*. He frees us from the need to be perfectly faithful and from the need to save ourselves. Daniel knew this on a profound level, and that's why he prayed, even when he knew it could lead to his death.

The way God offers us is a personal relationship with him, our Rescuer. And it is indeed better.

Prayer: Jesus, thank you for rescuing me. Draw me nearer to you.

Reflection Question: In what ways have you tried to save yourself?

---

1. Forrest Frank, "Your Way's Better," produced by Forrest Frank and PERA (River House Records, 2024).

The Cloud-Riding King

CHELSEA KINGSTON ERICKSON

Think for a moment about the most powerful kingdoms in our world—whether recognized governments or terrorist groups. Since God's creation of human beings, kingdoms have risen and fallen, giving way to new empires. But for a time, these powers hold influence over people made in God's image.

In Daniel 7, God gives Daniel a vision to encourage him and the other exiles living under Babylon's oppressive rule. Daniel's vision includes four bizarre-looking beasts who are like something out of a fantasy novel. Most scholars agree that the lion with a human mind (v. 4) represents Babylon; the bear with ribs in its mouth (v. 5) depicts Medo-Persia; and the four-headed leopard (v. 6) represents Greece. Most terrifying of all, the beast with iron teeth and ten horns (vv. 7–8) represents Rome, which will arise long after Daniel's life has ended.

The fifth and final kingdom in Daniel's vision is not represented by a terrifying beast, but by "one like a son of man," who rides on the clouds. In Exodus, the presence of clouds signifies the glory of the Lord—only God himself comes on the clouds (Exodus 13:21; 19:9; 40:34–38). The person Daniel sees moving toward the Ancient of Days (a name for God the Father) will be both human and divine. In other words, Daniel sees *Jesus*, and he sees that people of all nations and languages will worship this true king forever!

Jesus often referred to himself as the "son of man," and even said that he would come again on the clouds of heaven (Mark 14:62). And he is the Son of God, who conquered sin and all the powers of evil in the world through his death on the cross.

As we see all of the world's destructive kingdoms today, Daniel's vision reminds us that Jesus has come and will come again. One day, we will hear the host of heaven proclaim, "The kingdom of the world has become the kingdom of our Lord and of his Messiah, and he will reign for ever and ever" (Revelation 11:15).

Prayer: Thank you, Father, for already establishing the kingdom of Jesus. Help me wait in trusting expectation for the day when he will come again to make all things new.

Reflection Question: In what part of our world are you longing to see the everlasting kingdom of Jesus established?

Singing in a Foreign Land

ISAIAH A. MARSHALL

My grandfather's funeral is the first one I can remember. He passed when I was a junior in high school. Everyone in the room was weeping. I remember being perplexed because the music was joyful and tinted with hope, a hope I didn't yet understand.

In Psalm 137, exiled Israelites sit down by the rivers of Babylon and weep as they remember their homeland. They miss Zion like we miss someone who has died. Grief can feel like exile because you can never go back to the life you had before you lost the person you love. While the Israelites grieve, their captors force them to sing songs of Zion. They respond, "How can we sing the songs of the Lord while in a foreign land?" (v. 4).

It's hard to sing songs of joy when we're hurting. In times of difficulty, we often lose hope and feel trapped in despair, forgetting that God is present with us even in pain. But we are not left without hope. Jesus answers humanity's cry for deliverance. When Jesus entered Jerusalem, the people shouted, "Hosanna to the Son of David! Blessed is he who comes in the name of the Lord!" (Matthew 21:9). Hosanna means "save us." Their cry became a song of hope, like the songs at my grandfather's funeral. *Hosanna* is the prayer from our mouths to a God who hears our prayers and acts in our lives.

Jesus came to carry our grief and bring us a peace that surpasses understanding, comforting us in our pain (Philippians 4:7). As Isaiah writes, Jesus is "a man of sorrows and acquainted with grief" (53:3 ESV). Jesus knew the feeling of being an exile. Jesus grieved for his friend Lazarus (John 11) just as we do when we lose a loved one, and he grieved for our sin like we do when we miss the mark. Jesus experienced unimaginable grief when he hung on the cross, where he bore the sins of the world so we can be forgiven and experience him now and forever.

Our Savior meets us in our foreign lands of grief, offering us comfort and hope. We can cry out to Jesus in our pain, knowing he understands and brings healing. Through Christ, we're given a new song, a song of hosanna that reminds us of this truth: Our God saves.

Prayer: Lord, in my grief, remind me of your lasting hope. Be my sustaining hope on my most difficult days. In Jesus' name. Amen.

Reflection Question: When have you felt far from hope? How can you seek God's comfort today?

Looking Forward to the Day of the Lord

ERICSON JOUBERT

When I was seventeen, my mother and I were driving behind a van that had the words "God is coming back. Repent, for the kingdom of God is at hand" spray painted on it. I had a panic attack when I read these words. I begged my mom to take me to our priest to confess my sins before it was too late. Although I had grown up in church, I saw God as a distant taskmaster, more wrathful than compassionate. I somehow missed the work of Jesus and felt it was ultimately up to me to save myself. It dawned on me: Before a holy and just God, I stood no chance of earning salvation, and that thought terrified me.

The prophet Joel warns God's people about a coming day of the Lord, in which God will judge the world. Joel depicts earth and heaven shaking as God comes with his armies to punish the wicked for their sin (2:1–11). Humanity's sinful condition puts every single person in history under immediate condemnation. Seems overwhelming, right? It is. This is why Joel says, "For the day of the LORD is great and very awesome; who can endure it?" (v. 11 ESV). The answer is . . . no one!

But Joel also tells God's people that the day of the Lord can be a day of hope if they will return to him with all their hearts (vv. 12–13). Like the dawn rising to meet the night, so God's judgment is met with God's divine mercy. God does not abandon Israel, but promises the outpouring of his Spirit to dwell with them (vv. 28–29).

This promise points to God's new way of relating to his covenant children. Through the death and resurrection of Jesus and the power of the Holy Spirit, God makes his dwelling within us. Those who trust in the name of Jesus receive the Spirit and by faith belong to him forever and ever. So what must we do to receive this good news? *We must call on the name of the Lord* (Joel 2:32). Jesus is the only priest you need. You don't even need to get better before you call on his name.

Prayer: Thank you, Father for sending Jesus to save sinners, and for your Spirit, who dwells with me now. Amen.

Reflection Question: Have you called on the name of the Lord to save you? Why or why not?

God Works in the King's Heart

KENDAL CONNER

Consider your favorite books, shows, or movies. Whether it's character, plots, or iconic scenes, all were imagined by an author working behind the scenes to craft the stories and people we love. As the author of creation, God has always been working, even when we may not see him.

The people of God are far from home in the book of Ezra. The people of Israel have been captured, living as exiles in a foreign land for a generation. Their homeland has been destroyed and the temple of their God brought to ruin. Has God abandoned his people?

Here God is at work in the heart of a pagan king, Cyrus of Persia. God sets in motion the plan to return his people home to Jerusalem by stirring the king to release the Jews from captivity. The king's decree happens through the Lord's hand. Once again, God saves his people and brings them back into the promised land. God is the author of creation and of salvation.

Although we cannot see it, we can trust that God is always at work—both for his glory and for the good of those who love him (Romans 8:28). As the true King over everything that happens, God can work even through sinful people. We can have faith that God will bring about his perfect story. Not one promise given to his people will fail, but every word of the Lord will come to pass (Joshua 21:45). This is our lasting hope.

No matter what challenges you face, God is still at work. He has not left you alone but has authored a way to salvation through Jesus. Keep trusting him. God will direct your path and finish the good work he began in you (Philippians 1:6).

Prayer: Father, thank you for your story of salvation, which you continue to work out today. Help me trust in you as the author and perfecter of my faith.

Reflection Question: How does knowing that God is always at work give you comfort in times of suffering?

Celebrating Today

ISAIAH A. MARSHALL

After the last runner crossed the finish line in the relay, my track team erupted in cheers. We had defended our state title. Though we were excited by the win, it felt almost like a sigh of relief, unlike the year before when our unexpected win had us celebrating the whole way home.

Something similar is happening as the exiled Israelites return to Jerusalem. Zerubbabel, a descendant of the kings of Judah, leads the charge to rebuild the temple, where they hope God himself will return to dwell. Zerubbabel first rebuilds the altar, where the priests will offer sacrifices to God. Now they need a place to gather. As the foundation is laid, the priests and Levites lead the people in worship and praise. The people rejoice as they sing, but the priests who remember the first temple weep loudly Why are they weeping during such a joyous occasion? It doesn't appear these are tears of joy. Instead, they are realizing this new temple is not going to measure up to King Solomon's.

I mean, winning a second championship is cool or whatever, but it's not the first. We often let past experiences overshadow the present, hindering our ability to celebrate the new thing that God is doing.

At Jesus' death, the temple veil is torn in two (Matthew 27:51). This tearing signifies a new thing God is doing through his Son as he establishes a new covenant with his people. No longer do believers sacrifice a lamb, because Jesus became the perfect lamb who died for our sins. No longer will the Lord dwell in a temple made by human hands (Acts 17:24), but all can now worship him in the Spirit and in truth (John 4:21–24).

Don't let the past keep you from appreciating what God is doing today. Like the returning exiles, rejoice in the Lord. If there are tears, let them be tears of joy because God is good.

Prayer: Lord, teach me to recognize your enduring love for me and to celebrate the work you are doing in my life.

Reflection Question: Have you ever compared your present with past wins or others' successes? How can you celebrate the new thing God is doing in your life through Christ?

First Priority

CAMERON COLE

In high school, I attended a morning Christian fellowship called First Priority. The name conveyed the most fulfilling way to live—making our relationship with Jesus the top priority in our lives.

In Haggai 1, God has a similar message for the Israelites. For more than seventy years, they have lived in Babylon as exiles due to their disobedience to God's covenant. Their enemies have destroyed Jerusalem and the beloved temple of God. Eventually, by God's sovereign grace, the Lord sets the people free from captivity and leads them back to Jerusalem, where he calls them to restore the wall, the city, and the temple.

However, the people have not prioritized the Lord, as evidenced by their neglect of the temple. God says in verse 4, "Is it a time for you yourselves to be living in your paneled houses, while this house remains a ruin?" God essentially says through the prophet Haggai, "You guys are prioritizing building fancy houses for yourselves while allowing my house to remain in ruins." Putting their own comfort and luxury above the reconstruction of the temple reveals that worshiping God and being faithful to him is a secondary priority. The people have bigger priorities than loving God.

God warns the people that this mindset will leave them with empty hearts, "You eat, but never have enough. You drink, but never have your fill" (v. 6). In other words, this lifestyle of not prioritizing God leaves your hearts unsatisfied and unfulfilled.

Many distractions lead us away from God. You may feel busy with school responsibilities or a demanding weekend job. Sports, band, or theater activities may take up a great deal of your time. Because of sin, we are prone to put these commitments before God. But Jesus urges his followers to seek his kingdom above anything else (Matthew 6:33–34). Remember, God designed your heart for him to be at the center of your life. Only prioritizing your relationship with Jesus will deliver true contentment.

Prayer: Jesus, you are worthy of being my first priority in life. Fill me with your Spirit so I will make you more important than anything else in my life.

Reflection Question: What do you tend to prioritize above your relationship with God—perhaps school, sports, popularity, or the like? What would it look like to prioritize your relationship with Jesus?

Even Better Than Silver and Gold

CHELSEA KINGSTON ERICKSON

Royal palaces like Buckingham, Versailles, and the Forbidden City capture our imagination in history and literature. The opulence of these structures points to the dignity of the people who live (or lived) within them.

Similarly, the Old Testament's descriptions of the temple include silver, gold, and other treasures in order to convey that it is the place of God's glorious presence. Or it was—until God departed from the temple and the Babylonians stole its sacred objects (Ezekiel 10).

As the people return from exile to rebuild Jerusalem and the temple, we can understand why they are discouraged. The former majesty of the temple is gone, and they are refugees attempting to restore it. But in Haggai 2, God promises that the new temple will surpass the first, and it will be a place of *peace*. God reminds the people that all silver and gold belong to him. He plans to draw the nations of the earth to himself to bring their material wealth into his temple. Naturally, the exiles believe that all God has said will come true once they finish building the temple. As it turns out, God has something in mind far better than a mere physical space. God will fulfill his words to Haggai through the gift of his Son. *Jesus* is the true treasure of all nations—the one who will fill the new temple with God's glorious presence.

At the very end of the Bible, we find a vision of the magnificent city God is building for those who love and serve him (Revelation 21:15–21). But in this city, there will be no need for a physical temple. Instead, God the Father and Christ the Lamb will dwell fully with God's people forever (v. 22), and the kings of the earth will bring their wealth and honor before the true King of kings (v. 26).

If you trust in Jesus for your salvation, your future is far greater than you can imagine. The splendor of God's own presence awaits you when he makes all things new.

Prayer: Lord, I often feel discouraged by the realities of living in this broken world. Help me lift my eyes to the glory that awaits me in heaven with you.

Reflection Question: Is it hard to imagine that eternity with God will be worth waiting for? Ask God to fill you with hope as you wait on him.

Wishing for Easy

CAROLYN LANKFORD

I breezed through math until tenth grade. Mrs. Sullivan made precalculus a nightmare for me. I experienced genuine panic every day in that class. So of course, my relief was overwhelming when I got kind Mr. Bench for Calculus. I just knew my breezy relationship with math would come back. Only it didn't. Math was still hard, and I never felt that breeze again.

The prophet Zechariah is writing to Israelites who have returned to their homeland after seventy years in Babylon. Coming home has been more challenging than joyful. The Israelites remain the subjects of a foreign king—this time, the king of Persia—and their holy temple is a pile of ruins. The task of rebuilding seems impossible. This homecoming has not met their expectations for a return to life as it once had been.

Zechariah proclaims God's words of ultimate victory and hope for his broken and floundering people. He is reminding them of God's promises—the same promises that remain trustworthy for God's people today. The Israelites hear through God's prophet Zechariah that they have a Savior, and he is good. His salvation is far greater than their expectations. This Savior is more powerful than their sin. He is going to restore the whole world, not just their nation.

Fast-forward five hundred years. Luke tells of Jesus' entry into Jerusalem on a colt (Luke 19:30–38) five days before he will be nailed to a cross. The people were expecting a military leader, but Jesus rides in not on a warhorse but on a donkey, symbolizing that he is a king of peace. He will fulfill God's promises made all the way back in Eden after Adam and Eve fell into sin.

Jesus does not save us by improving our circumstances, though he does know them and his will is for our flourishing. He saves us by forgiving our sins once and for all and establishing our everlasting place in his kingdom. This is good news for all of us, especially those who aren't feeling a breeze right now.

Prayer: Lord Jesus, help me trust that when my circumstances are hard, you are with me and your plans for me are good. Show me how I can rest in your trustworthy promises, knowing you are my Good Shepherd.

Reflection Question: Can you point to a time in your life when you've seen God keep his promises or work things out for the best in the end?

Ever Felt like You're Drowning?

CHARLOTTE GETZ

Have you ever been a babysitter? Imagine you're at the pool, and you're holding the hand of a little girl. She doesn't know how to swim, and she is terrified. As you take a step deeper, the little girl grips your hand even tighter. Who is keeping the little girl safe from drowning? Is it her own efforts in clinging to you? No. No matter how hard she clutches, you're the one who keeps her from drowning.

Psalm 119 is the longest chapter in the Bible, filled with heavy words like *commands*, *precepts*, *decrees*, and *upright*. It would be easy to see this psalm as a demand to do a better job following God's rules, or in the language of the above illustration, work harder to keep yourself from drowning. This psalm appears to be saying (but we know it isn't) that we need to be good for God to love us.

Even the most thoughtful Christians are tempted to believe that our best behavior, our faithful church attendance, our quiet times will earn God's love. But Psalm 119 reminds us that it's God who loves and saves us first, not the other way around. See how instead of saying "*I will follow* your decrees," the psalmist says, "*Teach me*, Lord, the way of your decrees" (v. 33, emphasis added). Instead of "*I* have understanding," he says, "*Give* me understanding" (v. 34, emphasis added). Instead of "*I will follow* your commands," he says, "*Direct me* in the path of your commands" (v. 35, emphasis added). Can you see the difference?

As the psalmist looks at God's perfect law, he sees his own sin and inadequacy clearly. He knows that the burden of doing all these right and beautiful things—to follow, to learn, to understand, to obey—could never be on his own insufficient shoulders. The burden is on God. It always has been.

Friend, your good deeds, your right behavior, are not what make God love you. God's people did not earn the arrival of Jesus. No. God came down to them (to us), despite their fear and faithlessness. He has had us in his hands from the beginning. God always knew he would come, regardless of what we do or do not do. Why? Because he loves us. Everything we long to do and be as Christians starts here: God loves us first. We love, we do, we are, because he first loves us (1 John 4:19).

Prayer: God, free me from the false belief that your love is dependent on my behavior as a follower of Christ.

Reflection Question: What is an area of your life in which you have believed that God's love is dependent on you?

More Than Words

MARK HOWARD

In ninth grade, I taught myself to play the drums. Two years later, I joined the church worship team. I wasn't talented enough to both sing and play, so for most of high school, worship came in the form of banging drums. Through that experience, I learned that it really is possible to worship without words. In time, I discovered I could praise God for his grace and truth given to us in Jesus through other means as well, like running and creating art.

Psalm 150 is the final song in the Bible's songbook, which exhorts everything that has breath to praise the Lord. It begins with a call to worship God in his sanctuary because of his power and greatness (vv. 1–2) and then encourage us to praise God with music and dancing. It moves from a form of worship that is limited in method and setting to something that can be done anywhere and anytime. It moves from the breath formed by singing to the breath that comes from exertion. It's a fitting way to close a lyrical book of ancient worship songs, for even as the book ends, our praise must continue as we go out into the world.

Centuries later, the apostle Paul urges the church to "rejoice always, pray continually, give thanks in all circumstances" (1 Thessalonians 5:16–18). This isn't possible if we only think of praying and praising with our voices or in church settings. We can worship more and more when we discover how to worship God in whatever we do.

I love gathering with other believers on Sunday to worship Jesus (Hebrews 10:25), whose sacrifice made it possible for us to be adopted into the family of God. Yet Sunday church is not the only time and place we are called to worship. God is worthy of our praise *always*. We are designed to praise the Lord *at all times*. We praise God as we listen in church and sing praises. We can also learn to worship as we walk the school halls, play a sport, doodle at home, or practice an instrument. In all things, we can let every breath and personal expression praise the Lord.

Prayer: Father God, thank you for giving me this body to praise you. Help me learn what it means to praise you in each moment.

Reflection Question: What is your favorite activity? What might it look like to praise the Lord as you do what you love to do?

Why Am I Here, Now?

KATIE POLSKI

Have you ever wondered why God has placed you where he has? Maybe you don't like your school or church and wonder why God doesn't make it easier to attend elsewhere. Or maybe your parents are divorced, and you're living in a new place that doesn't feel like home. It's not uncommon to go through seasons in which we wonder, *Why have you put me here, God?*

Today's reading comes from the book of Esther, which tells the story of a Jewish orphan who becomes the queen of Persia during the reign of King Xerxes. She must wonder why God places her in this foreign kingdom. At first, Esther conceals her Jewish identity from the king at the advice of her cousin Mordecai. But after a high-ranking official named Haman plots to annihilate all Jews, Mordecai urges Esther to reveal her true identity. He pleads with her to speak to the king on behalf of the Jews, even though doing so could mean her death (4:13–14).

Can you imagine how afraid Esther must have been? But Mordecai reminds her of an important truth: *God has brought her into this situation for a reason.* He has chosen Esther to be in a place where she can help save the Jews, which is exactly what she does. Esther bravely exposes her Jewish identity, as well as Haman's evil plan. And because of her willingness to be used by God "for such a time as this," the Jewish people are delivered.

In an even greater way than God used Esther, God sent his Son, Jesus, to be the ultimate deliverer from our sin. When we trust in Jesus, we can know for sure that none of our circumstances are ever wasted.

Even if your current situation is difficult, your circumstances are not a mistake. Perhaps God wants you to be a source of encouragement to someone who's struggling or to bring hope to a situation that seems hopeless. Like Esther, you may not always understand the full extent of God's plan. But trust that he has a purpose for you in every circumstance, and he will always give you just what you need. Seek God's courage and ask him boldly for his help. God is able to do *immeasurably more* than we can even imagine (Ephesians 3:20).

Prayer: Jesus, in places that feel uncertain, remind me that you have a purpose. Give me courage to trust in your perfect and loving plan.

Reflection Question: How can knowing that you are where you are "for such a time as this" change the way you approach your current challenges?

Group Project Gone Wrong

REBECCA HECK

Have you ever been on a group project with someone who said they'd contribute to the project, only to have them neglect their job, do it their own way, or otherwise fail the team?

The book of Nehemiah reads like a group project gone terribly wrong. One leader of the group (Nehemiah) is paired up with a bunch of people (the Israelites) who do not pull their weight. Nehemiah believes that the Lord deserves to be obeyed. He says yes to doing the hardest job there is—convincing others to obey God.

When Nehemiah discovers what happened to Jerusalem, he prays to ask God what he should do and then waits until God shows him. God gives Nehemiah the courage to approach King Xerxes of Persia, asking him to send Nehemiah and a group of priests to Jerusalem. As they rebuild the walls of their city, they begin to rebuild their relationship with God as well. The feel-good version of this story ends with new city walls and everyone cheering. In reality, it doesn't take long for the Israelites to once again live for themselves (Nehemiah 5:1–5). New city walls did not mean that everyone was ready to live for God. All along, Nehemiah asks God to remember what he has earlier promised the Israelites—to gather his people and provide a way for them (1:8–9). Nehemiah's prayers were answered ultimately when God sent his own Son into the world.

We see the pattern of Nehemiah repeated when Jesus confronts the religious leaders of his day. He calls them "whitewashed tombs" (Matthew 23:27) because they look good on the outside, but their hearts do not align with God's.

We're not so different from those who pretend to be righteous. But the most righteous One, Jesus, gave his life for us and for all the times we try to look good on the outside while our hearts are a mess. Thanks be to God! We can rest in the knowledge that Jesus' perfect life, death, and resurrection made us righteous in God's eyes.

Prayer: Holy Spirit, thank you for leading my heart toward what is right, even when it is hard. Help me rest in Jesus' work to forgive all of my sins.

Reflection Question: Have there been times when you've said yes to God, only to follow your own way instead? How has Jesus met you there?

Feeling Far from God

HANNAH DOW

We've all had times in our lives when we've felt distant from the Lord. Perhaps reading the Bible became stale or prayer felt routine. You may have felt guilt or shame over something and avoided God altogether. Worse yet, you may think you have to somehow earn God's love to get back into his good graces. At these times, restoring your relationship with God can feel impossible.

The book of Nehemiah, coupled with Ezra, tells the incredible story of the restoration of the Israelites to God after their captivity in Babylon. A small group of Israelites have returned to Jerusalem to rebuild the city walls and the temple. Their very lives are being restored alongside their relationship with God, yet the work of rebuilding feels overwhelming and will take generations to complete.

The Israelites will spend years reconstructing the city walls. Working in shifts around the clock, they labor with a weapon in one hand and a tool in the other because they are under constant threat of attack (Nehemiah 4:17). When the work is complete, they gather to read the law of Moses together. Every person old enough to understand assembles. Priests move through the crowd teaching and answering questions to ensure comprehension of God's Word. We have the privilege of hearing God's Word read aloud every Sunday, but for the Israelites, reading God's Word aloud publicly likely hadn't happened since before Babylon destroyed Israel more than 150 years before this gathering.

The result is a beautiful restoration, an outpouring of generosity within the community. The holiness of God cannot coexist with gloom. The people rightly begin by being sorrowful for their sin (8:9), but they are subsequently overjoyed at the renewed relationship with God (vv. 10–12). They live out David's prayer of repentance: "Restore to me the joy of your salvation" (Psalm 51:12).

The things that keep us from God are never of God. He is always seeking to restore us to himself. If this were not true, he would not have sent his one and only Son to die for the sins of this broken world. Hearing the Word of God will inevitably lead to the renewing of our faith and a sense of gratitude for God's great providence (Romans 10:17).

Prayer: Lord, sometimes I feel distant from you, and I don't know how to get back to you. Help me remember I don't have to earn your love.

Reflection Question: Using Romans 8:31–39 as a guide, remind yourself that nothing can separate you from the Lord.

Very Excited and a Little Scared

CAMERON COLE

I remember the night before my high school basketball championship game like it was yesterday. I was so nervous I couldn't sleep, and I almost vomited as we were heading onto the court. But at the same time, I was totally pumped. Joyful expectation and anxious anticipation battled for first place in my head.

Throughout the Old Testament prophets, the day of the Lord prompts both excitement and dread. Malachi refers to the day of the Lord as "great and dreadful" (4:5). This day involves God himself coming to the earth for a final visitation. Malachi says, "Then suddenly the Lord you are seeking will come to his temple" (3:1). The excitement comes from the reality that God will cleanse the world of everything that is wrong, crooked, and evil when he visits. He will make the world perfect again.

At the same time, all people are sinners, and the notion of a perfect judge coming to enact full justice means that the hammer can fall on anyone. Malachi asks, "Who can endure the day of his coming? Who can stand when he appears?" (3:2). The answer to this question is that no sinner can stand before a perfect, holy God. This aspect of the day of the Lord makes it dreadful and scary.

Jesus has taken away this fear. The New Testament uses the term *justified* to describe how the grace of Jesus provides forgiveness of sins and a saving righteousness from God (Romans 3:23–25). The word *justified* comes from the Latin word *justus*, which means "just," "upright," and "righteous." In other words, Jesus' forgiveness enables us to stand upright before a holy God when we see him face-to-face.

Jesus has eliminated the dread of seeing God. Because Jesus has justified those who belong to him, we can anticipate the day of the Lord with eager expectation. We can stand before God in confidence, peace, and joy.

Prayer: Jesus, thank you for coming to cleanse me from my sins so I don't have to fear your judgment. Help me admit my needs and confess my sins, knowing you will meet me with mercy and grace. Amen.

Reflection Question: How does this statement make you feel: "The Lord you are seeking will come"? Does it fill you with excitement and hope?

People Change; God Does Not

KENDAL CONNER

By fifth grade, I had called six different states home. I often joked that the one thing I could always count on was change. Deep down, I longed for consistency, imagining it would make me feel secure. In reality, change is inevitable for all of us.

This is why God's words in Malachi 3:6 are so powerful: "I the LORD do not change." While everything else is changing, the Lord never is. God is the same today as he was yesterday and as he will be tomorrow. What incredible news for God's people returning from exile!

God has kept his promise to return Israel and rebuild the temple, yet his people are still struggling with doubt. They see how the evil people around them are prospering (v. 15), and it leads them to question why they should continue to serve God. In the midst of their doubt, God reminds them it is only because of his faithfulness they exist as a people (v. 6). God's saving mercy is the evidence that he is trustworthy. Yet if they want even more proof, God offers it.

God tells his people to "test me in this" (v. 10). He challenges them to follow his commands and watch as his mercy and blessing flow to them. He wants them to test his nature, knowing he is unmovable in his Word and promises. So even though Israel continues to struggle with trusting the Lord's faithfulness, God makes it clear to them here: "Return to me, and I will return to you" (v. 7). He is unchangeable, and he offers an invitation to all who have wandered from him to return to his covenant faithfulness.

The Old Testament ends with a crucial reminder. God's people enter an extended period of waiting until a prophet like Elijah prepares them for his coming (4:5). Yet they are encouraged with a firm word from God: "I the LORD do not change" (3:6). No matter what, they can place their full trust in God's guaranteed faithfulness that ushers in the greatest news that would ever come to God's people: the arrival of the incarnate, unchanging, faithful one who is "the same yesterday and today and forever" (Hebrews 13:8)—Jesus, who is God with us.

Prayer: Father, in your unchanging nature, thank you for loving me. Help me more fully trust in your faithfulness today.

Reflection Question: How is the unchangeable nature of God good news for you today?

Jesus' Birth Announcement

CHELSEA KINGSTON ERICKSON

When my best friend, Sarah, and I both found out we were pregnant, we each privately worried the other would feel sad or left out. But when I finally called Sarah, she told me the same wonderful news. I still can hardly believe it, but we had our firstborn baby boys on the exact same day.

Luke introduces us to two cousins who share miraculous birth announcements. Elizabeth and her husband, Zechariah the priest, are elderly and childless, but an angel tells them they will have a baby, who will be a prophet like Elijah (Malachi 4:5), preparing the way for the Lord. Mary is young and engaged to be married. The angel tells her the Holy Spirit will cause her to become pregnant and have a baby named Jesus, God's own Son.

Elizabeth has wanted a baby for such a long time, but now she is very old. Meanwhile, Mary faces an unplanned pregnancy. She knows Joseph might call off the wedding, which would put her on the margins of society as a single mother. Both women could have responded with fear, anger, or disbelief. Instead, they welcome the angels' announcements as good news.

In the New Testament, the word for "good news" is *gospel*—the message that Jesus has come to rescue sinners and renew their relationship with God (Romans 1:16–17). When Mary and Elizabeth meet during their pregnancies, they become the first people in the New Testament to celebrate the gospel. Elizabeth feels her baby leap in her womb and is filled with the Holy Spirit. Recognizing that she is a part of a much larger story, Mary sings praises to the God who promises good to his people (Luke 1:46–55).

God invites us to respond to the gospel with the same kind of joyful obedience. Following Jesus will not always be easy. God will call you to say no to certain pursuits out of love for him. You will sometimes face rejection for your faith. When these things happen, remember the very *best* news: God sent his Son to rescue you, inviting you into his story.

Prayer: Father, sometimes I forget how good is the news that you sent Jesus. Please help me trust in you and celebrate your work in my life.

Reflection Question: How is the gospel good news in your life today?

When Truth Is Stranger Than Fiction

SYLER THOMAS

The Christian faith began in scandal.

Each Christmas season, we celebrate the miracle that Mary, Jesus' mother, became pregnant "through the Holy Spirit." But imagine you or one of your friends had to try to explain how you or they were pregnant.

When Joseph hears the news, he has a choice to make. The logical explanation is that Mary has been unfaithful to him, so he could reveal that to their community, subjecting her to what the Bible calls "public disgrace" (Matthew 1:19). Instead, he decides that the honorable thing is to call off the marriage quietly (the verse says "divorce" because an engagement was considered binding and required a formal divorce).

But a visit from an angel in a dream convinces Joseph otherwise and reveals that this baby is the Messiah, the long-awaited rescuer for God's people. In fact, the opening verses of Matthew 1 trace Jesus' genealogy—through Joseph—all the way back to David and to Abraham. The angel tells Joseph to name the child Jesus ("the LORD saves") because "he will save his people from their sins" (v. 21). This fulfills Isaiah's prophecy that a virgin will have a child named Immanuel, or "God with us" (Isaiah 7:14). "God with us" is a beautiful three-word summary of who Jesus is—our Creator who leaves heaven to be close to us.

Matthew 1 is one of many New Testament examples that the truth is stranger than fiction. If you were creating a religion, would you perpetuate the rumor that the cornerstone of your faith was born to an unmarried mother?

The truth *is* sometimes stranger than fiction. God *did* become a scandal for our sakes. Not only did Jesus' life begin amid rumors and innuendo, but it ended in scandal as well. Galatians 3:13 points out that anyone who hangs on a tree is cursed. God left heaven to be born of a virgin so that he could die in our place to rescue us and to be with us forever.

Prayer: Lord, thank you for loving me enough to send Jesus as a baby and allow him to be the curse that set me free.

Reflection Question: Other than the virgin birth, can you think of another aspect of Christianity that would be too spectacular to make up?

Even Better Than the Hype

ANNE SANFORD

Some things are overhyped. The new pizza place that everyone's raving about is just okay. The blockbuster film that got a bunch of Oscar nominations is actually bizarre. The five-star recruit your favorite team signed ends up being a bust. But every now and then, the hype is merited. Sometimes it even exceeds expectations.

Exceeding expectations is an understatement of what happens when the shepherds encounter the newborn Jesus. They are going about their normal lives when suddenly "an angel of the Lord appeared to them, and the glory of the Lord shone around them" (Luke 2:9). They are understandably terrified, but that's when the angel encourages them: Don't be afraid. This is *good* news. The Messiah, your Savior, is here!

These shepherds likely knew the prophecies about the Messiah, but I doubt they thought they'd encounter him in their lifetime. Certainly not through a direct announcement from an angel. So they had to go see. They found that their Messiah had indeed come, and they were ecstatic. They went away praising God because everything they had experienced was "just as they had been told" but assuredly even more amazing than they could have imagined.

We may sometimes find ourselves like the shepherds—afraid of an encounter with God. But if we seek him, if we run *to* him, even in our fear, doubt, and confusion, we will encounter a God who is "immeasurably more than all we ask or imagine" (Ephesians 3:20). Just like the shepherds, we will encounter the Messiah—the One who came, lived, died, and rose again to wipe out all of our fear, doubt, and confusion.

Prayer: Lord, thank you that no amount of hype can prepare me for an encounter with you. You are so much more than I can comprehend. Thank you for choosing to love me. Help me be like the shepherds—praising you for all I've seen you do. Amen.

Reflection Question: In what way has the reality of encountering Jesus been even better than you expected?

God with Us

DANNY KWON

When you were a child, did you ever get scared of the dark in the middle of the night? Maybe a sliver of light came from the night-light, but it wasn't enough to snuff out your fear. Of course, if it got really scary, you might call out to your mom or dad to comfort you. When they came to your bedside or even crawled into your bed to come close, their presence was calming and peaceful.

John 1:14 highlights God's relentless commitment to be close to his people. The words "made his dwelling among us" allude to God's glory—the awesome display of his character and presence—in the Old Testament. God's glory would appear to the Israelites, filling the tabernacle (Exodus 40:34–35).

Jesus has come to dwell even more personally with God's people. In Jesus, God takes on human form. Our eternal, holy, omnipresent God becomes a human being who lives among humanity. He takes up residence among us in the flesh. Jesus becomes Immanuel, *God with us.*

God's presence can sometimes feel like just a sliver of light coming from a night-light. While you know he is God, you may imagine he is somehow distant. In Jesus, however, God shows us that he is present and active. Even greater than a parent coming to comfort you in your fear at night, he is your loving Father who will never leave you nor forsake you.

As he ascends into heaven, Jesus tells his disciples, "I am with you always, to the very end of the age" (Matthew 28:20). He reassures them that his presence will continue through the gift of the promised Holy Spirit (John 15:26–27), who now lives in every believer, assuring us of Jesus' presence with us today (John 16:13; 1 Corinthians 3:16). His unwavering, devoted closeness offers grace and truth to comfort us in our dark and scary experiences.

Prayer: God, thank you for not only being a presence in my life but for coming to this earth as a man to show me that you are with me.

Reflection Question: How does knowing that Jesus is both divine and human and made his dwelling among us as his people bring you comfort?

The Christmas Villain

CHELSEA KINGSTON ERICKSON

Every great Christmas story has its villain: *It's a Wonderful Life*'s Henry Potter. *The Nutcracker*'s Rat King. *Home Alone*'s Harry and Marv. Dr. Seuss's The Grinch. *A Christmas Carol*'s Ebenezer Scrooge. And the original Christmas story has Herod the Great, the vengeful and paranoid ruler who killed one of his wives and three of his sons, along with many innocents, for fear that they would dethrone him.

Matthew's gospel sets Herod in sharp contrast with the Magi (elite Persian scholars). Their study of the night sky leads them to conclude that a king will be born in Judea. So they travel from Babylon to Judea to ask Herod about this new king, causing his paranoia to flare. Herod consults with Jewish scholars, who tell him that God's promised messianic king will be born in Bethlehem. Herod instructs the Magi to go and report back to him so that he, too, "may go and worship him" (2:8). Herod is actually hatching a plan to kill the child, a fact God later reveals to the Magi in a dream so that they take a different path home.

The Magi find the young Jesus with his parents in Bethlehem. They bow down to him, offering expensive gifts of gold (recognizing his kingship), frankincense (used by priests, signifying that Jesus is the greatest priest, God's Son), and myrrh (used for burial, acknowledging that Jesus will die). These pagan stargazers understand who Jesus is and worship him.

Because of Herod's wicked plot, Jesus and his parents flee to Egypt and live there as refugees until Herod dies. In going to Egypt and then returning to Judea, Jesus traces Israel's own exodus and exile. While Jesus escaped Herod's wicked plan, he did not escape evil forever. He took evil upon himself on the cross thirtysome years later to deliver us from sin and the ultimate villain, Satan.

Until Jesus returns to make all things right, evil still has a hold on our world. But the true King of Israel, the one the Magi worshiped, will one day overcome evil's grip. He will dethrone every earthly king and rule over God's kingdom of justice and mercy forever.

Prayer: Jesus, what a comfort that you have walked in my shoes. Thank you for being the priest-king who came to die for me, conquering sin and Satan.

Reflection Question: What does this darker side of the Christmas story show us about God's good character and plans?

The Wild Ride of Faith

MARK HOWARD

Roller coasters make me feel unsafe. I can't help but think, *Will the harness hold?* Life can be like a roller coaster too. It's filled with twists and turns, and sometimes the bottom drops out beneath us—a diagnosis, a divorce, a death. It's easy to wonder if Jesus still holds us tight.

Mark's gospel starts like a roller coaster too as it swerves from verse to verse. He begins by announcing news about Jesus the Messiah, the rescuer for God's people. He calls this message "the good news." In Greco-Roman culture, the term "good news" (*euangelion*, or gospel) was used for proclamations about Caesar. Heralds would tell the good news of Caesar's military victories or the birth of a royal son. Calling Jesus "Messiah" also evokes generations of Israel's longing for a king to deliver them from their enemies and establish God's kingdom. To use these terms about Jesus is shocking, which adds to the thrilling start of Mark's narrative.

We meet Jesus with his cousin John, who is called "John the Baptist" because he dips people in water as a sign of ritual cleansing when they turn away from sin. John baptizes Jesus, and the Holy Spirit descends on Jesus as the Father speaks: "You are my Son, whom I love; with you I am well pleased" (1:11). This proclamation is a mash-up of three verses that highlight who Jesus is and what he's about. He's a king in David's line (Psalm 2:7); a beloved son, like Isaac was to Abraham (Genesis 22:2); and Israel's justice-bringing servant (Isaiah 42:1).

The good news has a jarring twist. Jesus is the promised son of Abraham, but he's being prepared for sacrifice like Isaac was (Genesis 22). He is King of kings, but also the servant who will be crushed for our sin (Isaiah 53:5). Jesus is the Messiah, but salvation will come through suffering. The Father is pleased with him because, unlike the other people John baptizes, Jesus never sins.

Because Jesus comes to fulfill all the promises God has made to Abraham, David, and the prophets, we are safe on life's wild rides. We don't have to be afraid when the bottom drops out. We can rest in God's secure love displayed in Jesus (Romans 5:8), from which nothing can separate us (8:35–39). No matter what happens today, remember how tightly you are held. Let God's love fuel your joy on your wild journey of faith.

Prayer: Loving God, draw me near by the power of your Spirit.

Reflection Question: Read Romans 8:35–39. How does knowing the strength of God's love change your experience of hard times?

Even Jesus Was Tempted to Sin

REBECCA HECK

When you think about temptation, what past moments come to mind? Do you feel exhausted by your thoughts? Is there shame? Confusion? Guilt? Apathy?

Jesus knows what it feels like to face temptation. In Matthew 3, we read about Jesus' baptism, which is followed by a forty-day fast. At the end of these forty days, Matthew tells us that the Holy Spirit leads Jesus into the wilderness to be tempted. God allows Jesus to face the devil's evil tactics. Satan makes three attempts, beginning each one with the sinister words, "if you really are the Son of God." With this question, Satan calls Jesus' identity and God's goodness into question, just as he did with Adam and Eve in the garden.

Satan uses temptation to get us to wonder about God's goodness too. So is God good to you? The answer is always yes, because Jesus "has been tempted in every way, just as we are—yet he did not sin" (Hebrews 4:15). In Matthew 4, each time Jesus is tempted by Satan, he resists by quoting Scripture and standing firm in God's Word.

This is good news for us because as Jesus faced his own temptations, he was also taking on ours. While he experienced every temptation as we do, he met them without sinning against God and others. Because Jesus was able to say no to temptation, we benefit from the outpouring of his strength. We receive the same power to say no to our temptations through the life-giving support of the Holy Spirit.

When you are in the midst of temptation, practice asking yourself, *Is God good to me?* Because the answer is a resounding yes, you can hold your head high, knowing that temptation will not be the end of you. Your great high priest has conquered it for you and sends the Holy Spirit to carry you toward his goodness again and again.

Prayer: Lord Jesus, thank you for enduring your own temptation so that I would not give in to mine. Protect my heart, mind, and soul from the things this world says can fill and heal me, and instead turn my eyes toward you.

Reflection Question: Where in your life does Satan try to tempt you away from believing in God's goodness? With whom can you share the burden of your temptations so you remember you're not alone in them?

Accepting the Invitation

MARK HOWARD

Do you read user agreements before clicking "accept" for new apps? I usually just skim the headlines and ignore the fine print. I think many of us do the same when deciding to follow Jesus. But Jesus invites us to "come and see" what following him means. He promises to give us what we need to persevere in faith.

In his gospel, John tells of four people who decide to follow Jesus after discovering a headline about who Jesus is. Andrew joins after hearing John the Baptist call Jesus, "the Lamb of God," the one who "takes away the sins of the world"(John 1:29). Excited, Andrew finds his brother, Simon Peter, and tells him, "We have found the Messiah" (v. 41), or the long-awaited rescuer. After Philip meets Jesus, he tells Nathanael, "We have found the one Moses wrote about in the Law, and about whom the prophets also wrote" (v. 44). Nathanael declares Jesus to be the "King of Israel" (v. 49).

These are incredible—and true—claims, but to figure out the depth of what they mean, each person will have to accept the invitation to "come and see" Jesus in order to follow him. Eventually, Andrew, Simon Peter, Philip, and Nathanael will each discover that the journey with Jesus, while filled with moments of power and glory, also includes misunderstandings, confusion, and hardship. Some who start to follow Jesus will leave as they begin to understand the cost of discipleship. Even one of Jesus' closest friends, Judas, will eventually betray Jesus before hitting "delete" on the discipleship app.

The call to "come and see" is an invitation to participate in the glorious life of God himself, but it is also always a call to wait, endure, and persevere in faith and hope. The way of Jesus isn't always easy, but it is the way to true life (John 6:68). It includes the cross, but it doesn't end there. Three days after his crucifixion, Jesus' broken body was made new with resurrection life. One day, Jesus will return. He will complete the new creation he began in his resurrection. This is why we follow Jesus, even when it gets tough: The story ends with good news. Jesus' invitation to each of us is to "come and see" for ourselves.

Prayer: Holy Spirit, draw me ever closer to Jesus and give me grace, courage, and endurance to follow wherever he leads.

Reflection Question: What has surprised you most on your journey with Jesus? Why?

What a Wedding!

SKYLER R. FLOWERS

How well do you know Jesus? Do you know him personally? I want to introduce you to him in the way he often introduces himself in the Bible—through his miracles.

When Jesus performs miracles, his actions aren't random. His miracles tell us about who he is and what he has come to do. In the first of Jesus' miracles, he is on a mission to reveal his identity and his ministry (John 2:1–12). His mother notices that their host has run out of wine, and she tells Jesus to fix it. His response shows we can trust that his determination is for us and our salvation. Jesus asks the servants to fill six stone water jars that were reserved for ceremonial washing—a washing that gives people access to the temple. By transforming the water, Jesus declares that a new way to be with God is beginning. Jesus' mission is to bring his people into the presence of God, not by their ability to cleanse themselves, but by *his* cleansing of them.

In Jesus' day, grooms were responsible for wine at weddings, and this groom fails to provide fully. Jesus' miracle is a sign that not only will he cleanse his people, but he will do so in abundance. He will always give us everything we need, even when we fall short. To know Jesus is to know his gracious provision that never runs out.

There is a lot to know about Jesus—historically, culturally, theologically—but Jesus' miracles always teach us to know him personally in his power. Especially in his first miracle, we see Jesus as the hope of salvation for the whole world, who loves us and loves to provide for us. This is only an introduction. But get to know Jesus, and you'll discover a relationship overflowing with love.

Prayer: Father, thank you for sending Jesus to rescue us and reveal himself to us. Help me enjoy a relationship with him through your Word.

Reflection Question: Why does Jesus use miracles to reveal himself to us? How can you grow to know him better in your life?

How Can I Be Born Again?

KATIE POLSKI

Have you ever held a newborn baby? When my oldest was born, she was just five pounds! Here's the thing—no baby chooses to be born. No infant says, "I think I'll make today my birthday." Birth is not something you *do*; it's something that happens to you.

In today's Bible reading, Jesus has a conversation about a different kind of birth—a spiritual one. As a Pharisee, Nicodemus knows the law well and is respected for it. But he's curious about Jesus, so he asks him about his teachings and miracles. Jesus' response is unexpected: "No one can see the kingdom of God unless they are *born again*" (John 3:3, emphasis added).

Of course, Jesus isn't talking about physical birth. To be born again means that God gives you a brand-new heart—a new way to think, live, and love him. When you trust in Jesus and decide to follow him, God's power enters your life, awakens your love for him, and makes you a child of God. Notice that Jesus doesn't say to Nicodemus that salvation comes by cleaning yourself up. If he did, we might be tempted to think we're able to save ourselves. But he says, "Be born again," something that we humans cannot do for ourselves. When Jesus gives us new life in God's Spirit, our eyes are opened to see the kingdom of God, which God promised through the prophets. Jesus says this kingdom comes through his ministry, and when we are born again in him, we get to be part of it.

Your status in God's kingdom isn't something you achieve; it's something you receive. A few verses later, John says, "God so loved the world that he gave his one and only Son, that whoever believes in him shall not perish but have eternal life" (v. 6). God sent Jesus to pay the penalty for your sins and give you a new heart. Your spiritual birth is the beginning of God's transforming work in you, which will be completed with him in eternity (Philippians 1:6).

Your salvation isn't based on going to church or being a good person. It's not something you inherit from your parents. True faith results from Jesus changing your heart and giving you the desire to follow him. Remember that being born again is something God does in you, giving you eyes to see his kingdom.

Prayer: Jesus, thank you for offering me new life. Help me to trust and live as someone made new by your grace. Amen.

Reflection Question: Have you been trying to fix your life on your own instead of trusting that Jesus helps you become born again?

Never Thirsty Again

JENNIFER M. KVAMME

My guess is you have felt the pain of being excluded. You've probably done things—or had things done to you—that brought shame. And you've probably experienced deep longings that seem to never quite be satisfied.

The woman in John 4 experienced these things. She feels ashamed, excluded, and thirsty, and Jesus sees her and strikes up a conversation as she draws water from a well. We learn that she married five men and is now living with someone who isn't her husband, and in her culture, all of that is particularly shameful. She is a Samaritan, a half-Jew, excluded from temple worship and community in Jerusalem. Every day, she avoids her neighbors as she goes to the well for water.

She wants to slip by unnoticed and just fetch her water, but Jesus doesn't let her stay in the shadows. He knows she is thirsty, not just for water, but for acceptance, for joy, for love—for real life. He gently brings up the pain of her past to let her know he sees her. He offers to give her overflowing life from the inside out, through his Spirit, so that she will never again be consumed by shame or longing. The Samaritan woman listens to Jesus. She leaves her water jar at the well and runs to tell her whole community about this man who knows everything about her and includes her anyway.

I'm not sure what longings you experience most or where you go to fill them. But I do know that, outside of Jesus, nothing satisfies for long. Friends are fickle. Injuries happen. Influence is temporary. Trophies collect dust. If we keep looking to achievements, relationships, or approval to fulfill us, we'll continue to be thirsty. But Jesus offers us the same invitation he offered the woman at the well: *Drink my living water, and you'll never be thirsty again*. This water washes away shame and brings an everlasting life and joy that can never be taken away. It satisfies forever.

Prayer: Thank you, Jesus, for meeting me in my places of deepest shame and greatest longing. I want to experience your living water welling up inside me, satisfying my thirst and giving me real life. Amen.

Reflection Question: What would it look like for you to drink deeply of Jesus' living water and not be thirsty again?

What Is the Good Life?

CLARK FOBES IV

When you imagine the good life, what comes to mind? What blessings do you envision having? Many of us might imagine hanging out on a beautiful beach with someone we love or being able to buy whatever our heart desires. Social media, with captions including #blessed, has promoted a vision of the good life that centers around material pleasure and comfort.

In Matthew 5:1–12, often called "the Beatitudes," Jesus presents his own version of the blessed life. However, his definition of blessing runs contrary to the world's. We often think of blessed people as those who have all they could ever want. Those who are blessed in Jesus' kingdom, however, are not those who *have* but those who *need* (vv. 3–6), not those who have received from the world but those who receive from God and give to others (vv. 7–12).

Jesus is not simply making a statement about blessing; he is declaring the truth about his kingdom and his people. Jesus welcomes those who have been rejected, are looked down on, and are pushed to the margins of society. Jesus lifts up those who receive from God and pour themselves out for others. The Beatitudes—and the Sermon on the Mount as a whole—reveal the nature of the gospel and God's kingdom. The gospel calls us to fully depend on Christ for our needs—both spiritual and material—and to live for him in our pursuits. Being a citizen of Jesus' kingdom means laying down our pursuit of the world's blessings and finding our greatest blessings in him alone.

At first glance, this kind of blessing may sound bleak because many of us are blessed by the standards of this world. But the Beatitudes are an invitation to recognize the fleeting nature of the world's blessings. Being a citizen of Jesus' kingdom calls us to greater blessings of honor and hope that will not pass away. When we've been filled with Christ's blessings, we can live to bless others through what we've received in Christ.

Prayer: Lord, help me see the fleeting nature of the world's blessings and depend entirely on you for everything. May I rest content in what I have already received and will still gain in your kingdom.

Reflection Question: How do the blessings of Christ lead you to stop pursuing the blessings of the world?

Yes, No, or Not Yet

LIZ EDRINGTON

When I was in high school, I often prayed for God to heal my parents' marriage. My house was full of yelling. My mom worked two jobs to make ends meet. *God seems pretty pro-marriage*, I thought. *Why wouldn't he want to make theirs better?*

This Bible reading from Matthew 18 brought my high school prayers to mind. This time it's a desperate father seeking the only one who can do the impossible. He can't even wait for Jesus to finish teaching. He interrupts the whole scene, asking Jesus to bring his daughter back to life. This father doesn't try to offer the perfect prayer or pretend to be superspiritual. He presents the situation and turns to God wholeheartedly. Honestly. Vulnerably. He is a picture of what it means to come to God like little children (Matthew 18:3).

This is the invitation of Jesus: *Come to me just as you are. Desperate. Mad. Sad. Hopeful. Discouraged.* He will *always* hear and care. And yet he will not always say yes. His response to your good prayer, like mine for my parents' marriage, could be a no. Or it could be a not yet. Notice that Jesus doesn't heal the girl until the house has been cleared. He works in his own way and timing.

No matter God's immediate response to our prayers, he invites us to trust him, to wrestle with him (as we see in the Psalms) and to continually discover more of who he is as our good Father. Ultimately, what is best for us may not feel like it's the best. But we can look at God's unchangingly good, just, and loving character in the person of Jesus. We can know that God's priority is to see his love reshape every part of us, his beloved children (1 John 3:1–3).

Well-known pastor Timothy Keller wrote, "God will either give us what we ask or give us what we would have asked if we knew everything he knows."[1]

Prayer: Lord, help me trust you when you answer no or not yet. Show me your goodness along the journey.

Reflection Question: How has God met you in a *no* or a *not yet*?

1. Timothy Keller, *Prayer: Experiencing Awe and Intimacy with God* (Dutton, 2014), 228.

The Lightest Burden of All

CONNIE LEUNG NELSON

What sorts of expectations do you carry—of others or of yourself? Expectations feel like pressure to *do* what you have to do (make a high grade, win, get invited), or even to *be* who you have to be (well liked, well thought of, a perfect Christian). Expectations can feel like burdens.

In Matthew 11, Jesus calls himself the giver of rest for those who are tired and burdened (v. 28). But instead of giving us rest by zapping our burdens away, Jesus says that when we come to him and take *his* yoke upon our shoulders, we'll find that what is on our shoulders isn't heavy at all, but light. A yoke is a wooden frame that farmers put on their oxen's shoulders, attaching them to a plow. It restricts movement and isn't at all a symbol of a burden-free, carefree life. So why does Jesus say that following him is his *yoke* on us?

Following him is not carefree. We cannot ignore him or do whatever feels good to us. Jesus even describes following him as taking up a cross (Matthew 16:24), meaning we will often suffer as he did. But Jesus is inviting us to see that the yoke of following him is *easy to carry*—not because our shoulders are strong or because obeying him is easy, but because of *the kind of master Jesus is.*

Jesus is gentle and lowly (v. 29 ESV), the opposite of harsh and unyielding. His love for us does not waver based on how perfectly we obey him. He asks us to follow him because he knows we need him at every moment, like sheep need a shepherd. And he loves us, so he, the Good Shepherd, gave himself for us to save us (John 10:11). He cares so deeply for us, he invites us to cast our burdens on him (Psalm 55:22) and promises never to leave us (Matthew 28:20).

Jesus asks us to wear his yoke, not to burden us with expectations, but to invite us to *remain under his care.* Knowing who Jesus is, we would never want to become free of his yoke or out from under his care. Following Jesus is not easy, but it's the lightest non-burden burden of all.

Prayer: Lord, you know what is burdening me right now. Thank you for loving me and being my Shepherd. Give me courage and strength to obey you.

Reflection Question: What kinds of burdens or expectations are heaviest on you right now?

Jesus Calms the Storm

CLARK FOBES IV

For all the technological advances mankind has made to heal diseases and improve human flourishing, one thing we still cannot control is natural disasters. Storms have a tendency to reveal what we truly believe—about life, our sense of being, and especially about God.

In Mark 4, Jesus' disciples encounter a storm on the sea of Galilee. Though many of them are skilled fishermen, this storm is so severe that they fear for their lives. In their distress, the disciples call on Jesus as "Teacher" (v. 38) to do something. Mark uses this title to show the type of faith the disciples have had up until now. In facing the storm, they believed Jesus was simply a good teacher who could teach them *how* to survive. They are shocked when Jesus commands the storm and winds to cease.

Jesus demonstrates something about himself the disciples have not yet understood: He is not simply a teacher, but rather the King of all creation. This powerful act causes the disciples' fear of the storm to be eclipsed by an even greater awe of Jesus.

When we face storms in life, our natural tendency is to plead with Jesus for a way out. But Jesus leads the disciples directly into the storm on the boat. His desire is not that they will avoid all storms of suffering. Instead, Jesus uses storms to show he is more than a good teacher; as the Son of God, he is in complete control and has power to save.

Mark's language about the violence of the storm echoes Jonah 1, where sailors throw Jonah into the sea to calm the storm. Though Jesus calms the storm from the boat in Mark 4, the allusion back to Jonah points to the way Jesus will be thrown into a storm when he suffers on the cross. By suffering for us under the storm of God's wrath, Jesus ensures that we will not perish as we face our own storms. And we will never have to face them alone. The powerful God of the universe is in the boat with us.

Prayer: Jesus, thank you for being powerful over all suffering. Thank you for weathering the storm of God's wrath on the cross and assuring me of your presence through any storm I face.

Reflection Question: How can the storms in your life right now help you know Jesus more?

Lunch for Five Thousand

CONNIE LEUNG NELSON

How would you react if you witnessed a miracle?

Mark 6 tells the story of Jesus' miraculously feeding five thousand people. We aren't told *how* five loaves and two fish multiply to feed so many; it takes some imagination to fill in the gaps. Maybe as the disciples were distributing the bread and the fish, the bottom of the basket was never seen until thousands of loaves and fish were pulled out of it. Or maybe portions of bread and fish kept regenerating as the food was passed around. No matter how the events unfolded, Jesus truly performed miracles.

As a child, I was excited to hear that Jesus could do amazing science-and-physics-defying things. But as I got older, I didn't know what to think of miracles. I had heard testimonies from missionaries and doctors who witnessed miracles—astonishing healings or people rescued from life-threatening situations against all odds. But in my own life, pets or loved ones got sick and died. Floods and tornadoes claimed innocent lives. I wondered whether God chose not to intervene with a miracle because of something about me or my prayers. Without realizing it, I had mistaken miraculous intervention as proof of Jesus' attention and care for me, or maybe as a sort of reward for praying right.

Jesus tells us how to think about his miracles: "Do not believe me unless I do the works of my Father" (John 10:37). Miracles like the feeding of the five thousand prove to us that Jesus is God in human flesh. But Jesus' *love* for you and me—a love that existed before we were born (Ephesians 1:4–6), a love that is never determined by what we do or don't do or pray or don't pray—is proven through his death on the cross to save us from our sins.

We don't know why God chooses to act with miracles only rarely. But we do know that our all-wise heavenly Father works in all things for the good of us his children (Romans 8:28). His care for us may or may not include miraculous interventions, but it will always include the everyday ways he meets our needs.

Friend, God's love for sinners is a miracle in itself. Jesus' loving sacrifice is enough to sustain us when we don't get the miracle we hope for. We can come to him with both our desires and laments, knowing he cares about it all.

Prayer: Father, help me see all the ways you have cared for me and answered my prayers in the past and still answer them today.

Reflection Question: What needs can I bring to God today?

Take Heart

ERICSON JOUBERT

One episode of the miniseries *Obi-Wan Kenobi* finds a young princess Leia and Jedi Master Obi-Wan on the run from the feared Inquisitors. Leia asks Obi-Wan, "How does it work—the Force? What does it feel like?" Obi-Wan turns toward her and asks if she's ever been afraid of the dark. Leia nods her head yes, and Obi-Wan asks, "How does it feel when you turn on the light?" Leia replies, "I feel safe." Obi-wan says, "Yes, it feels like that."[1]

We can all understand what it's like to find relief in a stressful situation. Light can provide comfort when you're lost and need to know where to go. A hug from a friend can reassure you after a hard day at school or work.

Matthew tells of a time when the disciples are out on the water fishing between roughly three and six in the morning. Jesus has told the disciples to meet him on the other side when they finish their work. As they sail onward, the wind and waves around them grow increasingly powerful. The disciples suddenly see a ghost walking toward them on the water! Jesus quickly assures his friends that it's him. Who else could defy the laws of gravity by walking on water? Jesus comforts his terrified friends: "Take courage! It is I. Don't be afraid" (14:27).

Jesus echoes the words God had spoken to Abraham, Moses, and Joshua (Genesis 15:1; Exodus 3:12; Joshua 1:9), reminding the disciples that he is God's own Son. Only Jesus, through whom all things were made (John 1:3), can display mastery over creation. Jesus invites the disciples to experience his presence and peace, even in the most stressful of situations.

Hearing Jesus' words, Peter is convinced he can meet Jesus on the water. When he walks toward Jesus, however, he begins to sink. Jesus lovingly rebukes Peter: "You of little faith . . . why did you doubt?" (Matthew 14:31). Jesus wants Peter to see that he is the one the winds and waves obey. When we find ourselves in situations that overwhelm us, we can look to Jesus for comfort and strength.

Prayer: Lord, help me face my fears with courage and trust in you. Thank you for strengthening me in my greatest hours of need.

Reflection Question: How does knowing the presence of Jesus comfort you in stressful situations?

---

1. "Obi-Wan Explains to Leia How the Force Works | Obi-Wan Kenobi (2022)," YouTube, June 1, 2022, www.youtube.com/watch?v=KtXH-Wh7nRU.

Follow the Leader

KYLE HOFFSMITH

Did you ever play "Follow the Leader" when you were younger? One child goes to the front of the line and walks through the classroom or the playground while everyone else follows along. The person at the front of the line decides where to go, when to turn, and when to stop.

Following another child in a game is one thing, but following Jesus through life is another. When we read the Bible, some things Jesus says sound confusing, like his instructions to take up the cross in order to be his disciple. His words and his life show us what he means.

First, Jesus invites you to deny yourself. This means you are not the most important person in the world. Second, join Jesus in bearing a cross (Luke 9:23). Each day, ask for his help to put God's desires for you ahead of your own, just as Jesus did (Matthew 26:36–46). Lastly, follow him wherever he leads alongside other Christians he puts in your life. Jesus goes on to say that if we don't follow him, we gain all that the world has to offer but lose our souls—the deepest part of who we are—and that if we lose our lives for his sake, we will find true life (Luke 9:24–25).

It makes sense that we would follow Jesus rather than ourselves because of who he is. It's not as though we are following another child around a playground; instead, we are following the King of the world who knows what is best for our souls—the King who "humbled himself by becoming obedient to death—even death on a cross" (Philippians 2:8).

Because we follow such a humble servant-leader, we can trust he knows what is best for us. Beyond this, knowing that Jesus paid the punishment we deserve for our sin shows us that we can trust him. Following Jesus is costly, but he promises it will be worth it as we find true life in him. Will you let him lead you?

Prayer: God, thank you for the reminder that my life is ultimately not about me but about following Jesus. Give me the strength to follow him today. Amen.

Reflection Question: What are the hardest areas of your life to deny in order to fully follow Jesus today?

Jesus, the Bread of Life

REBECCA HECK

For decades in his small Indiana town, my grandfather volunteered for a ministry called Bread of Life. When I close my eyes, I can still see the van, logo printed on the side, and my grandfather climbing in and out of the front seat as he delivered food and supplies to those who needed it. The image sticks with me because it reminds me that my grandfather cared about others and did everything he could to tangibly help with whatever he had.

Each of the gospel writers describes a time when Jesus miraculously fed thousands of people who came to hear him teach, meeting their physical need of hunger. In John 6, the people whom Jesus had miraculously fed can't get that experience with Jesus out of their heads. But Jesus calls out their true motives. He says they weren't coming to find him because they saw his power as God, but because he had fed them and now they were hungry again (v. 26).

The Bible speaks again and again to the importance for believers to care tangibly for their neighbors, just as Jesus did. At the same time, John 6 shows us that Jesus is calling for a deeper hunger from his followers—a hunger not to satisfy our physical needs but to know and worship him as the one true God. The people ask Jesus for tangible blessings, but as the Bread of Life, he wants to satisfy the deepest questions and longings of their souls.

Jesus calls us to seek him as the one who gives eternal salvation and everlasting dignity and hope. When we do, we find that our soul hunger is fed in full and our momentary desires no longer hold as much importance. We are free from striving for the next best thing and instead can rest in the eternal provision of Jesus' perfect work for us.

Prayer: King Jesus, forgive me for not seeing how much I need you in every moment of my life. I praise you for how you care for me through food, shelter, family, and friends. Deepen my faith, so that in seeking you, I will find you and be filled.

Reflection Question: In which areas are you seeking God so he can provide for each moment instead of asking him to provide for a lifetime?

A Mountaintop Experience

JOEY TURNER

I took my phone out of airplane mode, and the messages poured in. "You guys okay?" "Are you near the volcano?" My family had just arrived in Sicily, home of Mount Etna, which had erupted for the first time in six years. A few days later, we ascended the mountain and stood in awe of its height, beauty, and power.

We arrive at Matthew 17 remembering that this is not the first time God has appeared in glory, displaying his character and presence to one of his prophets. In Exodus 34, God's prophet Moses ascends Mount Sinai. God meets Moses, speaks to him, and passes by. Moses descends with a glowing face. In 1 Kings 19, God's prophet Elijah is on Mount Horeb. God meets Elijah, speaks to him, and passes by. Elijah covers his face while meeting with the Lord.

In Matthew 17, God's final prophet, Jesus, ascends a mountain with Peter, James, and John. Jesus is *transfigured* before them, meaning that his face shines like the sun and his clothes become as white as light. Moses and Elijah, long deceased, both appear and talk with Jesus. God proclaims, "This is my Son, whom I love; with him I am well pleased. Listen to him!" (v. 5).

God's people were supposed to listen to his prophets—messengers of the heavenly King. When a good king hears about subjects who are disobeying his rules, he sends a messenger to warn them of what will happen if they continue to disobey. God's prophets communicate blessings of covenant-keeping obedience and punishments of covenant-breaking disobedience.

God sent Jesus as his divine messenger. On the cross, Jesus both fulfilled covenant-keeping obedience and suffered the consequences of our covenant-breaking disobedience and therefore securing the blessings of obedience for us. Jesus himself is the very presence of God with us. He is God's last and greatest messenger, who not only delivers God's news to his people but is also the best news for God's people through his sacrificial death and life-giving resurrection.

Throughout history, God repeated the theme of a prophet on a mountain, so that when we get to Matthew 17 we will stand in awe of Jesus, God's special prophet. Now we repeat the message of the final messenger, Christ, to a world longing for freedom from sin and death.

Prayer: Father, thank you for revealing yourself through Jesus so I might know you. Help me to listen, understand, and obey.

Reflection Question: What are some ways you can listen to God?

Jesus Came for the Lost

DAWSON COOPER

I remember learning that a boy liked me in middle school. I was thrilled, maybe a little nervous, as I anticipated a girl like me dating a boy like him. *Someone wants to spend time with me! Get to know me! Thinks I'm cute!* We all want to be pursued, don't we? But pursuit can get derailed. You break up, and you don't feel wanted anymore.

In Matthew 18, Jesus uses a parable to describe God's pursuit of his people. A shepherd is taking care of one hundred sheep. When one of the sheep strays, the shepherd leaves the ninety-nine to search for the one. When he finds the lost sheep, he rejoices greatly.

Jesus' rural audience would have been familiar with the risks and rewards of keeping track of sheep. Going after one that wandered away doesn't seem logical. Wouldn't it make sense for the shepherd to stay with the ninety-nine that are safe and hope the one finds its way back? But that is not God's way. God pursues his people whatever the cost. He saves them from the punishment of sin and death through the life, death, and resurrection of Jesus. Isaiah 53:6 says, "We all, like sheep, have gone astray, each of us has turned to our own way; and the Lord has laid on him the iniquity of us all." To save the lost sheep, it cost God his Son. Once saved, we are kept.

Even as "little ones" who believe, we are prone to wander, to choose our own path. We find ourselves feeling lost, disconnected, or perhaps hopeless that God would want us back in his fold. But to God, we were never truly lost.

God does not leave even one little one. He seeks the lost, retrieves them, and rejoices over them. God's love for his people is unconditional and eternal, never fickle like our love. God's pursuit of us depends only on his longing love for us, which he has proven once and for all by sending Jesus to save us.

Prayer: Lord, thank you for pursuing me even when I am prone to wander. Keep me close to you through your unfailing love and grace.

Reflection Question: How does God's desire to pursue you at great cost, even when you stray, affect your relationship with him?

Don't Worry About What the Crowd Thinks

CHELSEA KINGSTON ERICKSON

As a basketball player, Michael Jordan achieved GOAT status, with six NBA championships for the Chicago Bulls and ten scoring titles. But after his father died in 1993, the legendary player gave it all up to pursue his dream of playing professional baseball. Jordan didn't play well in the minors, and he received a lot of criticism—most notably, a *Sports Illustrated* article slamming his performance. When asked about the criticism, Jordan said he didn't really care about what people wanted him to do. The important thing was that his father had encouraged him to pursue baseball.[1]

In John 8, we see Jesus offer a similar response to his critics, the religious leaders. One day, while Jesus is teaching in the temple courts, the Pharisees begin to question what right he has to teach them. Jesus tells them that the Son of Man will be "lifted up," referring to the kind of death he would die—and then overcome—on our behalf.

Jesus doesn't need to worry about what the religious authorities think he should be doing; God the Father has already told him, and he does it willingly. He goes to the cross, demonstrating his full obedience to his Father. In his life, by always pleasing God the Father, Jesus does what we have failed to do. In his death, he pays the penalty for our sin. In rising again, he makes a way for us to live with God forever.

God calls us to obey him, but we grow in pleasing God as we look to Jesus for his power to transform us (2 Corinthians 3:18). If you have trusted in Jesus, then you don't need to worry about what others think you should be doing. God your Father has already shown you.

Prayer: Thank you, Father, for sending Jesus to live, die, and rise again in my place. Thank you that his obedience makes it possible for me to be called your child. Help me not to worry about approval from others, but to rest secure in your acceptance of me. Amen.

Reflection Question: Where are you most tempted to seek acceptance from others? How could God's acceptance of you through Jesus make a difference?

---

1. Jason Guerrasio, "Michael Jordan's Final Conversation with Dad Prompted His First Retirement from the NBA to Play Baseball," *Business Insider*, May 10, 2020, www.businessinsider.com/michael-jordan-fathers-death-prompted-retirement-baseball-the-last-dance-2020-5.

The Good Shepherd

KATHERINE PRECHT STINE

Lions, bears, thieves, thorny bushes—these are just a few of the dangers to sheep we read about in the Bible. Without a shepherd to care for them, sheep are completely vulnerable. The Bible says that just like sheep, we need a caring shepherd too.

Jesus, the Good Shepherd, answers that need. When Jesus goes from town to town teaching, healing, and proclaiming the good news of the kingdom, he looks at the crowds and "had compassion on them, because they were harassed and helpless, like sheep without a shepherd" (Matthew 9:36). Jesus sees us in our defenseless state—spiritually dead and unable to save ourselves from punishment for sin—and he intervenes to save us into abundant life forever with him.

We see more of this life "to the full" (John 10:10) with the Good Shepherd described in Psalm 23. In receiving abundant life, we will lack nothing. He will give us rest, provide for all our needs, and comfort and protect us. Ezekiel 34 tells us that God will rescue his sheep from all their scattered places, that he will "search for the lost and bring back the strays, bind up the injured and strengthen the weak" (v. 16).

Sometimes the threats of the Enemy to steal, kill, and destroy may seem very real to you. At other times you may not notice your need for a shepherding Savior. The call is the same either way: Remember that your Savior knows you and helps you know him. Listen to your Good Shepherd's voice and follow him wherever he leads you. Your great God "tends his flock like a shepherd: He gathers the lambs in his arms and carries them close to his heart" (Isaiah 40:11). Above all, his posture toward you is one of a love so powerful that he deemed you worthy of laying down his own life that you may live with him forever.

Prayer: Father, show me my deep need for you and remind me of your provision for everything I need. Thank you, Jesus, for laying your life down for me and for being my Good Shepherd.

Reflection Question: How does it encourage you to know that Jesus is your Good Shepherd—compassionate and protective toward you as he holds you close to his heart?

How Can I Be Good Enough?

KARISHMA SRIRAM

I've always been a high achiever. I wanted to get perfect grades, play the viola perfectly, and be the perfect child, friend, sister. It wasn't until high school that I realized, *I'm not perfect.* To my teenage self, this was jarring. What could I do to be good enough?

The lawyer here asks a similar question—what do I have to do to inherit eternal life? (Luke 10:25). He is able to recite the Scripture "Love the Lord your God . . .," checking off in his mind that he already loves the Lord with all his heart, soul, strength, and mind. He asks who his neighbor is, implying that it's another thing to check off the list when completed. The lawyer is trying to earn his right standing with God—loving God perfectly, loving his neighbor perfectly. He wants to earn his salvation. He thinks he *can* be perfect. But he can't. I can't. No one can.

Jesus tells a story (vv. 30–35). A man is attacked and lies dying by the side of the road. Who will respond with compassion? Shockingly, it's not the priest or the Levite (members of the religious elite) who stops to help. Instead, a Samaritan assists in the man's recovery. Most of Jesus' listeners do not regard Samaritans worthy of their time, seeing them as half-Jews. By featuring a marginalized person as the hero of his story, Jesus challenges the lawyer's assumptions about who will inherit eternal life.

Like the lawyer, we are unable to justify ourselves. How are we good neighbors? Should we pick and choose whom we should love as our neighbor? Jesus' work on our behalf enables *all* of us to love everyone around us in a radical way.

Prayer: Thank you, gracious Father, for offering me eternal life through faith in Christ. Thank you for your Son, Jesus, whose perfect life in my place compels me to show mercy to others.

Reflection Question: How are you tempted to rely on yourself instead of resting in God's grace?

We All Need God's Grace

ANNA MEADE HARRIS

As a big sister, I still remember how much more my little brother got away with than I did. I was busy following the rules . . . and resenting how my parents loved my mischievous brother as much as they loved me. So I recognize myself in Jesus' parable about two brothers (Luke 15:11–32). The older thinks he deserves his father's love, and the younger knows he doesn't. Yet both are equally loved.

The story begins with the younger brother asking for his share of his father's wealth. It's an insult to his dad. Asking for an inheritance before the person dies is kind of like saying you wish that person would die. Taking the money, the son "set off for a distant country and there squandered his wealth in wild living" (v. 13). Nearly starving, he has to take a job feeding pigs (note: Jews are forbidden to touch pigs). Cut off from his family and in defiance of his culture, the younger brother may as well be dead.

Remembering that his dad is rich, he wonders about returning home as a servant. He doesn't know that dad has been longing for his wild-living, much-loved son to return. In a display of joy unheard of for a man of his status, the father runs to hug his son, restores his sonship, and throws a lavish party to celebrate his homecoming.

But big brother is *not happy* that baby brother is warmly welcomed. "All these years I've been slaving for you and never disobeyed your orders" (v. 29). *Dad, you never even gave me a goat to barbecue with my friends, but here you are, throwing a huge bash for my worthless brother.* The father's grace toward his rule-breaking younger son offends his self-righteous, rule-following older son, making it harder for the eldest to accept his father's love.

If you're a rule follower like me, you need God's grace. If you're a rule bender—or breaker!—you need God's grace. You don't have to be "good" to make God love you (you can't keep all the rules anyway); nor can you be so "bad" that he stops loving you. Either way, God loves you because you belong to him. When you come home to him, accepting your total dependence on Jesus for salvation and all you need, he throws a party because he is so happy (v. 10). God is *always with you* and *all that he has is yours.*

Prayer: Father, help me not to judge your grace toward others. Fill me with gratitude for your grace toward me.

Reflection Question: How does it make you feel to know that God celebrates your salvation with a great big party?

The God Who Cries

LIZ EDRINGTON

I recently watched the live-streamed funeral of my friend Laura, who had lost an intense four-month battle with cancer. It was brutal not to be able to be with my friends to grieve together.

In the story of Lazarus in John 11, *the one who will defeat death also cries over death.* Have you ever imagined what it was like for Mary and Martha to see their hero cry? They had total confidence in his power to heal. They asked him to come, having an unshakable hope in his ability to work a miracle. Instead of snapping his fingers and immediately bringing Lazarus back to life, Jesus *enters into* the grief. With his tears, Jesus acknowledges the heaviness and wrongness of death. He doesn't ask the mourners to "remember the good things about Lazarus's life." He doesn't quote Scripture to try to get them to look on the bright side. Instead, he lets the situation allow him to be "deeply moved in spirit and troubled."

I mean, c'mon, Jesus. They're already devastated. Now you're going to go and get all distraught too? Won't crying just make it even worse? No, it won't. Jesus enters into their suffering wholeheartedly and shares in it.

Jesus' response is convicting. I'd often rather give advice than allow my heart to be moved by someone's struggle. I'd rather suggest something helpful than join in the sadness. But Jesus invites us, as he is, to be honest about how horrible sickness, brokenness, and death are. We get to look *at* him as our example. And yet we also get to look *to* him as the resurrection and the life (v. 25). His empty tomb means death will never be the end of the story for those who believe in him. We can be sad over all the brokenness in this world, but we never grieve without hope (1 Thessalonians 4:13). Our hope is based not on our feelings, but on a living God who defeated death once and for all.

Prayer: Jesus, help me be honest about the sad, hard, and broken things in my life and this world. Help me trust that you enter into my sorrow and grieve with me.

Reflection Question: What story in your life would Jesus be sad about, even if you have a hard time being sad about it?

Jesus Loves Kids

ANNE SANFORD

I recently visited an art museum that had an exhibit of ancient artifacts. A small clay figurine caught my attention. If I had found it on the street, I wouldn't have given it a second glance. But because a curator with a better eye and more knowledge than myself deemed it worthy for display, I found myself examining it with interest.

Like museum curators, Jesus has the divine ability to see value and worth where others do not. Jesus' disciples are rebuking people for bringing children to see him (Matthew 19:13–15). The disciples have been with Jesus throughout his ministry. They have seen him work miracles and care for the poor and the sick. You would think they'd get Jesus' mission by now, but in this instance, they miss it.

Jesus sees and cares for the vulnerable (Matthew 5:5). He sees and cares for those who can offer him nothing in return (20:28), because in Jesus' own words, he came "to seek and save the lost" (Luke 19:10). These children who were brought to Jesus held no great value in their society, but they mattered greatly to him. They also allowed him the opportunity to show his followers, once again, what the kingdom of heaven looks like (see Matthew 5:2–12).

Being a teenager is tough for a million reasons. One of them is that you're no longer a child but you're also not an adult. It's easy to feel lost in that in-between stage. It's easy to feel unseen and unknown. But you are seen. Your Savior, Jesus Christ, knows you and loves you with a perfect love. When you feel lost or vulnerable or like you have nothing to offer, I pray you will remember that Jesus loves you so much that he died and rose again to save you from your sins. You matter to your Savior.

Prayer: Lord, when I feel lost or unseen, remind me of your great love for me. Give me eyes to see others who may not feel loved or known, and give me courage to share your love with them. Thank you for loving me enough to give your life for me. Amen.

Reflection Question: What are ways you feel seen and known in your daily life? How do those point you to Jesus?

Only Jesus Satisfies

HUEY LEE

I still remember when I got my first smartphone—the first Apple iPhone. I naively believed that my iPhone would make my life more meaningful, efficient, joyful, and connected. In a matter of days, however, I found myself more distracted, dependent, and isolated. The allure of this piece of technology overpromised and underdelivered—no fault of its own.

One day, Jesus encounters a rich man who had it all—fame, money, success, popularity (Mark 10:17–22). He may well have been the pride and envy of his community. Yet we see this wealthy and influential leader in his community run up and kneel in desperation before Jesus. The rich are not accustomed to running, let alone kneeling before anyone. Not only that, his question in verse 17, "What must I do to inherit eternal life?" exposes a deeper reality—namely, that he is experiencing a sense of emptiness. He has it all in the eyes of the world, and it isn't enough. This sobering exchange between this man and Jesus reveals a restlessness that no amount of worldly achievements and accolades can satisfy. When we trust something other than God to give us significance or meaning, it's only a matter of time before that thing leaves us wanting more. We may feel sad, anxious, or even depressed because that thing isn't fulfilling us.

The early church father Augustine of Hippo said, "You have made us for yourself, O Lord, and our heart is restless until it rests in you." We regularly need to be rescued from the possessions and people we center our lives on that we think will give us satisfaction, significance, and security. This rescue cannot be found in anyone else but God.

Jesus had the true riches and greater glory in heaven. Yet he gave it all up willingly and sacrificially so that we might gain true and lasting satisfaction and significance, secured for us by his life, death, and resurrection. Jesus rescues us by his grace and invites us to find our joy and hope in the only One who will never disappoint us.

Prayer: Lord, I am prone to looking to the people and things of this world for my worth and satisfaction. Rescue me by your grace, and help me fix my eyes on Jesus, who will never fail me. Amen.

Reflection Question: What is something or someone that has taken too much prominence in your life and left you empty and restless?

A Short Man in a Tall Tree

CONNIE LEUNG NELSON

I used to dream I would meet my favorite artists, who would somehow take notice of me and we would become friends. It's a little embarrassing, but I think I understand a bit of what Zacchaeus hopes for when he climbs a tree to get a glimpse of Jesus in Luke 19. And Zacchaeus gets much more than a glimpse. Jesus spots him and says, "I must stay at your house today" (v. 5). But Jesus' action upsets the crowds, who dislike Zacchaeus because of his reputation for dishonest dealings. They judge Jesus for being "the guest of a sinner" (v. 7). Zacchaeus then turns to Jesus and makes a public promise to pay back whatever he stole fourfold and to give half his possessions to the poor (v. 8).

Pay attention to Jesus' response to Zacchaeus. Jesus does not say, "Because you have decided to do good, you're saved." He says, "Today salvation has come to this house . . . for the Son of Man came to seek and to save the lost" (vv. 9–10).

Jesus is clear. *He* is Zacchaeus's salvation; salvation is *not* found in Zacchaeus's act of paying back stolen money. Jesus seeks and saves this lost man by noticing him, asking to stay with him, and ultimately going to the cross for him. Zacchaeus may have climbed a tree to try to see Jesus, but Jesus had known his name and that he would go to his house way before he walked into Zacchaeus's line of sight. Jesus' death on the cross wipes away Zacchaeus's *every* sin so that God's wrath would not fall on him. Jesus completely saves Zacchaeus.

In the same way, Jesus sought us and saved us completely by his perfect life and his death on the cross. Jesus' disciple John says, "This is love: not that we loved God, *but that he loved us* and sent his Son as an atoning sacrifice for our sins" (1 John 4:10, emphasis added). Jesus' love for us existed before we could even do one act of obedience. Jesus asks us to obey him because it is our way of responding to God's goodness in Jesus, who first loved us. Because our Savior demonstrated his incomparably great love in coming to seek us, and save us, we don't obey to be saved; we obey *because* we are saved.

Prayer: Lord, help me see how much I continue to need you. Help me see how much you love me, and give me the strength to obey you.

Reflection Question: How would you tell the story of your salvation with Jesus as the hero?

Here Comes the King!

KENDAL CONNER

I loved walking home from the bus stop when I was in middle school. As I came into my driveway, I would look up at my bedroom window where my dog would be wagging her tail in excitement. As soon as she saw me, she would run down the hall and eagerly wait for me at the door. This simple act made me feel so loved.

In Mark 11, the people wait for Jesus and welcome him because his entry into Jerusalem is a story of return and celebration. The passage begins with Jesus and his disciples on the Mount of Olives. The Mount of Olives is the mountain east of the city mentioned by the prophet Ezekiel in his vision (11:23). Ezekiel sees God's presence depart from the temple before its eventual destruction by the Babylonians. Ezekiel's vision was significant in the history of God's people because even after they rebuilt the temple under Zerubbabel, God's presence had yet to return.

Until Jesus. Not only does Jesus come down to Jerusalem from the Mount of Olives, but he rides into the city on a donkey, fulfilling a prophecy given by Zechariah (9:9). In this moment, Jesus reveals himself as the king "righteous and victorious" and the very presence of God—God incarnate—returning to his people. So as the Israelites turn their eyes to the Mount of Olives—the very place where the presence of God rested after departing the temple—they are witnessing his return. What a moment of celebration!

The celebration did not last, however. The shouts of "hosanna" will soon fade as the Jewish leaders and Roman authorities conspire to lead Jesus to the cross. Yet through this very cross, Jesus establishes his kingly throne forever. Just as the temple was once destroyed, so will his body be also. Unlike the first temple, however, in three days Jesus will rise, never to be destroyed again. Because of Jesus, the presence of God now dwells in his people through the Holy Spirit. In Jesus, God is near now, and one day, he will come again. What a return and what a celebration that will be!

Prayer: Father, thank you for sending your Son to defeat the power of death and lead me back into relationship with you.

Reflection Question: How does remembering God's act of sending Jesus encourage you in the moments when God feels distant?

The Most Important Commandment

MIKE MCGARRY

"Which is the greatest commandment?" The lawyer who asked Jesus this question assumed faithfulness could be measured by keeping the "right" commandments (Matthew 22:36). We, too, try to figure out how good is "good enough." But to do so completely misunderstands the point of the Law and the Prophets.

"The Law and the Prophets" is a way to speak about the Old Testament. Instead of making a list of most important commands, Jesus calls his followers to love God with their whole selves and to love their neighbors as generously as they care for themselves (vv. 37–40). He refuses to separate the acts of loving God and loving others. They are two expressions of the same love, flowing from our whole heart, soul, and mind. If we do this, then we're keeping "all the Law and the Prophets," which is impossible for us to do. Loving God is hard because it's so easy to doubt his goodness in this confusing world. Loving our neighbor is difficult because we're sinful, selfish people who often find that our neighbors can be really annoying.

This is why the Bible reminds us, "We love because [God] first loved us" (1 John 4:19). We know what love is and we know how to love because of the way God has loved us through Jesus Christ.

Some of us can hear "love God and love others" as a demanding whip, rebuking all our doubt and selfishness. But this isn't an example of Jesus saying, "Do better! Try harder!" We love God with our whole selves because he is worthy of everything we have to give. We love our neighbor, even when it's costly, because we have received the costly love of Jesus through the cross and empty tomb. He *sets us free to love* by defeating our sin, *shows us* what love looks like, and *gives it to us* so that we can share his love with others.

Prayer: Lord Jesus, give me your selfless love. Fan into flame in me a deep and abiding love for you and let it lead me to love others in your name.

Reflection Question: How is Jesus the best example of the perfect love of God and love for people? How can looking at Jesus shape the way we follow him?

Washing Feet

KENDAL CONNER

One of the most memorable scenes in *The Lord of the Rings: The Return of the King* film is the coronation of King Aragorn. As the new king walks through the crowd, the hobbits do what subjects are expected to do in the presence of a king—they bow. However, the king stops them, and in an unimaginable act, *bows to them*. He does not demand humility from them, but rather humbles himself before them. All who witness the king's act follow suit—bowing to those who were once considered the lowest of the low. Wow!

Even this unthinkable act pales in comparison to what Jesus' disciples felt seeing him bow before them to wash their feet (John 13:4–5). Peter's first reaction is to try to stop Jesus. Peter knows washing feet is a dirty job meant only for a servant. While Peter isn't wrong to be shocked by Jesus' humility, he misses the point.

Knowing that his death is quickly approaching, Jesus gathers his disciples to prepare them for what is about to happen. Jesus would soon enact the greatest display of humility in all of human history. The one true King of kings would humble himself by taking on the penalty of a criminal—a penalty he did not deserve—and dying a humiliating death on a cross (Philippians 2:8). Why would a king do such a thing? Jesus knows that through this act of humiliation, he would ultimately humiliate death itself, defeating its power by walking out of the grave—alive!

When Jesus washes his disciples' feet, he is preparing them for the inauguration of God's kingdom that is coming, but not in the way anyone expected. It would be an upside-down kingdom, a kingdom in which the king willingly brings himself low in order to raise up others.

Like Aragorn leading the crowds at his coronation, Jesus is giving an example for his disciples to follow. If the master humbles himself, how much more should his servants? Jesus, the ultimate example of humility, asks us to humble ourselves to serve others—knowing that in the kingdom of God "those who exalt themselves will be humbled, and those who humble themselves will be exalted" (Matthew 23:12).

Prayer: God, thank you for humbling yourself to the point of death on a cross so that I may be raised to new life in you.

Reflection Question: How can you serve others this week?

The Last Supper

KARISHMA SRIRAM

Lunchtime was my favorite part of seventh grade. I used to head to my usual table, knowing that my closest friends would join me. We'd eat—sometimes sampling one another's meals—share stories, and laugh about funny moments in class. But I remember a day when a friend had been invited to a birthday party and I had not. Suddenly, sharing food and stories was harder; we avoided eye contact.

Imagine Jesus, who knows that Judas will betray him, sharing a meal with Judas, even as he is planning to *die* for Judas (Mark 14:17–25). Jesus even dips bread into the same bowl as Judas. The Passover meal points to the way Jesus will give his body and blood for believers as the truest and purest sign of his love. Jesus loves the very man he knows will betray him—the man who turns him in to the Roman authorities, sending him to the cross.

God's love is unlike any love we are able to muster ourselves, no matter how hard we try. I wasn't even able to look my friend in the eye at that lunch table, much less to share food with her, to *love* her. But Jesus is perfect in love, in holiness, in goodness, in kindness. I am not. In his perfect love, he died for us on the cross. He has rescued us and brought us into relationship with our perfect God.

Jesus calls us to become more like him so that maybe one day, I can look across the table at my friend and give even 0.00001 percent of the love Jesus has given me. Through the Lord's Supper, we commune with Christ and our church family—even those we find hard to love.

Prayer: Lord, thank you for Jesus, who came to this earth to love me beyond what I can understand. Thank you for his death and resurrection that gives me hope of life forever with you. Make me more like Christ every day. Amen.

Reflection Question: How do you need Jesus to give you his love for someone today?

Staying Connected to Jesus

REBECCA LANKFORD

In *Finding Nemo*, the clownfish Nemo and his dad, Marlin, live inside a sea anemone. This detail is true to the natural world. Clownfish need sea anemones to survive. The anemone protects the clownfish from predators and provides food scraps for the clownfish to eat. At home in the anemone, the clownfish has everything it needs to flourish.

Spoken just hours before his arrest and crucifixion, Jesus' words to his disciples in John 15 tell us that we were created for a similar but deeper kind of life-giving relationship. Jesus explains that when we remain in him, the vine, we, the branches, cannot help but thrive spiritually and bear fruit for his glory.

No one has ever seen a gardener duct-taping a branch to a vine. The branch is naturally connected to the vine simply by being a branch. When connected to the vine, the branch cannot help but sprout new life. Similarly, we are connected to Jesus not because we choose him, but because he chose us. Our deep, unbreakable union with Jesus is a product of his grace toward us. When we place our faith in Jesus, we become intimately united to him, such that we become one with him and our lives are now "hidden with Christ in God" (Colossians 3:3). Just as a branch receives nutrients from the vine, being united to Christ means we receive the nutrients of his wisdom, power, and constant presence in our lives.

Notice that Jesus uses the word *remain* eleven times in seventeen verses. Not *visit* or *stop by*, but *remain*. Jesus invites us to enjoy and cultivate the life-giving union we have with him when we are united to him by grace through faith.

While there is no formula for deeper intimacy with Jesus, daily remaining in him may mean spending time with him in prayer, listening to his Word on the way to school, or taking a walk to enjoy the beauty of his creation. Feeling far from Jesus does not change the reality that Christians are united to him forever, for nothing can separate us from his love (Romans 8:39).

Prayer: Jesus, thank you for being the true vine and for loving me so much that you have permanently united me to yourself. Help me remain in you, in your Word, and in your love. Use me to bear fruit for your glory.

Reflection Question: What are some ways you can cultivate deeper intimacy with Jesus each day? How is he inviting you to remain in him today?

Jesus Prays a Desperate Prayer

CHRISTINA FOX

Our family once visited Israel and walked among the olive trees in Gethsemane, where Jesus went the night before his arrest. Some of the trees we saw were alive there on the night Jesus asked his friends to join him when he prayed.

Gethsemane is on a hillside, and from its vantage point, one can see the Temple Mount across the valley in Jerusalem. The temple of Jesus' day is not there now, but one can imagine what he might have seen as he bowed and prayed three times that he would not have to endure God's just punishment for our sins. He would have seen plumes of smoke billowing out from where lambs were sacrificed for sin—all the while, knowing he would be the final sacrifice.

Have you ever faced something fearful? Something you dreaded? Jesus understands. These verses show Jesus feeling intense fear and anguish as he anticipates the cross. Jesus isn't merely fearing the loss of his life; he anticipates bearing the weight of all our sins as he takes God's wrath for us. In fact, the word *Gethsemane* means "oil press." Here Jesus is truly "pressed" by the weight of our sin.

Meanwhile, his closest friends cannot even stay awake to pray, comfort, and show him compassion (Matthew 26:40–45). Chances are we've all had friends who let us down when we needed them most. Jesus' friends abandon him. He feels all alone with no one to help him (Psalm 22:11). Even so, he continues forward to the cross, dying for those very failures.

Jesus faced the anguish of the cross, cried out to the Father in prayer, and accepted the Father's will. He did so for you and for me. Our Savior knows the fears and sorrows we experience. He knows what it's like for friends to fail. Still, he willingly bore the weight of our sins so that we might be forgiven. Jesus' heart is for us.

Prayer: Lord Jesus, though I've felt fear in my life, I can't imagine what you felt at Gethsemane. Thank you for accepting the Father's will and for enduring the cross so I can be forgiven for my sins. Amen.

Reflection Question: What does it mean to you that Jesus understands the fears, sorrows, and betrayal you've felt?

Betrayed

MARK HOWARD

I vividly remember worrying as a teenager that God would get tired of my repeated failures and stop loving me. Maybe you know the feeling. I still sin more than I care to admit, but I no longer worry about losing God's love. The story of Jesus' arrest is a part of the reason.

By this point, Jesus has spent three years pouring himself out for others. He has patiently taught, prayed, and shown incredible feats of insight and power. He knows his death is approaching, and we're told he is in anguish to the point of sweating blood (Luke 22:44). It's a low point. But it's about to get worse.

Jesus realizes that while he is pouring out his soul in prayer, his friends have fallen asleep. They aren't there for him when he needs them most. Then he sees Judas, a close disciple, approaching with some people whose goal is Jesus' death. It's one thing to be betrayed, but it's so much worse to be betrayed by a friend. And Judas does so with a kiss.

When the other disciples wake up to what's happening, Peter grabs a sword and attacks (John 18:10). For years, Jesus has taught that he is not the sort of Messiah who builds his kingdom through violence, yet Peter still doesn't get it. Then Jesus turns to those who have come to arrest him—the chief priests, the officers of the temple guard, and the elders. They should be welcoming Jesus with open arms as their Savior and God, but they treat Jesus like a common criminal as they come at him with weapons of war.

Yet Jesus willingly endures the cross so that all who failed him might be saved. Even as he hangs on the cross, betrayed by his friend, abandoned by his disciples, and murdered by the people he came to save, Jesus cries out, "Father, forgive them, for they do not know what they are doing" (Luke 23:34).

The apostle Paul writes, "God demonstrates his own love for us in this: While we were still sinners, Christ died for us" (Romans 5:8). God already knows your faults and loves you anyway. There is nothing we can do to make God stop loving us. Turn again to him today and find rest in his love.

Prayer: Forgiving God, thank you for your unfailing love. Help me trust in you and share your love with the world.

Reflection Question: How does the story of Jesus' arrest change what you think about the love of God?

Betrayed Again

FAITH CHANG

I don't know what it is about people getting hurt that makes us laugh, but the many "fail" videos on the internet prove that most of us enjoy a bit of slapstick. Something about these unexpected, over-the-top, cringe-inducing moments is just funny. But some fails are too painful to watch, where people are hurt or deeply shamed. We all have moments when we've messed up badly. Moments we'd never want posted publicly, like Peter's epic failure in John 18.

Jesus has been arrested and is being subjected to a rigged trial in the high priest's palace. Outside in the courtyard, Peter tries to blend in. Three times that night, Peter is confronted about knowing Jesus. Three times, he insists he doesn't. Then a rooster crows, which hits Peter hard. Peter had earlier boasted that he'd *never* disown Jesus, even if everyone else did. He'd told Jesus he'd *die* for him. But Jesus had known better: "Before the rooster crows, you will disown me three times" (13:38). Peter remembers this and weeps.

End of scene. But not the end of Peter's story. John includes an account of Jesus' trial sandwiched between Peter's denials (18:19–24). Unlike Peter, Jesus stands strong when questioned, and all the way to the cross, where he will die for the sins of the world, including Peter's boasts and denials.

Have you ever disowned Jesus? Maybe you passed up an opportunity to share your faith because of fear. Maybe you've done things a Christian should never do. Perhaps like Peter, you've thought you were better than others. Though you may feel ashamed and afraid, don't lose hope.

After the resurrection, Jesus forgives and restores Peter (21:15–17). Filled with the Holy Spirit, Peter becomes a bold messenger of the gospel who eventually dies for Christ. Like Peter, you are not defined by your worst moments. Though your love for God may waver, God's commitment to you never changes. He knows all your failures—past, present, and future—and *still chooses you*. He died for the sins you're ashamed of and promises to forgive and change you. Your story is not over yet.

Prayer: God, thank you for being faithful even when I fail you. Transform me and give me courage to try again.

Reflection Question: What difference does it make to know that God knows all your failures and yet will not give up on you?

Innocent, but Found Guilty

ISAIAH A. MARSHALL

Think about a time when you went along with a group to do something, even though it felt wrong. In high school, I found myself in this position countless times, going along with a plan I knew wasn't right. Peer pressure is real. Will you follow the crowd, or will you follow what God says is right?

Matthew 27 describes Jesus' trial before Pilate, who serves as governor and judge. An angry crowd of jurors stands by. Accused by the religious leaders of claiming to be king of the Jews, Jesus stays silent while the crowd pressures the governor. Since it was customary to release one prisoner for the crowd, Pilate asks, "Which one do you want me to release to you: Barabbas, or Jesus who is called the Messiah?" (v. 17). The rowdy crowd chooses Barabbas, known to be a big-time criminal. In harmony, they chant "Crucify him" at our beloved Savior.

Caught between duty and the pressure of the mob, Pilate symbolically washes his hands, absolving himself of the decision. Yet he succumbs to the crowd's demands, releasing Barabbas and condemning Jesus to crucifixion. Pilate's choice is driven by fear, the weight of public pressure, and a desire to avoid further conflict.

Jesus' trial before this angry mob leads to his crucifixion. Little did the crowd know that when Jesus is lifted up on the cross, he is being lifted up to his throne where he reigns and is robed in majesty (Psalm 93:1). Some of those watching would soon discover the truth: The Son of God will not be defeated.

Crowd mentality is common in our school halls. The desire for acceptance may steer us away from what is right, even when deep down we know the truth. If we're honest, we've all been like Pilate, tempted to follow the crowd to please people. God knows, and he sent his Son to die for all the times we would choose popularity or conflict-avoidance instead of him. Praise the Lord, we know the truth Pilate didn't: We no longer have to chase after acceptance or strive for approval because God's acceptance found us through the love of a wounded Redeemer. When you face peer pressure, remember that Jesus stands with you and gives you courage to follow him.

Prayer: Lord, give me courage to choose your truth over the easy way. Help me resist peer pressure and stand firm in your love and justice.

Reflection Question: When have you felt pressured to follow the crowd? How did you respond? Talk to God about that experience.

Jesus Makes a Way for Us

HUEY LEE

After all that I've done, will God still love me? As a young Christian I was aware of my sin. I disobeyed his good commands, denied his truth, rejected his love, and often felt indifferent to the call to follow him. I struggled to feel assurance of God's love for me because of my failures and shortcomings. Can you relate?

In Mark 15:16–37, we read about the suffering Jesus endures on the cross. Every detail of Jesus' suffering and death is infused with meaning, serving as a window through which we see the love of God for sinners like me and you. As the apostle John reminds us, "This is how God showed his love among us. . . . [He] sent his Son as an atoning sacrifice for our sins" (1 John 4:9–10).

We see this love powerfully on display when Mark tells us what happens in the temple. The curtain in the temple in Jerusalem hangs heavy and thick, almost as thick as a wall. In the first temple, when God dwelt in the Most Holy Place, this curtain separated the people from his very presence. Only the high priest could go behind that curtain, and that only once a year. But at the moment Jesus dies, this massive curtain rips from top to bottom, as if God is saying, *I'm making a way where there was no way.*

The torn curtain in the temple means that through Jesus, the way into God's presence is flung open to us. There we find grace, mercy, and forgiveness for our sins. By faith in the crucified Christ, we can honestly, humbly, and boldly bring him our broken lives and our sin-bent hearts, fully confident that we will never be abandoned or turned away. The torn curtain assures us that God invites us into his presence. The cross assures us that God's grace and love are within reach.

Prayer: Lord Jesus, the cross assures me of your deep and abiding love, regardless of what I've done. Help me through your grace to live a life that pleases and honors you. Amen.

Reflection Question: In what ways are you tempted to doubt God's love for you? How does the torn curtain invite you to rest in his love for you?

The Tomb Is Empty!

ASHLEY KIM

When I was little, I lost my parents in a grocery store. They were next to me one moment, gone the next. Panicky and frantic, I scanned the aisles in search of some familiar figure. Everything felt unfamiliar and unfriendly. Where could they have gone? Why did the grocery store suddenly feel so big? I remember the sudden flood of relief when I found my parents—or realized they were there all along.

I wonder if the disciples felt a similar disorientation when Jesus died. Surely they were bewildered—wasn't Jesus the Messiah? Surely they were frightened—who were they to trust now?

John 20 tells us about one of Jesus' followers, Mary Magdalene. She recognizes, early on Sunday, that the stone in front of Jesus' tomb has been rolled away and his body is gone. This Mary brings the disciples to the tomb. As she returns to the tomb, she is afraid that a grave robber has come in the night and stolen his body.

Nothing could comfort Mary. Then she sees two angels, who ask her why she is weeping. She can only answer, "They have taken my Lord away, and I don't know where they have put him" (v. 13). The sight of angels would be shocking, but Mary hardly reacts. Even more shocking, Mary comes face-to-face with Jesus. Again, her grief blocks out all else. She cannot even recognize the one she seeks.

But Jesus is patient. "Why are you crying?" he asks, coaxing her to recognize that she no longer has cause for grief. "Who is it you are looking for?" It is as if he is saying, "Fear not. I'm here." When Mary still does not understand—when she assumes he is a stranger, perhaps the gardener—Jesus merely says her name: "Mary." At the familiar sound of *his* voice, her fear and grief melt away.

Death brings pain and loss because it means separation from the people we love. But not even death can separate us from the love of God in Christ (Romans 8:38–39). For us, like Mary, one of the great comforts of Jesus' resurrection is that we never have to be parted from him.

Prayer: Jesus, you are victorious over sin and death. Help me trust that you are always with me, even when I feel alone.

Reflection Question: How would your life be different if you always remembered Jesus' resurrection?

Good News for Doubters

MAC HARRIS

When I was in college, my campus minister encouraged us to take a personality test that would identify our spiritual strengths and weaknesses. This test also connected each of us to a particular biblical character who shared similar traits, and we all reported back with our results. As we went around the room, many people were excited to say names like Moses, David, Mary, Abraham, and so on. But when it was my turn to share, I couldn't help but recoil: *Doubting Thomas.*

A nickname is worth a thousand words, and Thomas—one of Jesus' closest friends and disciples—remains infamous for doubting whether Jesus had actually risen from the dead. Today, so many of us (including me) look down on Thomas for his reservations: *How could he doubt? Didn't he see the miracles? Didn't he hear Jesus' predictions?*

But when we look at Jesus' response, he is *far* kinder to Thomas than we are. Rather than rebuking his friend, Jesus reaches out his nail-pierced hand and says, "Put your finger here; see my hands. Reach out your hand and put it into my side. Stop doubting and believe" (John 20:27). Stunned, Thomas can't help but exclaim, "My Lord and my God!" (v. 28). One of the clearest confessions of Jesus' divinity in the entire Bible comes from the Bible's most famous doubter.

When we avoid or wallow in our doubts alone, they fester and grow. But when we bring them out in the open, talk about them with others, and lay them before Jesus, he is delighted to draw near and meet us in those doubts (even though he may not do so right away). In these illuminating few verses, we see God's gentle heart for us in our doubts, and we are freed to ask real, honest questions without fear or shame. There is good news for doubters like you and me: The tender touch of Jesus melts our skepticism into wonder, joy, and worship.

Prayer: Father God, I confess my doubts. Draw me deeper into your love and grace rather than deeper into my own head. Reveal yourself to me as more beautiful and believable than before. In Jesus' name. Amen.

Reflection Question: What is a question or doubt you think about often? How do you think God would respond to your doubts?

Supper with the Resurrected Jesus

CHELSEA KINGSTON ERICKSON

The next time you're watching a movie or your favorite TV series, notice when the actors eat. Movie directors widely recognize that having actors eat on screen humanizes them. Similarly, in Luke 24, two disciples understand that Jesus has risen from the dead when he shares a meal with them.

On the day of Jesus' resurrection, two of his followers travel from Jerusalem to the village of Emmaus. As they talk about Jesus' death, Jesus himself approaches—only they don't realize it's him. Cleopas explains dejectedly that the man they thought would redeem Israel has been crucified and that some of Jesus' female disciples had found his tomb empty earlier that morning. Jesus corrects Cleopas and his friend, saying they should know that God's Messiah would suffer, die, and rise again. Then Jesus leads a Bible study, showing how all the Hebrew Scriptures point to him. The men still don't recognize Jesus, but they invite him to stay with them in Emmaus. When Jesus breaks bread for the meal, they suddenly see him for exactly who he is—their Lord, the One who had given his own body for them on the cross (1 Corinthians 11:24).

Maybe you've wondered how the Old and New Testaments are related. Luke's inclusion of this encounter helps us see Scripture as one masterful story. When Jesus refers to "Moses and all the Prophets" and later the Psalms (Luke 24:44), he's using shorthand for the whole Old Testament. He tells the disciples that *all of it* reveals him as the long-awaited Savior the world needs.

Although you and I don't get to experience the fullness of Jesus' physical presence with us (yet!), the witness of Jesus' friends assures us that through him, all of God's promises have finally come true (Luke 1:1–4). And one day, we will see him face-to-face (1 Corinthians 13:12).

Prayer: Lord, thank you for your Word, which reveals your Son, Jesus. Help me recognize Jesus for who he is—the risen Lord and the fulfillment of every promise you have made.

Reflection Question: How has reading the Old Testament helped you to see the ways the Bible points to Jesus?

The Purpose of Your Life

CLARK FOBES IV

As a child, I often wondered about the purpose of school. I asked my mom why I couldn't just play all day. In her typical Korean-immigrant fashion, she scolded me and said that studying led to good grades, which would get me into a good school, earn me a good job, and eventually make me money.

We often question the purpose of the things we do. Purpose brings meaning to even the most mundane tasks, like going to school and studying. Purpose defines why we do what we do, but also who we decide to *be*. In Jesus' final words to his disciples, he gives them a purpose that transcends any earthly or material gain.

Following his resurrection, Jesus meets his disciples on a mountaintop. Despite their doubt that he is truly the Messiah (Matthew 28:17), he declares authority not just over creation but over his own people. This authority gives him the right to define the purpose of every believer, which he reveals in this passage—to make Jesus known and to walk with him.

While much can be said about the Great Commission, Jesus' commands are a call to live *for* Christ and *with* Christ in the world. He dealt with sin and shame on the cross and rose victorious from the grave. So Jesus promises that for all who believe in him, he will be with them "to the very end of the age" (v. 20). This purpose doesn't just end with us, however, as if the main goal of the Christian life is simply to know Jesus more. Jesus gives us his presence that we would "make disciples." Put simply, the purpose of the Christian life is to make Jesus known to the ends of the earth as Jesus makes himself known to us to the end of the age.

The next time you question the purpose of your life, consider how all that you do can declare the gospel to those around you and deepen Jesus' work within you.

Prayer: Father, remind me that everything in my life has meaning and purpose because of Christ. May I live every day with the goal of knowing you more deeply and making you known to others.

Reflection Question: How does this dual purpose of walking with Christ and making him known change how you approach every activity today?

You'll Have to Wait

KATIE POLSKI

I was stuck on a plane that was delayed for a long period. One by one the complaints began, as passengers asked if they could get off the plane. The flight attendants responded calmly, "I'm sorry, you'll have to wait." Once we were cleared for takeoff, the pilot explained that due to severe weather conditions, leaving at the original time could have been dangerous. The delay was part of a bigger plan for our well-being.

In Acts 1, Jesus' disciples are also waiting, wanting to know when God will restore Israel and make their life new and better. They think Jesus is going to immediately set up a physical kingdom on earth. Instead, he is about to ascend back to heaven. What the disciples don't quite understand is that God's kingdom is about grace and salvation, not about earthly power. So, Jesus says to them, *You'll have to wait*. Jesus promises that as the disciples wait for the fullness of God's kingdom, they will receive power from the Holy Spirit.

We read that Jesus is "taken up before their very eyes," with a cloud hiding him (v. 9). Jesus' ascension confirms his identity as the promised Messiah (Mark 14:62). As they wait for him to return, the Spirit will enable them to spread the gospel in their hometown and then all the way "to the ends of the earth" (Acts 1:8). They will carry the good news that God sent his Son, Jesus, so that anyone who believes in him can have eternal life.

We, too, experience times of waiting on God. Maybe you're waiting for a change in your circumstances, healing in a relationship, or clarity about your future. God has a purpose for you *now*. His delays are always part of his bigger plan for our lives. God can and will use you by the power of his Spirit to share the love of Jesus. He's equipping you to be his witness in your school, your family, your community, and beyond. You don't have to wait until everything is perfect.

Our ascended Savior, who reigns with God, will one day return to establish a perfect kingdom. All we have longed for will be restored. Until that day, let's wait with purpose.

Prayer: Jesus, thank you for your perfect timing. Help me trust in your plan as I wait. Empower me by your Spirit to be a bold witness for you.

Reflection Question: What are some areas in your life where you feel like you're waiting? How can you be a witness for Jesus now?

Filled with the Holy Spirit

JOEY TURNER

No calendars. No watches. No computers or notifications. No pens and no paper. Instead of these conveniences, God gives his people feasts to help them remember. The Passover Feast recalls the exodus of God's people from Egypt. The Feast of Weeks, known as Pentecost in Greek, remembers the giving of the Law, and the Feast of Booths remembers Israel's wilderness wanderings.

In Acts 2, the people of God are gathered in Jerusalem for Pentecost. Pentecost means "fiftieth" in Greek, and it represents the fifty days between Passover and the Feast of Weeks. Pentecost celebrates God's covenant with his people and the harvest of their grain, grapes, and olives.

Except this Pentecost is different. The Passover has now been fulfilled in the life, death, and resurrection of Christ. Pentecost had always been celebrated by God's people to remember the terrifying scene of wind, fire, and thunder on Mount Sinai when God gave Israel the first covenant (Exodus 20). God's Spirit now comes down in wind and fire and allows all those who speak different languages to understand each other. God is establishing a new covenant with his people.

In giving his people the Holy Spirit, God also reverses the Tower of Babel (Genesis 11), where he confused the language of the people who were focused on their own mighty works. But the diverse peoples gathered at Pentecost miraculously understand one another and tell of the mighty works of God. They are filled with the Holy Spirit, just as Jesus has promised.

The new harvest season has come (Matthew 9:37), and this time it's a harvest of souls, people who hear the good news of Jesus Christ, turn from sin, and believe. The new covenant has also come, and God's law will be written not on stone tablets but on human hearts (Ezekiel 11:19). The first covenant was of the law, but the second covenant with God is of the Spirit. The law reveals our need and inability, but the Spirit meets our need and makes us competent (2 Corinthians 3:3–6). If you belong to Jesus, the Holy Spirit lives inside you to remind you of all that God has said to you through his Word (John 14:26). The Spirit enables you to see your whole life inside God's redemptive story.

Prayer: God, thank you for the Holy Spirit. Thank you for including me in your harvest. Amen.

Reflection Question: What comfort do you have in knowing that God has established a new covenant by his Spirit?

A 3-D Glasses Moment

REBECCA LANKFORD

The most important part of a 3-D movie is to wear 3-D glasses (duh!). With the glasses on, the 3-D effects come to life and you can enjoy the movie as intended. Without the glasses, however, the whole screen looks fuzzy. You can "watch" the movie, but it doesn't make much sense, nor is it enjoyable.

In Acts 8, an Ethiopian royal official has a "3-D glasses" moment. In the ancient world, some royal officials called eunuchs were forced to have a procedure that rendered them unable to have children. Aside from the physical pain, eunuchs also lived with the emotionally painful reality of never having families of their own. It's no wonder this man might have been drawn to the comforting words of Isaiah 53, even if he was not yet able to fully comprehend them.

Before Philip comes alongside the eunuch and teaches him about Jesus, Isaiah's words are as good as a 3-D movie with no glasses. But everything changes when Philip explains that Isaiah is talking about Jesus. He shows the eunuch how *all* of God's Word points to Jesus' life, death, and resurrection on behalf of sinners.

Because the eunuch doesn't know about Jesus, he is confused about who was "led like a sheep to the slaughter" (Isaiah 53:7). When Philip shares the gospel with the eunuch, he is able to see that Isaiah was prophesying about Jesus, the Lamb of God, who would be slaughtered when he died to pay for the sins of the world.

When we read the Bible, it's important to remember that *every* part of Scripture is meant to point us to Jesus and his life, death, and resurrection on behalf of sinners (Luke 24:44–45). Reading God's Word in light of the good news of Jesus is like putting on 3-D glasses. Things come into focus, and we can get a better sense of the grand story. While it's not always easy to see how a passage points us to Jesus, it's always worth it to press on and to ask the Spirit to show us the good news of the gospel.

Prayer: Jesus, thank you for Philip and his ministry. Thank you for the Ethiopian eunuch, who is a testament to how you transform lives by your Word and through your Spirit. Thank you for your living Word that tells me who you are and what you have done for me. Amen.

Reflection Question: Has God ever used someone like Philip to open your eyes to the good news of Jesus? What was the experience like?

Surprising Grace

KATIE POLSKI

In high school, I had a friend who was an atheist. He enjoyed arguing against Christianity, so after one of our long debates, I thought, *There's no way he'll ever become a Christian.* I saw him several years later, and he surprised me with his testimony. After many months of conversing with a Christian mentor, my friend had given his life to Jesus. I was skeptical that he would ever believe, but God did his miraculous work, as he does in everyone who is saved.

In Acts 9, we find an unexpected conversion story. A Christian-hater named Saul (later called Paul) is on his way to Damascus to persecute believers when he falls blind after encountering Jesus along the way. In a vision, God tells a believer named Ananias to visit Saul. Can you imagine how afraid Ananias must have been? He is a Jesus-follower who is told to go visit a Jesus-hater! But Ananias obeys God. When he arrives, he treats Saul with kindness and respect, revealing God's plan to use Saul to spread the gospel far and wide. Those who knew Saul as a persecutor of Christians would have been highly skeptical that he would ever change.

Who in your life would you least expect to come to know Jesus? Maybe it's a sibling, a cousin, a friend, or even a parent. The truth is that no matter how far someone has strayed, no one is beyond the reach of God's grace. The gift of eternal life is for all who believe in Jesus and who desire to follow him (John 3:16). God is in the business of transforming lives, *no matter how unlikely it appears that someone will come to faith.*

Apart from God's grace, no one would come to faith in Jesus (Romans 3:10–12). Our job, through the power of the Holy Spirit, is to share the good news about Jesus—even with those we least expect would give their hearts to him. We can't predict how things will turn out, but we can trust Jesus to use us to spread his love. When you're skeptical, remember that the Holy Spirit can soften even the hardest hearts. God's love and forgiveness are available to all, and our role is to be faithful in sharing the good news.

Prayer: Lord, thank you for your power to transform lives. Help me to be bold in sharing your love, and may your Holy Spirit use me. Amen.

Reflection Question: Who in your life is resisting Jesus, and how can you pray for them?

Am I Allowed to Eat This?

JOEY TURNER

There it sat in front of me. Large, steaming, and in my bowl. Looking at the person next to me, I asked, "What is it?" They replied, "Guinea pig." *Okay, well, this is new,* I thought. As a college student on a mission trip in Ecuador, my first lesson was that in many rural parts of the world, squirrels, rabbits, guinea pigs, and other small creatures are sources of protein. As a suburban-raised kid from the Midwest, all I could think was, *Am I allowed to eat this?*

In Acts 10, Peter learns, by way of food, that God is doing a new thing. Peter has a vision of all sorts of creatures and hears a voice say, "Get up, Peter. Kill and eat" (v. 13). He is confused because these animals are all ceremonially unclean under the covenant law of Moses, meaning God's people were not permitted to eat them. The voice says three times, "Do not call anything impure that God has made clean" (v. 15).

While Peter is contemplating this vision, the Spirit tells him to go with three men who have come looking for him. Peter learns that a Roman soldier named Cornelius, a God-fearing man, has sent the men to bring Peter to Cornelius's house. Meanwhile, Cornelius has gathered all of his friends and relatives to listen to Peter.

Peter proclaims the good news of Christ's death and resurrection to Cornelius and his household, and the Holy Spirit works powerfully so that the crowd comes to saving faith in Jesus. Through the vision of the animals and the experience of preaching in Cornelius's house, God shows Peter that he is doing a new thing. Now people of all nations will be included in God's family—not by keeping the law of Moses, but through faith in Christ.

Under the law of the old covenant, when a non-Jewish person trusted in Israel's God, they had to be circumcised and observe all the food regulations God required of his covenant people. So the new believers initially assumed that Gentiles who trusted in Christ would need to observe those same rules. But God tells Peter he is doing a new thing through Jesus, establishing a new covenant. Jesus has perfectly fulfilled the law of the Old Testament on our behalf. In Jesus, people of all backgrounds can come to God by grace through faith alone.

Prayer: God, thank you for welcoming all people to you by faith in Jesus.

Reflection Question: How is it good news that God calls people from all nations?

When You Feel Left Out

SKYLER R. FLOWERS

Life can feel like it is defined by who is in the in-crowd and who is not. Where people sit in class and what brands they wear may establish clear boundaries of inclusion and exclusion. Feeling like you're left out is lonely and hurtful. But for those who are in, the pressure is often too much to bear. If you don't keep up outward appearances, you may find yourself on the outs!

In Acts 15, a serious debate has ignited within the church centered around this very question: Who is in and who is out? Some believe the non-Jews (called Gentiles) have to behave like the Jews to be saved. You may believe in Jesus, but you're still not one of us, they say. The other group, led by Paul, Peter, and James, sees that this conclusion misunderstands the work of Jesus.

The Christian faith teaches that being "in" has nothing to do with performance. You can't look a certain way, act a certain way, or talk a certain way to be in the in-crowd. Instead, as Peter says in verse 11, "We believe it is through the grace of our Lord Jesus Christ that we are saved."

In the Christian faith, there is no in-crowd and out-crowd. Rather, the gospel shows us that we are *all* worthy of exclusion by our sin. Apart from Jesus, we *all* reject God, which separates us from him and from salvation. But when Jesus died on the cross, he took the full punishment for our sins. Jesus did everything necessary to move us from out to in with the people of God.

So when we feel alone, we can remember that in Christ we have been brought into his church, his family, his love forever. He even lives in us by his Spirit (John 14:17). We don't need to fight to fit in; we can rest in the work of our Savior, who holds us close.

Prayer: Lord, I thank you that Jesus has opened the floodgates of God's grace to all people. When I feel alone and excluded, remind me of the grace of the gospel and the work of the Spirit. Let me show others your expansive inclusivity by my words and actions. Amen.

Reflection Question: Why do people often default to making others feel excluded? How can we live out the gospel's inclusiveness in our lives?

God Is Here, and So Am I

ISAIAH A. MARSHALL

In 1992 at the Barcelona Olympic Games, Derek Redmond ran the 400-meter semifinal for Great Britain. Two hundred meters into the race, he pulled his hamstring. Barely able to stand, he got up and limped around the track. His father ran from the stands, wrapped Derek's arm around his neck, and helped him to the finish line.

In Acts 16, we learn how God uses Paul and Silas to come alongside someone in distress. Paul and Silas find themselves in prison after driving a demon out of a slave girl (v. 18). Even in chains, Paul and Silas pray and sing hymns to God as their fellow prisoners listen (v. 25). Suddenly, a violent earthquake shakes the prison, flings the doors open, and unfastens every chain (v. 26). It's a vivid picture of what Jesus did on the cross, breaking the chains of sin for all who believe.

When the jailer sees the open doors, he assumes the prisoners have escaped. Fearing punishment or disgrace, he prepares to end his own life. But here is the good news: God works in miraculous ways through those who follow him. Paul sees what the jailer is about to do and shouts, "Don't harm yourself! We are all here!" (v. 28). God uses Paul and Silas to show his power. Not only do they stop a man from harming himself, but God also uses them to draw the jailer to saving faith in Jesus (vv. 30–34).

At times we all carry guilt, shame, and failure that make us want to give up. Like the jailer, we think our failures are final. Hopelessness whispers in our ear that our problems are too big and that we're unworthy of love. But there is no problem too big for God. He overcame your sin on the cross and defeated death so that you can live.

When we see others caught in despair, we can echo Paul's words: "Don't harm yourself! We are all here!" (v. 28). God uses us to bring hope and draw others to saving faith in Jesus. Each of us is called to be the type of friend who says, "God is here, and so am I." Like Derek's father, who helped him finish his race, we walk alongside those who are hurting and point them to Jesus, the One who never leaves.

Prayer: Lord, help me notice the pain of those around me and spread your love as I trust your power.

Reflection Question: Who in your life God is calling you to serve?

How Can I Grieve with Hope?

MARK HOWARD

It hurts when someone we love dies. Grief can be overwhelming. While death may be a normal part of our world, Scripture tells us this is not how it should be. Paul writes 1 Thessalonians in part because death has visited the church in Thessalonica. Paul wants to remind them that they don't need to "grieve like the rest of mankind, who have no hope" (4:13). Just as Jesus walked out of the grave, all who have died trusting in Christ will also experience resurrection.

The imagery Paul uses is that of a returning victorious general, a familiar image to the Thessalonians, since their city was home to a Roman military base. When a general returns from battle, his coming is announced by a shouting herald and blaring trumpets. He's accompanied by soldiers who carry the spoils of war. The town empties as the people go out to meet the victors and usher them back into the city to celebrate.

Paul uses this picture when he writes about the future return of Jesus "with a loud command, with the voice of an archangel, and with the trumpet call of God." It's the symbolism behind the dead in Christ rising first, followed by the living being "caught up together with them in the clouds" (vv. 16–17).

Rather than a picture of Christians escaping earth, we see here God's people going out to meet the victorious Jesus and his mighty soldiers, carrying the spoils of heaven's victory over sin and death coming to this world. It's about God's people suddenly receiving their resurrection bodies as all things are made new. This day "will come like a thief in the night" (5:2), a scary moment for those clinging to the darkness of this world. But for the Christian who is awake to the reality of Jesus' return, while the exact timing is unknown, our surprise will quickly shift to joyous celebration without end.

Creation is marred by sin, and "the wages of sin is death," but praise God, "the gift of God is eternal life in Christ Jesus" (Romans 6:23). This hope shapes our grief. It's bittersweet—bitter because death is wrong, but sweet because we know how the story ends. So yes, grieve when death comes. But remember that death is not final. Jesus will return, "and death shall be no more" (Revelation 21:4).

Prayer: Come, Lord Jesus! Complete what you began in your resurrection.

Reflection Question: What might grieving with hope look like, knowing that death is not the end?

Odd Beliefs Versus Anchored Hope

MICHAEL GOLDSTEIN

Have you ever believed something that turned out to be completely false? When I was little, I got the idea that all dogs were boys and all cats were girls. It gets worse! I believed that dogs and cats got together to have babies, and they either came out as baby boy dogs or baby girl cats. Pretty wild, huh?

Many unbelievers have silly, misguided, or downright false ideas about God, Christianity, and the Bible. You may have heard or read a few. In 2 Thessalonians, the apostle Paul addresses some of these false beliefs. He writes to a church that had been shaken by a distortion of the truth about Jesus' return. Some were terrified, thinking they had missed it. Others were dismissive, thinking their lives didn't really matter.

Paul reassures them by reminding them of what is true: "God chose you as firstfruits to be saved through the sanctifying work of the Spirit and through belief in the truth" (2:13). God *chooses* them for salvation (see John 15:16) but is also *sanctifying* them—making them like Jesus and setting them apart for his special work. Their salvation comes through believing the truth of the gospel, the good news of Jesus' death and resurrection for sinners. While false teachings cast doubt about their future, this truth anchors their confidence in Christ.

Paul then reminds us that we can find this truth in "the teachings we passed on to you" (2 Thessalonians 2:15). Passed down to us through the apostles' writings, truth is found in the Bible. Unlike the ever-changing ideas of our culture, the Bible is consistent, reliable, and life-giving. It proclaims the truth about who God is and what he has done to save us in Christ.

To *stand firm* and *hold fast* to these teachings means to cling tightly to the truths of Scripture like a free climber gripping a rock face with all their strength. We are constantly surrounded by messages that distort or contradict God's truth, and so we must turn to Scripture daily as our foundation for what is real. Paul tells us that when we do this, God will "encourage your hearts and strengthen you in every good deed and word" (v. 17). Regular reading of the Bible and trusting its authority will ground us and empower us to live faithfully.

Prayer: God, I commit myself to study and listen to your Word. Help me hold fast to the good news of Jesus Christ.

Reflection Question: What habits can you build to make Scripture a regular part of your life so you stay confident in the truth about Jesus?

Faith Alone

VINCE GREENWALD

Repetition is powerful. We remember things we hear over and over again. I still hear my seventh-grade football coach saying, "Quit your lollygagging," because he said it a gazillion times. I still hear my dad saying, "If you live your life to please your heavenly Father, you'll never have to worry about pleasing your earthly father," because that line played on repeat in our house.

Paul writes to churches in Galatia that have grown fuzzy on the good news of the gospel. He repeats a key word several times to help them understand. To be *justified* means to be declared righteous in God's sight. When we trust in Jesus, we are accepted by God because of what Jesus has done. God sees Jesus' perfect record instead of our sinful one.

First, Paul teaches that no one is *justified* by keeping God's law. Paul states it three times in two verses in Galatians 2 (vv. 16–17). Why? Because if you believe that doing good works will make you right with God, you will miss Jesus, who has offered the *only* way for any of us to be right with God.

Next, Paul teaches that justification comes by faith in Jesus Christ. Three times Paul drills into this core gospel truth: Being right with God comes *by faith* in Jesus Christ (vv. 16–20). Paul emphasizes this truth because justification comes by faith alone through Christ alone.

You might wonder what the big deal is. *Paul, I get it. You don't need to repeat yourself. I've heard that since I was in Sunday school.* But here's why repetition is needed. Our hearts are bent toward self-justification. We are always looking to achieve what can only be *received*. We want to work for wages, but God, in the gospel, offers salvation as a free gift through Jesus Christ alone.

Here's the gospel shift that must occur in every Christian heart: *Stop looking to what you can do for God, and start looking to Christ's finished work.* You could never save yourself through your efforts. But Jesus Christ lived a perfect life, endured the cross and the judgment of God, and rose again to defeat death. Paul was right. We need it on repeat. No one will be justified by their works. Justification comes by faith alone in Christ alone.

Prayer: Lord, thank you that salvation is found not through my strivings but through my Savior. Help me live by faith alone in Christ alone. Amen.

Reflection Question: What would it look like to keep this gospel truth in front of you daily?

How Do I Walk by the Spirit?

EMILY HEIDE

When my daughters were toddlers, fighting was an hourly occurrence. When my patience was waning, I would make both of them get into the same XL T-shirt. Their heads would poke through the neck hole I had enlarged with scissors. They were forced to play together in the same space.

Once you begin following Jesus, the power of the Holy Spirit takes over your heart. Your heart is made new. But it does not immediately overtake the flesh. The Spirit and the flesh are like opposing bodies in the same XL T-shirt—neither one wanting to concede to the other. "The flesh desires what is contrary to the Spirit, and the Spirit what is contrary to the flesh" (Galatians 5:17).

How do we learn to walk by the Spirit (v. 16)? Walking implies continuous action in a forward direction. Just as a baby painstakingly learns to walk by using her legs, so a Christian slowly learns to walk by the Spirit—a process we call sanctification, or becoming like Jesus. The more you lean into relationship with God and understand his love—through prayer, worship, and studying his Word—the more your faith will deepen, take root, and grow. The result? The fruit of the Spirit—"Love, joy, peace, forbearance, kindness, goodness, faithfulness, gentleness and self-control" (v. 22).

Two important things: (1) Love is always listed first, because "the greatest of these is love" (1 Corinthians 13:13), and (2) "fruit" is singular, not plural. Bearing the fruit of the Spirit means your overall character is changed. You begin to display the characteristics listed. And even when the fruit of the Spirit is evident to those around you, your struggle with sin will continue, calling you to repent and ask for forgiveness. You can walk forward in faith because Jesus has already died for the sins of yesterday, today, and tomorrow. Because of his great love, you can walk in the Spirit, abiding in him until he returns.

Prayer: Lord, help me walk by the Spirit, choosing you over the temptations of this world. Help me live a life filled with the fruit of the Spirit, bringing glory to you and sharing your love with those around me.

Reflection Question: Which characteristics of the fruit of the Spirit are hardest for you to display? Ask for God's help today.

Foolishness or the Power of God?

CURTIS ZACKERY

Imagine a new trend at school that everyone's into, but it seems silly to you. Some of your friends are all about it—buying the latest merch, posting about it, and trying to act as if they belong. You just don't get it. To you, it's ridiculous, like people are just following along because they think it'll make them cool.

Then you realize that someone you trust and respect seems to be into this thing. When you share your skepticism, your friend explains that the trend is a movement based on something deep and meaningful. At first, you're still suspicious, but you start to understand its true value over time. You start to see that this trend is leading people to act differently and is creating positive change in your school. You realize it's not just a fad; it's powerful.

In Paul's first letter to the Corinthians, he encourages them to hold fast to what they know to be true about Jesus, despite cultural resistance. Paul teaches them that Jesus Christ is the source of salvation and the world's hope, and the group he writes to believes it. But through the ridicule of others, the Corinthians begin to lean on their human instincts. Paul calls them to remember their hope in Jesus, regardless of how the watching world views it.

Paul's teachings in 1 Corinthians 1 are just as relevant today as it was when he wrote them. As we follow Jesus, our choices won't always make sense to the people around us. For example, the actions of loving your neighbor as yourself, blessing your enemies, and serving the needy are countercultural. When others don't understand the way we live, it can cause us to lose our excitement in following Jesus.

But remember, the message of the cross is that Christ died so we might be forgiven and live for his glory alone. The power of the cross helps us hold fast and not waver from our dedication to him. The hope is that those around us will shift from viewing the cross as foolishness to seeing it as a sign of their freedom in Christ.

Prayer: Thank you, Jesus, for your work on the cross. Keep me firm in my faith in you. Give me courage as I invite those around me into the freedom of salvation.

Reflection Question: Why do you think the message of the cross is seen as foolishness by those who don't follow Jesus? How can we help others see its true power and significance?

Who's the GOAT?

VINCE GREENWALD

We live in an age of likes and views, influencers and celebrities. I bet you and your friends have different opinions about who is the best of the best.

You may be surprised to know that a similar dynamic was found in the early church. In the Corinthian church, believers are identifying themselves with the leader whose teaching they follow. Some are saying, "I follow Paul," and others are saying, "I follow Apollos." And the apostle Paul is having none of it. Paul's point is clear. Even the very best Bible teachers are simply servants. They are merely tools that God uses to accomplish what *only he can do.* Paul uses blunt language here to communicate this point, even going so far as to say, "Neither the one who plants [Paul] nor the one who waters [Apollos] is anything" (1 Corinthians 3:7).

What does this have to do with us? Two things. First, let's be grateful for those who pastor us and serve us but refrain from idolizing them. If you are a Christian, you weren't saved by your local church pastor or your favorite Christian musician or writer. God alone saved you by his grace. No one praises the oven after a great meal; they thank the chef. No one praises the scalpel after a successful surgery; they praise the surgeon. So don't focus your praise on the planters or the ones who water your faith. Praise *God* from whom all blessings flow.

The second takeaway is the call to imitate Paul's mindset of humility. As we walk with Jesus, God uses us to help others grow. He gives us opportunities to plant and water, and it's an incredible joy to see God use us in the lives of others. But spiritual pride is a real danger. Paul's attitude should be our attitude: We are just servants; *God gives the growth.* He does what only *he* can do in saving sinners. You don't have to be Superman or Superwoman. Be faithful, and trust God to be God. And praise him for it!

Prayer: Lord, thank you for giving the growth. Help me come to you, abide in you, and bear much fruit through you. Amen.

Reflection Question: Where have you seen the celebrity dynamic at play in your life or in the church?

Love Is the Goal

LIZ EDRINGTON

Confession: I really like to be right. Sometimes winning an argument becomes more important to me than my relationship with the person I'm talking to.

It's like Paul knew exactly what I needed to hear when he wrote his letter to the Corinthians. I need to be reminded that *love* is the primary goal, not being right. Not winning. God gives us all of our gifts—intelligence, creativity, people skills, a knack for problem-solving, athleticism, and more—to love others and love him.

It can be all too easy to assume that arguing my position is the loving thing to do. We get wrapped up in wanting to prove we're smart, win competitions, be liked, get into college, and maybe even be really good Christians. Yet as 1 Corinthians 13 tells us, even if we're being really generous, volunteering a lot, and sacrificing for God, if we aren't motivated by genuine love for God and others, we've missed the point.

The apostle John wrote, "This is how we know what love is: Jesus Christ laid down his life for us. And we ought to lay down our lives for our brothers and sisters" (1 John 3:16). We're given a really clear definition of what love is. It isn't just a feeling, nor is it just an action. It's Christ-fueled and Christ-shaped. It's prioritizing someone over ourselves. Grieving with those who grieve. Using what we've been given to bless others.

When we realize our efforts have been far more about *us* than loving the one in front of us, we can remember that God forgives us through the ultimate act of love the universe has ever seen. Jesus' death on the cross while we were still sinners (Romans 5:8) means God's love comes to us when we can't stop needing to be right, when we're stubborn, selfish, numbed-out, annoyed, hypocritical, or people-pleasing. In him we have perfect love. And that is everything.

Prayer: Lord, thank you for showing me what love truly looks like through the life of Jesus. Let me believe that you love every last part of me.

Reflection Question: Think of a time you experienced the love of Jesus through someone else who prioritized you, empathized with you, or gave something up for you.

Clarity, Not Confusion

EMILY MENENDEZ

Is following Jesus confusing or complicated? You may be in a season when obedience feels hard (I'm there right now too). Or maybe you are confused about something you've read in the Bible or heard in church. Today's reading offers us brilliant clarity about the fundamental good news that makes us Christ followers.

Jesus Christ lived the perfect life, then died, and three days later rose from the dead. Our faith is first and foremost about this historical event. Jesus rose from the dead and appeared to hundreds of people. At the time Paul wrote to the Corinthians, there were still people alive who had seen Jesus and could tell you that his resurrection was genuine. It's the simple but incredible truth you must know to follow Jesus. Paul goes on to say, "And if Christ has not been raised, our preaching is useless and so is your faith" (1 Corinthians 15:14). If Jesus did not defeat death, we should feel sorry for Paul and his friends because everything they based their identity on would be a lie. Without the resurrection, our faith falls apart. But with the resurrection, our faith is grounded in an unshakable historical reality. Everything else about the Christian faith flows out of this truth.

Our God loves you so much that he stopped at nothing to defeat death to rescue you from sin and invite you into an eternal relationship with him. Therefore you can trust God with all the details of your life—and even your confusion and doubts about your faith. He has proven that he is trustworthy, faithful, and determined to show you his love.

So fix your eyes on Jesus, the author and perfecter of your faith, who endured the cross for you (Hebrews 12:2). Remember that he is a God of clarity, not confusion. Rest in the reality of the resurrection.

Prayer: Lord, thank you for living a perfect life, dying on the cross, and rising from the dead. Thank you that because of the truth of the resurrection, I can trust you with my life. I submit my life to you. Fill me with confidence in this good news and cover me with your peace.

Reflection Question: Do you believe that Jesus rose from the dead? If so, what impact will it have on your life this week?

Wondering About Heaven

SYLER THOMAS

In my first year as youth pastor at my church, the children's ministry invited me to join the fourth grade Sunday school class one morning. The prompt was, ask the pastor anything. Two things I remember most: (1) how many of the questions were about what heaven will be like, and (2) how many of my answers were "I don't know!"

From Jesus' interaction with the Pharisees recorded in Matthew 22, we know there will be no marriage in heaven. Revelation 21 teaches there will be no sadness, as God will wipe away our tears. The same chapter also indicates that the sun won't be necessary, for heaven's light source will be provided by the glory of God. But in terms of whether there will be internet (I hope not), pets, food, video games . . . we just don't know.

In today's Bible reading from 1 Corinthians 15, Paul gives insight into what our bodies will be like in heaven, making it quite clear that they will be *different* from our earthly bodies. In fact, he compares our earthly bodies to seeds, implying that death is necessary for us to gain heavenly bodies. When we consider death, we mostly contemplate the loss involved. But Paul's perspective is much more hopeful: In the same way a seed dies and then produces something much greater, so will the end of our earthly bodies produce our much greater spiritual bodies.

Paul says the "sting of death is sin, and the power of sin is the law" (v. 56), meaning that our sin, revealed by the law, condemns us. That's the bad news. The good news is found in the next verse: "He gives us the victory through our Lord Jesus Christ" (v. 57). Because Jesus conquered death through the cross, sin and death do not have the last word. No matter the difficulties we face in life, the glory that awaits us in heaven will make it all worth it.

Prayer: Lord, even though I don't fully understand what heaven will be like, I'm grateful I can know that it will be glorious.

Reflection Question: Does knowing that God is preparing a spiritual body for you in heaven give you hope? Why or why not?

Comfort in Suffering

LIZ EDRINGTON

"It's no big deal. I'm totally fine," I told my teammates as blood streamed from my nose. I shouldn't have been sitting in the truck bed on the way to soccer practice. My face had gone through the back window, and now my nose was broken and I had a concussion. But man, was I quick to play it down.

It's hard to be honest with our pain, isn't it? We don't want to look weak, nor do we want others to make a big deal out of it. If our pain is coming from a wound that can't be seen—maybe as a result of a mean comment, a friend letting us down, going through a breakup, or continual tension at home—it's even more difficult to own.

Unlike us, God doesn't ignore our pain or pretend it isn't real. Instead, he *meets us* in our suffering, as 2 Corinthians 1 shows. Paul writes about the relationship between suffering and the power of the Holy Spirit. He shares that he thought he was going to die on his trip to Asia (v. 8). His situation is beyond his ability to cope. Yet Christ helps him endure and reminds him he isn't alone. Paul is united to God and to the body of Christ, who share in both his sufferings and his comfort.

Christianity is honest about suffering. In fact, it tells the true story of a God who suffers. Jesus experiences friends who let him down (Matthew 26:38–40). He is bullied by religious leaders (Luke 11:53–54) and misunderstood on a regular basis (Matthew 15:15–16). In the end, he is murdered in the most awful way. He suffers on the cross so that suffering will never have the final say over our lives. He leaves us with the Holy Spirit, also known as the Comforter (John 14:16 KJV), to walk with us now. We are *never* left alone in our pain.

For me, comfort has rarely involved the removal of my pain. Instead, I have been seen, known, and loved in my hurt. This happens for each of us through the body of Christ when friends come to be with us—to listen, empathize, and pray. They bear our burdens through the Holy Spirit (Galatians 6:2), which inspires us to do the same for others. We get to offer the comfort the Lord has offered to us. Praise God.

Prayer: Lord, please give me courage to share my suffering and receive comfort in my deepest places of pain. Amen.

Reflection Question: What pain in your life might God be inviting you to share with someone who needs his comfort?

The Treasure in You

ISAIAH A. MARSHALL

Middle school was tough for me. Walking through the halls often felt like walking through a battlefield. Names were thrown like weapons: "Shorty" was common for me, but the one that stung most was "Lips." Even now, I wrestle with insecurity at times. It's easy to let hardship shape how we see ourselves.

Paul reminds us that our worth isn't defined by the challenges we face. Our identity is rooted in something far greater. He encourages the church in Corinth not to lose heart in their suffering. He describes believers as jars of clay. In ancient times, fragile clay jars held valuable treasures. Similarly, we carry something priceless within our frail human selves—the knowledge of God's glory through Jesus (2 Corinthians 4:6).

Though we hold this treasure, Jesus holds our lives in his hands. In spite of our sin and weakness, God gives us all-surpassing power to endure trials and not be destroyed. In fact, his grace is sufficient, and his power is made perfect in our weakness (12:9).

Like walking through school halls, we walk through a broken and fallen world where we will experience struggle. We may be hard pressed, perplexed, persecuted, and struck down, but we are never crushed, abandoned, or destroyed because of the treasure of the gospel (2 Corinthians 4:8–9). Our hardships don't define us; God's power within us does. Though we experience pain, it is temporary and ultimately points us to an eternal glory that outweighs it all (v. 17).

We've heard the saying, "Sticks and stones may break my bones . . ." but will names really hurt us? Of course they will. But they don't define us. Jesus understands mockery. As he hung on the cross, he was insulted and ridiculed (Mark 15:27–32). Yet three days later, he rose from the grave, defeating sin and death forever. And that same power that raised Jesus lives in us. Like jars of clay, we may feel weak and ordinary, but God's strength is within us. Whatever struggle you're facing, know this: You are not crushed, not abandoned, not destroyed. God's power is at work in you.

Prayer: Lord, when I feel weak and overwhelmed, remind me that your power is within me. Help me fix my eyes on what lasts, trusting that you are shaping me through every trial. Amen.

Reflection Question: What struggles or insecurities have been weighing you down? How can you shift your focus from pain to God's eternal truth?

A New Body in Heaven

KATHERINE PRECHT STINE

For a long time, I've longed to have the "perfect" body. I've struggled with my body in so many ways—from disordered eating and anxiety to infertility and battling cancer. So much of our world's (and my) focus is achieving glory for ourselves through our bodies. Whether it's training for peak athletic performance, finding the perfect skincare routine, or defying the reality of aging, we could spend our entire lives trying to perfect our bodies. God's Word points us in a different direction.

Paul calls our bodies an "earthly tent," that is, temporary dwellings (2 Corinthians 5:1). As the early church experiences persecution and martyrdom, Paul reminds them (and us) not to lose hope. When our earthly bodies pass away, we have an eternal, heavenly body built by God to look forward to. This is not to say we should neglect our bodies—God made our bodies good, in his image. Throughout the Bible, he calls us to honor him with our bodies. Paul urges us not to fear death, nor to idolize our earthly bodies, because what is coming is so much better.

For the believer, the death of the earthly body isn't the end of their life; it's actually the beginning of eternal life in the physical presence of God. We will be made new. Isaiah 35:4 reveals, "Then will the eyes of the blind be opened, and the ears of the deaf unstopped." In Revelation, God promises he will "wipe every tear from their eyes. There will be no more death or mourning or crying or pain, for the old order of things has passed away" (21:4).

When Jesus came in an earthly body, experiencing every challenge we face, he endured the ultimate pain of separation from God and defeated sin and death—all because he loves us and wants to live with us forever. The very best part of our new heavenly dwelling is not only that we'll be free of all earthly hurt, but that we'll be fully present with Jesus, face-to-face. So when the groaning of your earthly body feels overwhelming, remember that God gave you his presence through the Spirit as his guarantee of what is yet to come.

Prayer: Lord, give me faith to believe that what is coming is eternally greater than any bodily suffering I endure here on earth. Help me live by faith and not by sight.

Reflection Question: How does knowing that God promises you a heavenly dwelling with him bring you hope and peace?

We Are Christ's Ambassadors

CURTIS DUNLAP

You may know Benjamin Franklin as one of the founding fathers who helped draft the Declaration of Independence and the United States Constitution. You may also know him for his achievements as an inventor. What you may not know is that from 1778–1785, he served as the US ambassador to France and was instrumental in helping end the Revolutionary War. As an ambassador, his speech and behavior represented something bigger than himself.

God has called each of us to be his ambassadors, not just in a particular country, but in the world (2 Corinthians 5:20). We carry the message of the gospel as God's representatives. Paul explains that when we trust Jesus, God reconciles us to himself, forgiving all our sins. To be reconciled means to reestablish a relationship that has been disrupted or broken due to an offense.

Because of sin, God has a beef with us. Jesus' death on the cross removes this grievance for anyone who believes Jesus is the only way to a restored relationship with God. But that's not all. God calls everyone who has been reconciled to him through Jesus to share the message of the gospel in the hope that others will also be reconciled to God. What a privilege to be trusted with something so valuable!

Jesus, who is God, also models what it means to represent God in the world. Paul describes him as the "image of the invisible God" (Colossians 1:15), and the writer of Hebrews says he is the "exact representation" (1:3) of God's nature. Jesus displays what God is like in both word and character. We have been called to this same task.

Believe it or not, the credibility of this message entrusted to us is often tied to the credibility of the messenger. That may feel like a lot of pressure, but be encouraged: God chooses to work through imperfect people like us to reflect his perfect love. So ask yourself, *When people encounter me, do they feel like they're being drawn closer to God?* If the answer challenges you, don't lose heart. God gives you the Holy Spirit to help you grow in the likeness of Jesus so that others can see his love through you.

Prayer: Father, help me remember that the same gospel that saved me is powerful enough to save others. I want to live boldly for you and share the good news of the gospel. Amen.

Reflection Question: Can you think of a time when your actions either helped or hurt the way someone saw Jesus?

God's Strength in My Weakness

ANNA MEADE HARRIS

When Rick Hoyt died at the age of sixty-one, ESPN described him as a "marathon icon." Praised for his "courage, determination, tenacity and willingness to give of [himself]," Rick participated in more than one thousand races. Yet Rick was a quadriplegic, confined to a wheelchair. His father, Dick, pushed his chair every step of the way.[1]

In 2 Corinthians 12, Paul describes his ongoing battle with what he calls "a thorn in my flesh" (v. 7). Scholars differ on what that thorn might be—a physical challenge, a struggle with temptation, or anxiety over opposition to his ministry. Three times, Paul asks God to take away this painful thorn, and God's response is this: "My grace is sufficient for you" (v. 9).

Remember that the word *sufficient* means "enough." God wants Paul (and us) to know that no matter how painful a circumstance is, his grace—his unearned, lavish love toward sinners—is enough to carry us through. The weaker we are, the more we need God's strength to carry us through our own illnesses, temptations, and battles. In fact, God's power is *made perfect*—reaching its fullest potential—when we are at our weakest, relying solely on him.

If you wonder how weakness can display strength, think back to Rick Hoyt. In his own strength, Rick was unable to move his arms or legs, much less complete a marathon. But by yielding to his father's strength, Rick became a powerful athlete indeed. His father's might and endurance were more than enough to carry him and his son, so they both experienced the thrill of the race.

Though we hate to think of ourselves as weak, if we've ever felt deep grief or battled a sin we couldn't overcome, we know weakness. In history's most amazing act of love, Jesus *chose* weakness, taking on human flesh and allowing himself to be crucified. He set aside his limitless power to embrace being weak. But he didn't stop there. He conquered death for us. That's the kind of strength he gives anyone who leans on him.

Prayer: Father, I am weak. Help me accept your grace and strength.

Reflection Question: How can you look to your strong Father in weakness?

---

1. Associated Press staff, "Boston Marathon Icon Rick Hoyt, Whose Father Pushed Wheelchair, Died," ESPN, May 22, 2023, www.espn.com/olympics/story/_/id/37708647/boston-marathon-icon-rick-hoyt-father-pushed-wheelchair-dies.

Being "Good Enough for God" Is a Gift from God

MIKE MCGARRY

How good is good enough before God? Will God love me more if I'm worthy? Will God stop loving me because I sinned too many times? Romans 3 gives us hope, because it proclaims salvation as the gift of God rather than as a reward for good behavior.

Righteousness means "right standing" with God, meaning you are pure and holy in his sight. So how righteous are you, really? The way you answer reflects what you believe about sin. Maybe you're tempted to overlook sin since you're a good person. Maybe you treat it like a debt to pay off or as a character flaw to improve. But sin is rebellion against God, basically telling him you know more about what's good for you and for the world than he does.

Meanwhile, the gospel announces that sinners receive the perfect righteousness of Jesus Christ by faith, and Christ's perfect obedience becomes ours (v. 22). We don't gain God's acceptance through our own goodness or performance. Our sin has earned us his judgment, but when we are in Christ, we are more than forgiven; we're declared righteous and holy.

Before Jesus, only Jewish people were considered the people of God, but now all people (Gentiles, or non-Jews) can be justified freely by the grace of God through Jesus Christ. This is why the gospel is "good news. It is a gift, not a paycheck for good behavior. The gospel is an invitation to receive Christ's perfect righteousness. He is our hope and salvation, so we give our sin to him.

We don't have to cover up our sin, pretend it isn't there, or do more good deeds to balance the scales. We are accepted by God because we have confessed our sin to Jesus and received his righteousness as a gift. Now we can live with freedom because God saves sinners like us.

Prayer: Lord Jesus, I know I'm a sinner. I cannot pay for my sin, and you can't overlook it. Thank you for taking my sin and giving me Jesus' righteousness. Equip me to live with great joy and faith because of who you are and what you've done.

Reflection Question: How does the gospel call us away from trying to earn our salvation?

When God Allows Suffering

LUKE PAIVA

Has someone ever tried to encourage you with words like, "It's okay. God has a plan," but instead of comfort, it felt like a slap in the face? Sometimes the pain of this broken world is so intense that no well-worn phrase, no matter how true it is, can bring us comfort. Thankfully, the Word of God tells the story that does comfort us in our pain.

In Romans 5:3, we read words that may feel like a slap in the face: "We rejoice in our sufferings, knowing that suffering produces endurance" (ESV). Without the rest of the story, those words can feel cruel. But a closer read shows that God does not ask us to rejoice in the reality of suffering itself. Instead, he calls us to rejoice because *even though* we are suffering, our hope in Christ will never put us to shame. We can look to the cross, where Jesus loved us so perfectly that he died to give us life, and be sure that God will never leave us.

God tells us specifically in Revelation 21 that he is making all things new, doing away with evil and suffering forever. In the here and now, he will be with us to comfort us as we experience suffering. Through the Holy Spirit, he will move us to know his love more and be more like him. The cross proves that he will bring us through all trials and tribulations into his everlasting love. We did nothing to earn his love on the cross. Instead, we were still his enemies when he loved us to give us life for us. How much more can we trust in his love now that we are his children!

We can tell God we are suffering and ask for his mercy, peace, and help—even though we have nothing to offer in return. We are free to need Jesus. God promises us that his love is forever and that our hope in him will never fail. We can be honest about the pain of suffering and yet still rejoice because God is good, and his love never fails.

Prayer: Lord, thank you for showing your love for me by dying on the cross. Help me embrace your love and feel your comfort and peace, even in suffering.

Reflection Question: Can you see the love of Jesus for you on the cross? Will you trust that the love of Jesus will never fail you?

When I Hate What I Do

ANNA MEADE HARRIS

When I was a teenager, I went through a season of lying to my parents a lot. I made excuses for my behavior—they were too controlling and their rules were unreasonable—but I couldn't deny that I was deceiving my parents, and I felt terrible about it. However, the more I lied, the more I had to lie to cover up past lies. Deception became a habit that I wanted desperately to break but felt powerless to stop. Even as a Christ follower, I was disobeying God, doing the evil I did not want to do.

Paul's honesty here in Romans 7 is comforting. If Paul—the apostle to the Gentiles and author of thirteen letters in the New Testament—had a hard time with obedience, maybe God isn't surprised that I still struggle with sin. Paul teaches that even Christians will grapple with temptation, but sin no longer condemns us because the penalty we deserve has been paid by Jesus at the cross (Romans 8:1). What's more, Christ rescues sinners not just for our salvation but also for our transformation.

Here's a helpful metaphor: Juneteenth celebrates the emancipation of the final American slaves. All across the country, slaves were legally freed on January 1, 1863, but it took nine hundred days for that glorious news to reach every corner of the nation. The slaves were truly free but lived as captives until news of their emancipation could transform their lives and set them free from bondage.

A similar process is at work in a redeemed believer who comes to faith in Christ and receives the freedom to choose obedience to God in all things. They are no longer bound by sin, but it takes the rest of their life for that truth to transform every corner of their heart, mind, body, and soul so that they become a pure reflection of the image of Christ: "We all, who with unveiled faces contemplate the Lord's glory, are being transformed into his image with ever-increasing glory, which comes from the Lord, who is the Spirit" (2 Corinthians 3:18). Your transformation into Christ's image may seem so gradual that it seems like it's not happening at all. Yet, "[God] who began a good work in you will carry it on to completion" (Philippians 1:6). Thanks be to God!

Prayer: Father, thank you for your patient grace in my spiritual growth.

Reflection Question: Even as you battle temptation, how does knowing that God is working in you help you persevere?

No Condemnation for Those in Jesus

MICHAEL GOLDSTEIN

If you've ever traveled to another country, you learned quickly that there are different laws, customs, and expectations to follow. For example, American teenagers expect the right to vote at age eighteen, but if you emigrated to Brazil, you'd be thrilled to find out that you can vote at age sixteen instead.

Romans 8 describes how those who put their faith in Jesus are transferred from living under one *law*—sin and death—to another, namely, *the Spirit*. It's like moving to a new country with a completely different set of laws. The old ruler is called *the flesh* and has power over your mind, body, and desires, causing them to disobey God. This is because "the mind governed by the flesh is hostile to God; it does not submit to God's law, nor can it do so" (v. 7).

Living *according to the flesh* is why we find ourselves trapped in cycles of bad habits like gossip, anger, hatred, lust, selfishness, and pride. I remember in high school lying in bed at night feeling shame over some of the hurtful things I had said earlier that day. I would vow to do better, only to confess the same sins twenty-four hours later.

But God acted against the evil powers of sin and death by sending Jesus to abolish them. Jesus overthrew the power of sin by nailing it with him to the cross and claimed victory over death through his resurrection. When you receive the gospel of Jesus, you are set free from the power of sin so you can walk in the life and peace of God. This means you no longer live under the weight of guilt, nor are you powerless to change. Jesus saves you from condemnation and frees you to get rid of the sin in your life. He gives you a superior power, the Holy Spirit, who is his personal presence.

Living *according to the Spirit* is a whole new approach to following God that brings true transformation. It's like remembering you own a chainsaw after trying to chop down a tree with a pocketknife. Setting our minds on the Spirit gives us the desire and power to cut down sin in our lives so we look more and more like Christ.

Prayer: God, I praise you for Jesus, who has set me free from the old law of sin and death and transferred me to a new state of life and peace with you. Help me set my mind on the Spirit, so I can live according to your will.

Reflection Question: What one habit or attitude of yours makes you feel stuck? How can setting your mind on the Spirit help you move forward?

Adopted by God

JONATHAN LILLEY

It felt like a lifetime before our son finally said the word *Mom*. From the beginning, he called me *Appa*—the Korean word for Dad—and soon after, he added *Dad* in English. But *Mom* didn't come so easily. He was especially close to his foster mother in Korea, and losing her left a deep wound. So when we adopted him, he barely acknowledged my wife—grief had made attachment hard.

When he finally called my wife Mom, it caught us off guard in the best kind of way. It was just a word, but it held massive meaning. It was the first sign that trust and belonging were starting to grow. A similar picture is found in Romans 8. Before we know God, we live like spiritual orphans—unsure of where we stand, afraid of rejection, trying to prove our worth. But Romans 8 tells us that when we come to faith in Christ, we receive the Holy Spirit and are adopted as God's children. As his children, the Spirit leads us to cry out, "*Abba*, Father" (v. 15).

Abba is a deeply personal word. Children today might say "Daddy" or "Papa," but in Jesus' day, *Abba* was one of the first words a child would say to their father. Like "Daddy" and "Papa," this word spoke of intimacy, not distance; of safety, not danger; of belonging, not rejection. Through the Spirit, we're invited to call God by that name.

The Holy Spirit also helps us believe that this relationship is real. The Spirit testifies with our spirit that we are not slaves who live in fear of never having God's approval, but children who belong. Because of what Christ has done, we are fully loved, fully secure, and forever home.

Maybe you're always trying to prove yourself—to teachers, friends, or parents. Maybe deep down, you wonder if you have to do the same with God. Romans 8 says no. You don't have to perform for God's love. If you belong to Jesus, you've already been adopted. God isn't waiting for you to get it together; he has already brought you in. You can cry out to God with confidence, because the Spirit reminds you, *I belong here.*

Prayer: Father, thank you for making me your child, not because I earned it, but because Jesus made a way. Remind me that I belong to you. Amen.

Reflection Question: What are some ways you still try to earn love or approval from others or from God? How does being adopted by God change the way you see yourself?

God's Everlasting Love for You

DANNY KWON

Krazy Glue is a strong adhesive created in the 1970s that makes a super-sticky bond. As a kid, I heard several urban legends about Krazy Glue—stories about people mistaking the glue stick for ChapStick and getting their lips stuck together and a prank involving Krazy Glue on a toilet seat. Krazy Glue supposedly creates an unbreakable bond.

In Romans 8:31–39, the apostle Paul writes about God's love for us demonstrated in Jesus Christ. He says that God's love for us in Jesus is so sticky that nothing can ever break its powerful bond. Paul explains this everlasting love by saying that when we look at the way God gave Jesus up for us, we know for certain that God is for us.

Then Paul offers examples that could *appear* to break the bond of God's love for us—trouble, hardship, persecution, or various experiences of poverty (v. 35). His list also includes more ominous-sounding threats such as death, angels, demons, and "powers," which is a reference to spiritual forces of evil (v. 38). Paul is alluding to attacks on Christian faith during his lifetime, including various beliefs and other religions, such as Roman and Greek gods and the threat of persecution from the state. Paul insists, however, that *none* of these things can compel God to remove his love from us.

We may feel we have messed up so badly that God could not love us anymore. We may wrestle with doubt about who God is. We may experience seasons of grief or hardship that cause us to question God's love. In all of these experiences, Paul tells us we have nothing to fear: "I am sure that . . . [nothing] in all creation, will be able to separate us from the love of God in Christ Jesus our Lord" (Romans 8:38–39 ESV).

Because of Jesus' death and resurrection on our behalf, *nothing* can separate us from the love of God—not even our doubts. We have the eternal, unchanging, unbreakable love of God because of Jesus Christ.

Prayer: Father, help me be assured of your love for me in Jesus. Help me know that nothing can ever separate me from your love.

Reflection Question: How can Jesus' sacrifice on the cross assure you of God's love for you?

How Can We Be Saved?

MAC HARRIS

Some days I feel close to God, and it's easier to believe that Jesus loves me, died for me, and has already saved me. Other days I'm not so sure. Back and forth I go in my head, yo-yoing between assurance of my salvation and doubt. Growing up, this meant that every time I heard an altar call or retreat speaker asking if I wanted to commit (or recommit) my life to Jesus, I'd struggle internally. *Do I need to raise my hand again? Do I need to walk up front and ask Jesus to save me,* for real *this time? How can I know if I'm* really *saved?*

In Romans 10, Paul articulates the simplicity of the gospel: We are saved by the life, death, and resurrection of Jesus, not by our own efforts to do good and be good. At the same time, he offers us a comforting lifeline of *assurance.* In those moments when we wonder whether or not we are saved, Paul encourages us to look back to *who* Jesus is and *what* he has done: Jesus is Lord, and God raised him from the dead.

Importantly, Paul is *not* saying that "declaring" and "believing" make up some kind of two-step process we must perfectly follow in order to be saved. External professions of internal faith do not *earn* us our salvation. Rather, declaring and believing *reflect* the saving work that Jesus has already done within us. This means I never have to wonder if I've said the "right" words or believed with "enough" belief to be saved. It means I don't have to find assurance of God's love for me in the strength of my own faith, but rather in what Jesus has already done. And it means that even when my faith wavers, my salvation is not in question.

We are not saved by following a formula; we are saved only by the life, death, and resurrection of Jesus. When we put our hope in Jesus, we never again have to wonder how God feels about us.

Prayer: Father, I lay my doubts before you today. When my faith is weak, help me overcome my unbelief and reassure me of your unwavering love for me. In Jesus' name. Amen.

Reflection Question: How do you think God feels about you? How would living with a greater assurance of God's unwavering love for you affect the ways you think about him?

Don't Conform; Be Transformed.

CHRISTINA FOX

Have you ever known someone who seemed to change dramatically? Maybe a friend went through a growth spurt over the summer and returned to school taller and looking more like an adult. Or a friend tried a new hobby, and now it's all she wants to do.

The Bible talks about change in Romans 12—change that happens as we live out the realities of God's great mercy for us. Paul has spent the previous chapters in Romans explaining the gospel. He taught that we are all sinners in need of salvation. He explained that God saves us by grace alone through faith alone. There is nothing we can do to earn God's love. God gives us what we don't deserve—forgiveness of sin—because of what Jesus did for us through his perfect life and sacrificial death.

What does this mean for how we live our lives? That's where Romans 12 comes in. Paul says that because of what God has done for us, we respond by offering our lives to him. We are living sacrifices—not like the dead animals sacrificed on the altar in the Old Testament. Because of God's great mercy, we live our lives for him, honoring and obeying him in body and soul. This is how we worship God.

Paul warns us to be alert to what the world is teaching us. We are not to be conformed (shaped) by the world. We guard against this by renewing our minds—reading, studying, and meditating on God's Word. Scripture reshapes our thoughts and beliefs and helps us identify what is true and what is false. We test what the world tells us to see if it measures up against God's Word.

As our minds are transformed, we will know God's will—how he wants us to live for him. The more our minds are transformed, the more we honor him with our lives.

Prayer: Father, I thank you for your great mercy toward me. Help my mind to be transformed by your Word so I might know your will. Help me to be conformed not to the world around me, but to your truth. Help me live my life for your glory.

Reflection Question: What is the world teaching you and what does God's Word say in contrast? What does it look like to live for God? Who is an example you can look to?

Jesus Gets All the Credit

KYLE HOFFSMITH

Have you noticed how many activities in middle and high school have to do with your performance evaluation? In school you take tests where your success is measured by your score. College scholarship committees typically compare your academic ranking against other applicants. Those who sing and act the best get the lead roles in the musical. In sports, the best players are those who not only make the team but get the most playing time. It seems like everything you do is measured and analyzed.

Yet when it comes to our relationship with God, we don't become Christians based on what we do. This can be hard to understand when almost every other area of our lives is based on performance. We are so used to earning things through effort and actions. The apostle Paul wrote to the church in Ephesus, telling them that they are saved from their sins by God's grace instead of their own actions (2:8–9). Grace is countercultural, the free gift of God that you don't deserve but can experience anyway. These verses explain that you are saved by receiving the gift of God, which is Jesus.

You can't take credit for being a Christian today, and you won't be able to take credit for being in heaven one day in the future. Think about that for a moment. Unlike someone who gets a scholarship and thinks back to the hard work that helped them gain the award, those in heaven will *not* be able to think about how much they accomplished in order to get there. Heaven will have no proud people because only one person is responsible for those who are there, and that person is not you; it's Jesus.

The work required for you to become a Christian was already accomplished through the works of Christ—his life, death, and resurrection. This should be a relief, but also a reminder: You can now spend your life honoring him with what you say and do. Your actions do not earn your place in God's family, but they can serve as evidence that you already are a part of it.

Prayer: Dear God, in a world where I'm measured by how much or how little I do, help me remember that salvation is a gift. Remind me to rest in the grace you have given me in Jesus. Amen.

Reflection Question: How can you train your mind to trust the finished work of Jesus instead of trying to earn his love?

The Strength to Overcome

ERICSON JOUBERT

We love watching superheroes because of the feats they can achieve with their own strength. Bruce Wayne uses his intelligence to fight the criminals of Gotham as Batman. Tony Stark designs the Ironman suit and reshapes weapons technology worldwide. Princess Diana of Themyscira uses her power and resolve to stand against her foes.

But what happens when we find ourselves lacking the strength we need in desperate times? Anxiety overtakes you before you walk inside the classroom to take your test. Bitter disappointment seeps in when the college letter comes in the mail and it's not what you expected. Your sports coach treats you unfairly, prompting you to question your place on the team. When faced with trials, how can we find the strength we need to overcome?

In Ephesians, Paul writes to a church in need of God's strength to overcome their own challenges. Paul prays that "Christ may grant them to be strengthened with power *through his Spirit* in their inner being" (3:6). Then he shows the Ephesians that living by the Spirit gives them access to the armor they desperately need against the schemes of the enemy (6:10–20).

Paul uses an extended metaphor to describe how we prepare spiritually to face opposition and hardship in the world. We put on the belt of truth, which points to God's revealed character and will for our lives; the breastplate of righteousness, which Christ generously gives to believers; the shoes of readiness to preach the gospel; the shield of faith, which protects us from the schemes of the evil one; the helmet of salvation, which directs us to meditate on Christ's finished work in redemption; the sword of the Spirit, which is God's Word—all the while praying in the Spirit at all times.

Instead of fighting evil in their own strength (which is impossible), Paul calls the church to trust in the Lord's strength (v. 10). Christians fight sin through the Holy Spirit. Rather than striving for individual heroism, we place our trust in a God who fights our battles for us as we humbly rely on the Spirit's power.

Prayer: Lord, I pray for strength in my trials, given according to your immeasurable power through the power of the Holy Spirit. Amen.

Reflection Question: Where in your life can you see that you need God to be your source of strength?

Humility Shines

MATTHEW D. KIM

I knew two young people arguing over who was busier. The two bantered back and forth about who had more tests, papers, and assignments to prepare for—all to be completed the next day. It was almost comical as one tried to outdo the other in proving their busyness. Have you ever argued with another to showcase your significance?

Paul is writing here to believers who sometimes struggled to view others as more important than themselves. Paul tells the Philippian Christians that instead of focusing on self-importance they ought to pattern their lives after Christ who "did not consider equality with God something to be used to his advantage" (2:6). Instead, Jesus "made himself nothing by taking the very nature of a servant" (v. 7).

Social media convinces us to promote ourselves. We've been conditioned to boast and brag about who we are and about our accomplishments. While there's nothing wrong with hard work and gaining success, the way of Christ is the way of humility. We value and champion others for the sake of unity in the church.

Why is humility so important to Paul? Paul reminds the Philippians that they are to look different from their "warped and crooked generation" (v. 15). When we model our lives after Jesus, we're going to stand out. Here Paul says we're going to shine or sparkle like stars in the night when we live according to God's Word.

Over the years, I confess that I have needed to grow in humility. In the opening example, I was one of the two students competitively arguing over busyness. As I've grown closer to Jesus, he has patiently worked in my life, humbling me through the gospel. As the Lord and King of the universe, Jesus could have acted in pride and self-promotion. Instead, he became a servant and died on the cross for our sins. As we pattern our lives after Jesus, by his grace, we will shine as he did.

Prayer: Dear God—Father, Son, and Spirit—give me a spirit of humility that puts others first for the sake of unity. Help me become more like Jesus so that I will shine for you.

Reflection Question: What stands out to you about Jesus' humility in this passage? Where do you need to ask God to help you develop a humble posture toward others?

Paul's Résumé

DANNY KWON

If you've ever considered applying for a job or for entrance into college, you've written a résumé. A résumé lists accomplishments, including activities at school, church, or in the community; awards you've received; and experiences such as part-time jobs, internships, or service-learning trips. What a résumé cannot do is tell the full story about a person.

The apostle Paul has a résumé worth boasting about. At the beginning of Philippians 3, he lists his achievements, and they are quite impressive by the standards of his day. He is a circumcised Jewish man from the elite tribe of Benjamin and also a member of the Pharisees, a group that boasts in their specific understanding of the law (v. 6). Paul is an extremely accomplished person. But he says he counts all these achievements as a loss. In other words, he rejects these worldly accomplishments and calls them "rubbish" (literally, trash, or dung!) compared to the greatness of knowing Christ and being found in him. Paul proclaims that his righteousness, or moral standing, comes *not from his own efforts* but through Christ.

The world is constantly telling us to prove ourselves—academically, in sports or the arts, or even in our service to others. In contrast, Paul writes that we do not have "a righteousness of [our] own that comes from the law, but that which is through faith in Christ" (v. 9).

Isn't it a relief to know that our value and identity are found in something far greater than being impressive? They are grounded in Jesus' résumé, the One who lived, died, and rose again for us. If you belong to Jesus, you can know that you are loved, valued, and cared for. Your awards or accomplishments do not define you. Instead, Jesus gives you his own righteousness.

Prayer: Lord, help me find peace and rest in what you accomplished on the cross on my behalf and not in what I have or have not done.

Reflection Question: What would it look like to stop trying to be impressive? How can you rest in what Jesus has accomplished for you on the cross?

The Prize of Knowing Jesus

AKASH AHUJA

I live near Boston, a city known for many things—one of them being the Boston Marathon. Every April, the race attracts thousands of runners from all around the world. In 2025, 28,853 runners lined up in Hopkinton to begin their 26.2 mile journey to Boylston Street.[1]

Picture it—28,853 people at the starting line. Only one person can win the race and break the tape that stretches across the finish line; 28,852 people will be more or less forgotten, with one winner making headlines and receiving the unicorn-adorned medal.

Paul would have been familiar with the Olympic games—the original ones in ancient Greece, not the modern games that started in 1896. The description he gives of pressing on toward the goal invokes the image of a runner pushing themselves toward the finish line, much like Olympic athletes would. But there is an important difference between Paul's race and your average marathon. God's work has already gone before us in our spiritual race. In Philippians 3:14, Paul says God has *already* called him heavenward. In verse 16, he says we are living up to what we have *already* attained. He is running the race with the mindset and dedication of someone who wants to win, but he knows that first place has *already* been awarded.

Jesus Christ has run and won the race on our behalf. We can't possibly be the winners in our spiritual lives with God. Paul realizes this, but he's not giving up, even though first place isn't possible. He keeps pressing on, not resting in his past accomplishments and spiritual highs, but focusing on the destination—life in God's presence forever.

As you keep walking with Jesus, treat your faith like a marathon. Steadily move toward the destination, keeping Christ in the front of your mind. Celebrate your progress—God has already done a great work in you! But in all things, remain humble. Christ has won on your behalf and has freely offered you his victory. In your spiritual race, you're not trying to *earn* his love; you're just following—even running—in Christ's footsteps.

Prayer: Lord, help me run this race well, in gratitude for the grace you have already given me.

Reflection Question: What does the next mile of your race look like?

1. "2025 Boston Marathon Statistics," Boston Athletic Association, accessed December 30, 2025, https://registration.baa.org/2025/cf/Public/iframe_Statistics.htm.

Dealing with Anxious Thoughts

KATHERINE PRECHT STINE

"Don't be scared, but . . ." If you hear this phrase, your natural reaction is probably to be scared! What's the end of that sentence going to be? "Don't freak out, but . . . there's a giant spider on your shoulder!" or "Don't be anxious, but junior year is by far the hardest!"

Throughout the Bible, lots of people are told, "Don't be afraid," even as they go into scary situations. Think of Joshua heading into Canaan for battle, Mary finding out she will be miraculously pregnant with Jesus, or Moses seeing a burning bush.

With so many things in this world that can make us anxious, it seems quite impossible to follow Paul's command in Philippians 4:6. But thankfully, God doesn't just say "don't be anxious"; he reminds us why we don't need to fear and tells us what to do when we feel anxious. Look at verse 5. How can we handle our anxious thoughts? By remembering "the Lord is near."

When Jesus saves us from our sin, he doesn't just open the way to heaven; he makes it possible to have a real relationship with God every moment of every day. The God who defeated sin and death is with you always. When scary things happen, he provides peace. So when we feel anxious, we take every situation to God in prayer. We thank him for all he has done for us and ask him for help. He promises to give us his peace—peace that doesn't necessarily make sense to the rest of the world, but a peace that knows God is good, that he is in charge and is working in all things for our good. Instead of letting our thoughts spiral into anxiety, we have something new to focus on in verse 8: No matter what our situation is, we can lean on what we know to be true in Scripture, what God says is right, and what we admire about God. He is worthy of our praise!

Prayer: God, thank you for being present with me and giving me your peace. When I feel anxious, help me set my mind on the things that are excellent and praiseworthy. Amen.

Reflection Question: Are there things in your life that are making you anxious? How does knowing "the Lord is near" help quiet those anxious thoughts?

Jesus Is Bigger

SYLER THOMAS

Years ago, some friends of a high schooler named Rich played a prank on him by obtaining his spare car key and moving his car. Rich first noticed that his car was turned around after youth group. The next week, his friends moved it to a different spot and put a random CD in the player. Another day, Rich ran an errand with me. When we returned to *my* car in the parking lot, Rich walked past *his* car. "Hey, this is my car, Syler. Why is my car here?" At that point, his friends popped out, video camera in hand.

There had been a mystery as Rich's friends were invisibly at work. In our passage, the apostle Paul tells us how Jesus Christ makes the invisible God and his mysterious work visible to us.

In his letter to the church at Colossae, Paul explains Jesus' nature, saying that Jesus, the Son, is the *image* of the invisible God (1:15). In other words, if you're wondering about who the unseen God is, you can look at Jesus and know. Paul then shares that all things were created in Jesus and through Jesus, but also "for him" (v. 16). We can understand that all things were made by and through Jesus, but *for* him? That little word *for* indicates purpose, that the meaning of life is bound up in the fact that all creation exists *for* Jesus. Not in the way that an egomaniac needs everything to be about him, but in the way that all of life only makes sense when we understand that Jesus is who life is about.

Paul goes on to say that Jesus is "before all things and in him all things hold together" (v. 17). He's the head of the church. He is the beginning, and in everything he has "the supremacy" (v. 18). There's no one who has more authority, power, or status than Jesus. Why is this important? It means, among other things, that in whatever challenge you face today, Jesus Christ is bigger. It doesn't mean your challenge isn't a challenge. Rather, Jesus sees your challenge and says, *My supremacy means your challenge won't sink you.*

We often wish God were visible. *Why can't I see him?* You can. When we look at Jesus, we see God, the One who is supreme over anything we face, the One whose death on the cross is the once-for-all answer that God is not just good, but the greatest.

Prayer: Lord Jesus, help me know you are the image of the invisible God, supreme over all things—even my most difficult challenges.

Reflection Question: Why is it so hard to believe that Jesus is greater?

Jesus Gives Us Our Identity

REBECCA LANKFORD

Recently, in a workout class, the instructor confessed that she didn't feel like coming to class until she put on her workout clothes. Once she made the painful switch from slippers to tennis shoes, she was ready and excited to exercise. I'm sure you've had similar experiences, whether suiting up for a game or getting in costume for a show. What we're wearing tends to impact how we behave and how we feel.

In Colossians 3, Paul explains the new "clothes" the believers in Colossae are wearing. They have received Jesus into their hearts by faith. Now Paul shows them the realities of their new identity in Christ and how this identity transforms their lives. Paul reminds the Colossians that they are hidden in Christ, freely clothed by his life, death, and resurrection. Since they are united to Christ in his death and resurrection, their old selves have died with Christ, and their new selves have now been raised with him (v. 1). With this new clothing, they are called to live into the present realities of who they are in Christ.

Knowing who they are in Christ (chosen, holy, and beloved, to name a few qualities) dictates their behavior—never the other way around. This new identity in Christ is a gift from God that hinges on *Jesus'* perfect righteousness. Their new identities are as secure as Jesus' death and resurrection, and they can now operate in ways more suited to this new identity—with compassion, kindness, humility, meekness, patience, love, gratitude, and worship (vv. 12–17).

If you are united to Christ by faith, you, too, have a new identity that isn't based on what you do, have done, or will do, but on what Jesus has done for you. It is a gift from God that you daily get to walk in. Fully clothed in the righteousness of Christ, you are freed to take off your old self and put on the new self Christ has given you. In some cases, taking off your old self may mean asking God to help you say goodbye to old, comfortable habits that have hindered your fellowship with God and others. When you do, you'll find that true abundant life is found as you walk with Christ, seeking him and the things that are above.

Prayer: Father, thank you for clothing me in your perfect righteousness. Help me operate out of my new identity, putting on the new self.

Reflection Question: What are some ways you define yourself—the sport you play, the people you hang out with, the grades you make? How is your identity in Christ different?

A New Social Status

CLARK FOBES IV

When I was a middle schooler in the late 1990s, shoes were the greatest marker of social status. The cooler a kid's shoes were, the cooler they were. My family couldn't afford high-end shoes, but I saved up to buy my first pair of Nikes—my ticket to climbing the social ladder.

Much like today, the Greco-Roman world Paul lived in valued social position above all else. Power and prestige determined quality of life. The apostle Paul instructs the Colossians how to navigate this high-honor society. Rather than seeking to elevate their own social status, believers are to find their value in the kingdom of Christ.

In Colossians 3, Paul gives different instructions depending on social status. He urges those who are lower on the social stratum to practice submission. So wives, children, and even slaves are called to submit to their earthly masters. To us, submission seems like a call to give up our freedom, but in Paul's day, submission brought protection and provision to the individual and honor to the one in authority. By qualifying all of their submission as in the Lord, Paul shows that if we belong to the Lord and our honor comes from him, then we can submit freely without fear or worry. Paul's big idea is that believers live and work "for the Lord, not for human masters" (v. 23).

Paul then calls those in positions of authority to be gentle with those under them. Husbands, fathers, and masters are not to abuse their power, as authorities in their day typically did. Recognizing that they, too, are under a Master, they are called to reflect the fear and care of God. The gospel radically emphasizes care for the marginalized.

Whether we have very little honor or a lot, Paul urges us not to place our hope in social position. Recognizing we have a Savior who possesses all spiritual authority and honor in heaven but gave it up for us (Philippians 2:7–11), we can rest in the greater honor God bestows on us in his kingdom. With this inheritance, we are no longer enslaved to the social currency of the day but can live freely, wherever we find ourselves, for the glory of God and his kingdom.

Prayer: Father, thank you for my new standing in Christ. Set me free from the need to live for status in this world. Amen.

Reflection Question: How does the honor you have as a child of the King change the way you view your social status in this world?

Charge It to Me

ALEXIS ANDRE

Going to the library was a favorite pastime for my dad, my siblings, and me. I was an avid reader who loved to borrow books. But sometimes I lost those books. When I wanted to borrow more, there would be a charge on my account for the books I hadn't returned. Guess who had to pay those charges? You're right—my dad. No matter what, my dad paid paid the library what I owed and let me borrow new books.

In this letter, Paul writes to a wealthy slaveholder named Philemon. Slavery was widespread in Roman culture, and mainly came about through war or because of unpaid debts—not based on race. Philemon's former slave, Onesimus, has run away to Rome in search of freedom. Once he reaches his city of refuge, he encounters Paul. After spending some time with the apostle Paul, Onesimus believes the gospel of Christ; therefore, he gains a new Master. Based on Onesimus's confession, Paul writes to Philemon and urges him to accept Onesimus back into his home, not as a slave, but as "a dear brother" (v. 16).

Paul goes further in his plea for Onesimus by instructing Philemon to welcome Onesimus as he would welcome Paul and to charge any debt of Onesimus's to Paul's account. Paul is confident in sending a runaway slave back to his former master because Paul has heard about Philemon's "love for all [God's] holy people and [his] faith in the Lord Jesus" (v. 5). He trusts Philemon "to do what [he] ought to do" and release Onesimus from bondage (v. 8).

Paul's appeal for Onesimus's freedom is one of the strongest images of Christ's sacrificial work for us. Without Jesus, we, too, are bound to a master that is not meant to rule over us—sin. Through Christ's sacrifice on the cross, we can accept our rightful Master, who is God.

Despite all the times we stray from him, God welcomes us back into his fellowship through the work of his Son. All the wrong we have done is charged to Jesus' account. He took the blame and the punishment, so we can return to God (Romans 3:24–26). Living for God doesn't mean we will no longer make mistakes. But just like my dad kept paying my debt at the library, Christ's work on the cross continues to pay for our sins. We never have to worry about whether our Father will be there when we mess up. He always wants us to run back to him—our true Master who has forever freed us from sin's bondage.

Prayer: God, help me remember your grace when it's time to run back to you.

Reflection Question: What keeps you from believing you are free from sin?

Saying No to Ungodliness

SYLER THOMAS

One of my favorite children's books is called *No, David!* It features a mischievous boy zinging from one naughty behavior to the next—coloring on the walls, tracking mud into the house, jumping on the bed in his cowboy boots. The exasperated parents (understandably) try to keep him in line, saying "Come back here," "Not in the house," or simply, "No, David!"

Parents say no because they love their children. As kids grow, wise parents teach their children how to say no for themselves, even when it's hard. Our passage reveals that God's grace teaches each of us how to say no to the ungodliness around us.

The book of Titus is a personal letter from the apostle Paul to his ministry companion Titus, who has been sent to help the house churches on the island of Crete. Residents of Crete were notorious for sinful living. Paul instructs Titus to encourage Cretan Christians to live out their faith among the "evil" Cretans because *God's salvation-bringing grace has appeared* (1:12, 2:11). It is this grace, Paul says, that teaches us to say no to ungodliness.

In chapter 3, Paul lists all the different sins that characterize each of us before we begin to follow Jesus: "At one time we too were foolish, disobedient, deceived and enslaved by all kinds of passions and pleasures" (v. 3). In other words, we were evil, just like the Cretans. But then Paul says, "When the kindness and love of God our Savior appeared, he saved us" (v. 4). Not because we were pure and holy. Not because we were good. Only because of Jesus. God's grace displayed once and for all through Christ's sacrificial death on the cross is the historical event in the past that we can rest in, *and* we have something glorious in the future that awaits us—Christ's return. Notice that it's not God's judgment, wrath, or disappointment that teaches us to live holy lives; it's *grace*, God's favor, which we don't deserve and could never earn.

No, David! ends with a tearful David apologizing for breaking a vase and being comforted by his mother, who tells him, "Yes, David, I love you." Ultimately, the yes of God's love for us in Jesus is what gives us the power to say no to sin. Christ's "I love you" on the cross helps us reject sin's power as God works in us by his Spirit.

Prayer: Lord, give me strength to say no to sin through the power of your Spirit who lives in me.

Reflection Question: How do you handle temptation when it's hard to say no?

I Am the Worst of Sinners

JOHN ONWUCHEKWA

A. W. Tozer once said, "What comes into our minds when we think about God is the most important thing about us."[1] What we think about God shapes everything about us! But if we spend our time focusing solely on the good things Jesus did—the healings, the feedings, the teaching—but miss *why he came*, we may never actually trust him.

Paul makes what seems to be a crazy confession: "Christ Jesus came into the world to save sinners—of whom I am the worst" (1 Timothy 1:15). This isn't an exaggeration. Before he became the apostle who wrote much of the New Testament, Paul was a violent man who bullied Christians. If Christians had a yearbook and voted on the person they'd least expect God to love, Paul would've won unanimously. And yet this is exactly the point. Jesus didn't save him in spite of his past, but in a large part *because* of it. Jesus' act of saving someone like him is *the* way God wants to put the depths of his love on display. Paul wasn't the exception but the *example* of the type of person God saves.

That's why Paul uses present tense verbs, not past tense. He doesn't say, "I was the worst"; He says, "I *am* the worst." Not because he's sinking in shame, but because he knows how deep his need is—and how strong God's mercy is. He is living proof that Jesus didn't come for the put-together and impressive, but rather for the deeply broken.

Maybe you've got a past you'd rather forget. Maybe your mistakes feel too big and your faith feels too small. Romans 5:8 says, "While we were still sinners, Christ died for us." His love doesn't depend on your performance. It meets you right where you are.

Paul's story teaches us that no one is too far gone. If you've already trusted Jesus, never forget that you're still the one he came for. His patience didn't stop when you believed. It's still holding you, carrying you, calling you closer. You don't need to clean yourself up first; you just need to come.

Prayer: Jesus, help me remember that I don't have to be perfect to receive your grace, just honest enough to ask for it.

Reflection Question: How might your story—flaws and all—help someone else believe they're not too far gone to receive God's grace?

---

1. A. W. Tozer, *The Knowledge of the Holy* (HarperCollins, 1992), 1.

Qualified to Lead

DAVIS LACEY

There are a host of reasons people give for not becoming involved in a church. One of the most common objections has to do with the *people* in the church. In many cases, the true critique is that the *leaders* of the church are hypocritical. They may speak eloquently of Jesus, but they still fall short of exemplifying his character in their day-to-day lives. Some people wonder why anyone would willingly sacrifice time and energy to be involved in such a ministry.

In 1 Timothy 3:1–13, the apostle Paul lays out a series of qualifications for two distinct offices—overseers (also called pastors or elders) and deacons. Bible-believing Christians hold a variety of positions on the specific functions of these offices, but one truth is clear: Those who lead the church are called to exemplary Christian character.

There is a reason that character is at a premium for church leaders: Their chief responsibility is to serve as examples of Jesus (1 Peter 5:3). Peter clarifies the sort of example they are to set: "When the Chief Shepherd appears, you will receive the crown of glory that will never fade away" (v. 4).

Jesus is the Chief Shepherd. He is the true and better church leader. Those God calls to serve as pastors, deacons, and other church leaders are called primarily to be incarnate ("in bodily form") examples of Jesus through exemplifying the character ideals of 1 Timothy 3:1–13. When a church leader models these character ideals, we should be grateful for the ways this leader points us to Jesus. When a church leader falls short of these ideals, the gospel offers us hope.

Our salvation, our ongoing transformation, and our eternal hope are firmly and securely established based on the perfect, saving work our Chief Shepherd has already accomplished. The failures of our human leaders often have sad consequences and can cause us godly grief, but they do not threaten the salvation that Christ has graciously won for us. So they should not deter our willingness to be involved in churches that are led by imperfect examples of a perfect, all-sufficient Savior.

Prayer: Jesus, thank you for being the perfect leader I need. Equip those who serve as your undershepherds in local churches, and help them reflect your character.

Reflection Question: Do you know of a Christian leader who models the character directives of 1 Timothy 3:1–13? Encourage them with a specific example of how you've seen them model Jesus' character.

Do Not Be Ashamed

AKASH AHUJA

I grew up feeling like I stood out. I am a biracial immigrant who moved with my family across the world when I was young. We landed in a suburban Connecticut town that was 95 percent white, so I stood out like a sore thumb in elementary school. I was behind my classmates in speaking English and had a hard time relating to American traditions centering around the Fourth of July, Thanksgiving, and even Christmas. Being so different from my friends and peers became a reason to feel ashamed and even to be bullied. I didn't want to stand out; I just wanted to fit in.

Timothy also feels different. As a young person called to be a leader in the early church, he likely feels awkward as he lives out his faith and calling. Paul writes to encourage him that despite the challenges, Timothy can lead from a position of confidence, not fear. Paul reminds Timothy of God's salvation and calling through Christ, which is not because of anything any of us have done, but by grace alone. This is how Paul himself can preach the gospel without shame: "because I know whom I have believed" (2 Timothy 1:12). Our relationship with God empowers us to share the hope of Jesus with others.

Consider the contexts in which you feel different. It may be relatively easy to talk about Jesus and follow his commands when you're at church or youth group. But maybe you feel awkward doing those things around a certain friend or group. You may feel a little bit like how I felt about my cultural identity: It was easy to be Brazilian and Indian at home with my family, but I found it really challenging to embrace my cultures in other places.

Even if you feel shy about your commitment to God when you're at school or with friends, these verses remind you that the gospel gives you a reason to be bold instead of afraid. If you have trusted Jesus, you have the Holy Spirit with you. He gives power, love, and self-discipline. And in Timothy, you find a brother whom God called to lead, just as he has called you.

Prayer: Loving God, thank you for sending your Holy Spirit to give me courage. Help me stand firm in the gospel and live by it with confidence. Remind me every day that I am not alone.

Reflection Question: How can you take a small but brave step to be less timid in sharing your faith today?

The Bible Makes You Wise

LUKE PAIVA

In 2020, an estimated 64 trillion gigabytes of information were available on the internet. The estimate increased to as much as 175 trillion gigabytes by 2025.[1] More information is available in the world today than ever before in human history, and it is increasing exponentially. Somehow this increase has muddied the waters in our quest for truth. You can find information, evidence, and justification for nearly anything. How do we find true answers to our questions when the ocean of ideas only gets larger and more complicated each day?

The Bible reveals a speaking God who has declared himself "the way and the truth and the life" (John 14:6). God has created us to seek understanding and truth. He gives us his Word so that we may know him, know ourselves, and better understand the world. The Holy Spirit helps us understand all that God has said to us in his Word (2 Corinthians 2:10–13). God's Word is living and active (Hebrews 4:12) and transforms Christians through the power of the Holy Spirit. This is what we are designed for and crave. No other source satisfies our quest for truth like the Word of God.

God didn't give us the Bible to satisfy personal curiosity, but so that we may know Jesus and his love for us. You will not get every answer you want. You will not always get the depth of explanation you hope for. But you *will* meet the God you are looking for. You will be shaped more and more into his image as his Spirit works in you through his Word (2 Corinthians 3:18). God's Word will equip and transform you to follow Christ.

Do you want to draw close to God? Do you want to know him more and know what he wants for you? He has spoken in the timeless truth of his Word, revealing how we should live as his children. In the Bible, God has given the teaching, correction, and training in righteousness that orients us to himself (2 Timothy 3:16). His Word prepares us to be his people today.

Prayer: Thank you for not being silent. You have given me your Spirit and your Word. Draw me closer to you each day through your Word.

Reflection Question: How do you see God revealing himself and his love in the gift of Scripture?

---

1. "Has the Web Given People Access to Too Much Information?," History of the Web, February 13, 2025, https://thehistoryoftheweb.com/dialogues/has-the-web-given-people-access-to-too-much-information/.

Jesus Understands Our Weakness

JOEY TURNER

With a look of despair, my student asked a question I struggled to answer: "How do you know you will do what God requires of you in the moment he requires it?" Maybe you have wondered the same thing. It's one thing to say we'll do something difficult, like obey God or resist temptation. We can promise it, but it's another thing to follow through.

In Jewish Levitical law, the high priest is a mediator between God and human beings.. He enters into the Most Holy Place once a year on the Day of Atonement to make a sacrifice on behalf of the people. Jesus is the great high priest, the final mediator between God and man. He became the final sacrifice to "atone" for our sins so that we might be with God.

Because Jesus lived as a human being, he knows us. He knows how weak and ignorant we can be. He "has been tempted in every way, just as we are" (Hebrews 4:15), but unlike us, he never sinned. Also unlike us, Jesus fulfilled every commitment he ever made. He not only said he would suffer on our behalf, but when that day came, *he did it*. On the cross, he uttered the words, "It is finished" (John 19:30). Therefore, our hope is not in people, who may or may not fulfill their promises. Our hope and confidence are in a man who fulfilled what he said to the very end.

Jesus knows what it's like to endure. He is able to empathize with our weaknesses. He is our great high priest, the source of eternal salvation for all who trust in him. Christ's body and blood are the atoning sacrifice for our sins, making us eternally right with God. Our hope is not in our ability to do the right thing; our hope is in the fact that Jesus did what he said he was going to do when the hour came for him to suffer and die.

Prayer: Father, change my heart that I might rest in the finished work of Jesus each day.

Reflection Question: How does it help you in your walk with God to know that Jesus experienced temptation, just as you do?

Receive What Jesus Wants to Give You

AKASH AHUJA

Whether you lean iPhone or Android, smartphones are everywhere. You're probably less than three feet away from one right now. Most people you know have one, or at least have access to one. In the palm of everyone's hands is a piece of technology that would have amazed anyone thirty years ago but is now one of the most common items you can imagine. Yet a new version is released just about every year. You'll see the upgraded cameras and resolution and AI integration in advertisements everywhere. You may know someone who loves technology and enjoys getting a new smartphone every single year.

In Hebrews, we learn about a new high priest and a new covenant. The old covenant, explained in Exodus 19–24, is based on obedience. In order for the Israelites to live in relationship with God, they needed to obey a multitude of laws and offer sacrifices to make things right when they got things wrong. God gave his people chance after chance to follow him, but the people always disappointed. God knew his people couldn't ultimately obey his law on their own, so he promised a new covenant, or sacred agreement (Jeremiah 31).

But the new covenant in Jesus is not a small update. It's not new in the same way the newest iPhone compares to the last. The new covenant is better in the same way that a smartphone is better than two tin cans and a string. The new covenant isn't based on laws to keep and sacrifices to offer; it's based on the obedience and once-for-all sacrifice of Jesus. This covenant leads to fullness of life and a renewed relationship with God in a way that the old simply couldn't (Hebrews 8:7–13).

Have you upgraded to this new covenant? It's easy to say we have, but we can easily find ourselves treating God like the old model. We think we need to earn his love. We hide our sins from him instead of freely confessing and receiving grace. Our old way of thinking can sneak into our walk with God instead of letting Christ transform our way of thinking. As we mature in faith, a question we can keep asking is this: *Am I receiving everything Jesus wants to give me?* He offers a new and better covenant.

Prayer: Lord Jesus, thank you for the new covenant you made through your blood. Lead me into a deeper experience of your love.

Reflection Question: Are you trusting in the new promises of the new covenant, or are you trying to keep the law on your own terms?

Faith Is Believing What We Cannot See

KENDAL CONNER

I will never forget my first roller-coaster ride. As the youngest child, I had watched for years as my siblings enjoyed the thrills, eagerly awaiting the day I would be tall enough to join. Yet when the time finally came, my excitement turned into pure fear. Once I was strapped in, my dad took my hand and said, "Just have faith." Although I knew his intent was to bring me comfort, I yelled back at my dad, "How?" Faith felt like something I had to muster up out of my own strength, and it seemed impossible.

Hebrews 11 gives the clearest definition of faith in Scripture. It says faith consists of two things—assurance and conviction. First, faith is assurance of things we hope for. Another way to say this is that faith is not merely a wish, but the guarantee of what God has promised. Faith is God's gift to help us trust that what he says will finally come to reality (Ephesians 2:8). The author of Hebrews says that this gift of faith is what enables us to please God.

Second, faith is conviction of the things not yet seen. This means that faith is not blind; quite the opposite. Faith is a sure belief in what we know is true, even when we cannot yet see it. Conviction comes from knowing God and his Word, from having witnessed the power of God in other circumstances. In turn, we can stand in trusting belief in his power in every circumstance.

Not only does Hebrews 11 define faith, but it also offers tangible examples of true faith. Listed are men and women throughout Scripture who displayed the type of faith described in verse 1. Don't miss this: The author gives two distinct examples of faith lived out: (1) We read of people whose faith was displayed as they trusted God to deliver them from their circumstances, and then (2) starting in verse 5, the list continues with examples of people who displayed faith by trusting God even in the midst of their circumstances. They were persecuted and killed, yet they had assurance and conviction that God was better than anything in this world. *That* is great faith.

Faith is the assurance God will provide and a trusting conviction that he already has provided through his Son, Jesus Christ. We can walk by faith, knowing that God is the same " yesterday and today and forever" (13:8).

Prayer: God, help me grow in faith as I look to you as my full assurance.

Reflection Question: How does Hebrews 11 help you better understand faith? Which examples in this chapter encourage or challenge you?

Running the Race

DANNY KWON

Traditionally, one of the last events in the summer Olympics is the men's marathon. The event starts at various starting points, depending on the host city. In recent history, the event has concluded with runners entering the packed Olympic stadium, running their final few laps, and crossing the finish line. It's an awesome scene to see runners complete their course in a venue full of cheering fans.

Hebrews 12 starts with a picture of a "great cloud of witnesses," which feels like a stadium full of excited spectators. It is a picture of Christians from history who have gone before us in their lives with God, fellow believers who have walked with God in faith. Their presence testifies to the work of Jesus in the lives of many believers. The work of Jesus has not only impacted the lives of those who have gone before, but our verse speaks to the perfecting work of Jesus on our behalf too. The author of Hebrews invites us to look to the one person who can make us holy and pure—Jesus, the "perfecter of our faith."

On the cross, Jesus made atonement, cleansing us and paying our debt for our sins. Second Corinthians 5:17 says that Jesus, who had never sinned, *became* sin for us that we might become the righteousness of God. In a profound exchange, Jesus took on our sin and bestowed on us his righteousness. Praise God we don't have to be perfect. This is the work of Christ, who makes us more like him.

Jesus endured the cross for the "joy set before him," and that joy is—you guessed it—the great cloud of witnesses whose faith he perfects. One day, that great cloud of witnesses will include you and me. Saving us and living in eternity with us brings Jesus joy. Knowing that Jesus delights in us helps us run our own race of faith with the endurance he gives us.

Prayer: Lord, let me be at rest, knowing that while I can never be perfect on my own, you are forming me into the image of Christ.

Reflection Question: How can you find rest in Jesus' perfection instead of trying to be perfect in yourself?

God's Discipline Heals Us

ASHLEY KIM

Anyone who's had a major injury knows that recovery takes patience, time, and special care. Broken bones need to be realigned to heal straight. Sprained ankles require ice, rest, and often crutches. It's inconvenient and frustrating, but our bodies can only heal properly when we attend carefully to the conditions of recovery. Only then will what is broken be set straight.

Scripture often compares our spiritual deficiencies—our sinfulness—to bodily infirmities and weaknesses. Sin is like a disease. Spiritually, it makes us blind, deaf, and lame. It is a wound and a plague that is "incurable" (Jeremiah 30:12; Micah 1:9). When Jesus says he has come not for those who are well but for the sick, he means he came for sinners (Matthew 9:12; Mark 2:17; Luke 5:31). The gospel is a story of healing for desperately sick sinners.

Yet recovery from sickness or injury can often be a long process. Every Christian has been rescued from the death sentence of sin, but the Christian life is a lifelong recovery from the presence and effects of sin. Sin makes us crippled and immobile. The author of Hebrews tells us to walk along level paths, so that "the lame may not be disabled, but rather healed" (12:13). Like physical therapy for someone learning to walk again, healing from the crippling effects of sin means patiently and carefully learning to live righteously and wisely according to God's Word through his Spirit's work in us. True recovery requires often asking ourselves, *How can I walk in level paths? How can I protect myself from the dangers of sin? How can I practice a life of integrity?*

Healing is a long and often painful process. Medicine tastes bitter. Recovering strength requires exertion. Setting a bone hurts. Every grief and discomfort is the discipline of our Father, which is indeed unpleasant. But the author of Hebrews reminds us, using another analogy, that the pain and difficulty of Christian growth are worth it. Only later does discipline grant "a harvest of righteousness and peace," the fruit of enduring what feels unbearable in the moment. After discipline, after a long recovery, we enjoy the fruit of righteousness—the fruit of a healed soul.

Prayer: Father, thank you for being my true Physician, who knows and tends to my needs. Teach me to trust that you are growing and sanctifying me.

Reflection Question: What does a careful plan of healing look like for your soul?

Facing Trials of Many Kinds

CURTIS DUNLAP

It takes a lot for me to get angry. But here I was . . . furious. I felt completely disrespected. What made it worse was that the offense had come from a family member with whom I got along pretty well. As I wrestled to get my emotions under control I had one thought: *No matter how you respond, your actions must be pleasing to me.* Because I was so angry, I knew that this thought was the whisper of the Lord. So I had a choice: Would I let this person's hurtful comments justify a sinful response, or would I let God use this experience to grow me?

In James 1:2–4, James is addressing a group of Jewish Christians who were undergoing persecution. James wants them to understand that hardship in life does not mean that God is absent. Precisely the opposite. God cares about what we are going through. But he cares far more about who we are becoming.

James is communicating a profound truth that is often lost on us because we live in a culture that celebrates stress-free living: Growth requires adversity. God is purposeful in our trials. He uses even our hardships to produce things in us like endurance, which will eventually yield maturity. It can be hard to understand why, if God loves us, he lets us experience suffering. But sometimes we wrongly assume that God doesn't have a good reason for allowing hardship into our lives.

While Satan uses our suffering to tempt us to sin, God wants to use it to grow us closer to him. Even Jesus experienced the benefit of hardships. Hebrews 5:8 reads, "Jesus learned obedience through what he suffered." If Jesus was shaped through suffering, we shouldn't be surprised when God uses our trials to shape us too.

I learned from my experience that when we face trials with faith, something powerful happens: Our endurance grows, and with it, our character (Romans 5:1–5). And over time, that character makes us more complete . . . more like Jesus. Your pain isn't pointless. God is doing something in you, even when life feels unfair or confusing.

Prayer: God, help me see my trials the way you see them—as opportunities for gospel growth that will help my faith mature.

Reflection Question: What can you do to remind yourself that God is not absent in your suffering and that suffering is an opportunity for growth?

When It's Hard to Control Your Temper

MARY BETH JOHNSTON

"Where's your whoop whoop now?" I shouted at the stands after sinking a three-pointer. I'd had enough of the opposing team's parents cheering, taunting, and smack-talking that filled the air anytime our team missed a shot. Not to mention the flagrant fouls! This was seventh-grade basketball. Was I really expected to be more mature than the adults in the gym? My dad seemed to think so, based on the disapproving look he gave me from the stands. Yikes, now I was enraged *and* embarrassed. Not my finest hour.

I've always had a problem controlling my tongue and my temper. If I'm honest, I haven't always seen it as a problem. I can be quick to dismiss it as "venting" or "letting off some steam."

However, James tells us that the words we speak and the way we act deserve careful consideration. He tells us to be doers and not just hearers of God's Word (1:22). He says that if we listen to the Word and do not do what it says, we deceive ourselves and our religion is worthless (v. 26). Yikes again. We want to be people who know, love, trust, and follow Jesus, not just those who know about him. But that can be easier said than done.

To those of us who seem to have a really hard time living as God commands, James urges us to get rid of evil and "humbly accept the word planted in you, which can save you" (v. 21). Humbly *accept*—that word *accept* could also be read as *receive.* We are not saved by what we do, but by *receiving* God's grace, which is given to us through faith in Jesus. Jesus himself is the Word planted in us (John 1:1, 14). When we humbly receive him, Jesus is the One who helps us live according to his commands. Jesus is the One we turn to for forgiveness when we fall short. Jesus is the One we call on to save us, both for eternity and in our daily times of need.

Now that's something that deserves a whoop whoop!

Prayer: Lord, thank you for your saving grace. Help me to hear your word and follow you, Jesus. Amen.

Reflection Question: How are you struggling to live according to God's Word? Surrender these things to the Lord, and ask him to help you follow him.

Apple Trees Grow Apples

DAWSON COOPER

Imagine you are a farmer planting an orchard. If you plant an apple seed, you expect the tree that grows to produce apples. If it produces peaches instead, well, it must not have been an apple seed. The fruit produced doesn't match what was planted.

James is clarifying here in chapter 2 the relationship between faith and works, or the seed and the fruit. A Christian's works should demonstrate, or flow out of, their faith. Perhaps the people James writes to are struggling (like us) to have their actions match their faith.

Remember, we are saved by *grace alone* and *through faith* in Jesus Christ as our Lord and Savior (Ephesians 2:8). Jesus took the punishment we deserve for our sins, died, and rose again, reconciling us to God. He sends the Holy Spirit to live within us, refining us. There are no works in my past, present, or future that could merit my salvation—it truly is God's gift to us. Still, James clearly teaches that works are important to our faith. It's not one or the other.

When we become a new creation in Christ, we repent—or turn away—from our old ways to the Lord's ways. In practical ways, we should look different in how we live our lives. The Holy Spirit is like a seed, causing us to bear the fruit of being more like Jesus. We look more Christlike because the Holy Spirit is at work in us, not because we can be like Jesus on our own. As the Lord makes us more like Jesus, our lives will glorify him. Our works reflect not our goodness, but God's goodness through our salvation through faith and our restored relationship with God.

None of this would be possible if Jesus hadn't lived the perfect life of obedience to God. Though we fall short, Jesus did not. We will always be a work in progress on this side of heaven. Yet because of Christ's life, death, and resurrection and his gift of the Holy Spirit, we can be confident "that he who began a good work in you will carry it on to completion until the day of Christ Jesus" (Philippians 1:6).

Prayer: Lord, thank you for making me right with you through Christ. Turn me back to you quickly when my actions don't glorify you, and help me be patient as you transform me to be more like Christ. Amen.

Reflection Question: Where in your life do you find it hard to reflect your faith through your actions?

Watch Your Mouth!

ALEXIS ANDRE

"Watch your mouth!" snapped my mother and aunties to my cousins and me. If we heard this reprimand, we knew that whatever we had said was inappropriate for us children to say. Our parents' consistent directions regarding our speech and actions helped us learn who we were meant to be in the world. This sort of moment also happens in James 3.

James has been writing to his audience about the best ways to live in community with each other. Here in chapter 3, he instructs the believers about how they are meant to speak. He explains that although the tongue is small and seemingly insignificant, it has power to either bless or curse.

The problem is that some of James's readers are using their mouths to both praise God and curse others. James asks, "Can both fresh water and salt water flow from the same spring?" and "Can a fig tree bear olives, or a grapevine bear figs?" (vv. 11–12). In other words, God created springs to yield fresh water. Fig trees for figs. Grapevines for grapes. In this same way, God created human mouths to praise God and love their neighbors. To use our mouths to curse another image bearer is to work against God's design.

But if we're honest, our emotions get the best of us at times, and unkind words spew out toward our neighbor. If the tongue is as powerful and uncontrollable as James says, how are we supposed to master it amid anger or anxiety? Well, we can't without the help of the Holy Spirit. Through Ezekiel, God announces his plan to redeem his people: "I will put my Spirit in you and move you to follow my decrees and be careful to keep my laws" (36:27). And Jesus promises to send the Holy Spirit to help his followers (John 14:26) live according to God's standards.

Jesus offers us his perfect life in our place, and this is how God declares us right with him. Because we are his redeemed people, God still calls us to holy living. Through Christ's sacrifice and the Holy Spirit's power, we can live this kind of life, even in the way we speak.

Prayer: Father, thank you for the Holy Spirit. When the cares of this world stir up many words in my heart, thank you for giving me the power of your Spirit to speak words that point to you. Amen.

Reflection Question: How have you used your words to build up or tear down those around you?

God Gives More Grace

ANNE SANFORD

I'd like to speak for a minute to my fifteen- to eighteen-year-old self:

> Listen up, teenage Anne. I know you're feeling pretty proud of yourself right now. You don't struggle with any of the "big" sins. You have your regular quiet times of praying and reading the Bible. You get good grades. You serve in your community, and you're a leader in your youth group. You know you're not perfect. You asked Jesus to be your Savior so that one day you'll live with him forever. But if you're honest, you're pretty sure you could get yourself 85 percent of the way there and are grateful Jesus died to take you that last 15 percent.
>
> I've got news for you, sister. Life's coming quickly. Very soon your sin will be staring you right between the eyes. And in that moment when you become aware of the severity of your own sinful heart, you will look up and see Jesus. You'll expect to see him shaking his head at your disobedience. That's what you deserve, but it isn't what you'll see. You'll see him with arms wide open, walking toward you, saying "Come to me, you weary and burdened one, and I will give you rest." And in that moment, you'll truly understand this verse from James, perhaps for the first time.

Reader, I don't know if you identify with teenage Anne, or if you're thinking, *I blew it a long time ago. I'm extremely aware of my own sin*. Either way, as James teaches his readers, our God "gives more grace."

This world will humble you, and when it does, it will hurt. But the great news for Christians is that the gospel *also* humbles us, and yet the kind of humility that the gospel brings doesn't hurt—it heals. In your best and worst moments, "Come near to God and he will come near to you" (James 4:8). Take the advice of the old hymn: "Turn your eyes upon Jesus, look full in his wonderful face, and the things of earth will grow strangely dim, in the light of his glory and grace."

Prayer: Jesus, thank you for your grace. Thank you for humbling me through what you've done for me. Give me eyes to see your kindness.

Reflection Question: Can you think of a time you were truly humbled by what Jesus has done for you? Did it lead you into a closer relationship with him?

What Is It You're Hoping For?

CONNIE LEUNG NELSON

"I hope I make the team!" "We still have some hope of making it past this round!" "The hope of the championship rests on our best player!" We use the word *hope* in different ways. We say we *hope* when we mean we *desire*, when there's still a *chance*, or when we *trust in* someone to come through. In each case, we have varying levels of confidence that our hope will become reality.

The apostle Peter had much to say about a Christian's hope. In 1 Peter 1, he writes to early Christians who are suffering many trials (v. 6), including being ostracized for their faith and facing hardships from living in a fallen world.

Peter reminds suffering Christians that they have hope in every sense of the word. He assures us that our hope is living, immortal, and incapable of being lost. This is because Jesus, who never sinned, paid the penalty for our sins on the cross. He rose from the grave in victory over sin and death. His resurrection proves his ability to carry his people safely from this world, which is sick with sin and death. We can trust with utmost confidence that we are "shielded by God's power" at every moment of this life (v. 5), so that sin and death never have the last word.

While Christians want their suffering to end, there is an even deeper desire within us for goodness and glory. Peter assures believers that there is unshakable hope in this sense too. He describes an inheritance for believers that God keeps safely in heaven, one "that can never perish, spoil or fade" (v. 4). Believers will one day greet Jesus with "praise, glory and honor" (v. 7).

It's hard to keep going when you're overwhelmed by your troubles. It's scary not to know the future. But think about something hard you endured that ended up being good. How much more peace could you have had in the middle of the heartache had you known that a good outcome was right around the corner. That's the joy that Peter wants us to experience in this life now, even as we suffer (vv. 6, 8). It is a deep and abiding assurance that our hope, in every sense of the word, cannot fail. Our hope is Jesus Christ himself, who carries us through our trials now and will one day deliver us from suffering into glory.

Prayer: Father, help me rest in the knowledge that I am never without an impenetrable, living hope because Jesus rose from the dead.

Reflection Question: How does putting your full hope in Jesus to deliver you one day into his glorious presence change your thoughts or actions today?

You Belong

CLARK FOBES IV

Belonging is a fundamental desire of being human. We all want to be part of a group—a family, social group, or club, for example. Belonging drives much of our behavior and decision-making. As a teenager, I longed to fit in, even changing the way I dressed to try to feel included among the cool kids at my school.

Peter writes about the desire to belong when he addresses believers as "sojourners and exiles" (1 Peter 2:11 ESV). Because of their faith in Christ, the early Christians often experienced exclusion from Roman culture. In today's culture, holding the "wrong" beliefs can get you canceled—just another way of saying you're booted out of the group. What do we do when we feel like we stand out from the world, especially for believing in Jesus? According to Peter, we embrace our lack of belonging in the world.

Peter tells the early Christians that they are meant to be different—a "chosen race" and "holy nation" (v. 9 ESV). These images come from God's words to Israel about his purpose for them among the nations in the land of Canaan (Exodus 19:5–6). Peter applies them to the church to remind us that we *should* expect to feel different from those who don't know him. In fact, the more we feel like we don't belong in the world ("not a people"), the more we will learn to embrace our identity as "God's people" (v. 10 ESV).

As much as we long to fit in, following Jesus means walking in the footsteps of one who never belonged in the world. As a foreigner among human beings, Jesus came as God in the flesh, not so he might belong, but so he might prepare a greater belonging for his people. Through his rejection, Jesus accomplished salvation that makes us part of his people and his kingdom.

So when we feel out of place in this world, we are exactly where we ought to be, because we belong to a world to come. As we await God's coming kingdom, we can find comfort in belonging with God's family, the "spiritual house" he welcomes us into through Christ's work on the cross (vv. 4–6).

Prayer: Thank you, Father, for securing a new family for me in Christ. Remind me of my greater belonging with you and your people while I wait with hope for the world to come.

Reflection Question: How does your belonging with God and his people comfort you when you feel like you don't fit in?

How Do We Know What's True About Jesus?

CHELTEN L. CARTER

It's important to recognize the difference between what is real and what is fake. For example, when you use cash to buy items in a store, the cashier will sometimes examine the bill to confirm it is the real thing.

When we arrive at 2 Peter 1, the apostle Peter tells his readers that their faith is based on real events, not a fairy tale. Peter reminds them that he was with Jesus when he heard God the Father say, "This is my beloved Son, whom I love." Peter's words can be trusted because he knows what he heard and saw. He is pointing to something that is true of the New Testament as a whole: It was affirmed by those who actually walked and talked with Jesus.

Then Peter takes it a step further, asserting that believers can trust all of Scripture because Scripture originates from God, by the Holy Spirit, who works through humans to share his words. It did not come about through the minds of people.

In 2 Timothy 3:16, the apostle Paul agrees: "All Scripture is God-breathed and useful for teaching, rebuking, correcting and training in righteousness." We can be confident that Scripture is the Word of God. Whenever you wonder what God would say to you, you don't have to guess; you can simply go to his Word.

Prayer: Lord, when I'm confused, lead me to open your Word. Thank you for sending Jesus, the Living Word, to save me when I could not save myself. Help me cherish your Word, knowing that Scripture is your idea and not the product of human thoughts. Amen.

Reflection Question: In what ways do you need to live like Scripture is God's Word and not people's idea?

Jesus Wants to Friend You

MAC HARRIS

With some of my best friends, I communicate almost exclusively through videos, jokes, and memes we find on the internet. After nearly a decade of friendship, we understand each other's humor, and we keep in touch by trying to make each other laugh. It's not enough for me to laugh at a particular video or joke on my own; I want to share that experience with someone I love.

The apostle John, one of Jesus' closest friends, wrote several letters to Christians near the end of his life. In this first letter, he testifies to "what we have seen and heard" (1:3)—the perfect life, atoning death, and triumphant resurrection of Jesus—because this news is too good not to share.

John desires that others will believe in the Word of life—Jesus, a real human being who could be heard, seen, touched, and so on. But according to John, the Christian life doesn't stop at simply believing in Jesus because there are good reasons to believe in him (vv. 1–2). More than that, John wants people to *experience* Jesus and enjoy true relationship with him and other believers (v. 3).

John gets to invite his friends into eternal life and fellowship with other Christians. Most importantly, he invites them into a real relationship with the Trinity—Father, Son, and Holy Spirit—three Persons existing in perfect relationship as one God. In other words, John gets to share his friendship with Jesus with the people he loves.

God wants to know you and be known by you. He wants you to enjoy friendship with other believers, and he invites you into a relationship with him—the triune God. Just as you enjoy your friends here on earth, God wants to enjoy friendship with you and be enjoyed by you.

Prayer: Father, I am humbled at the thought that you want to know me and be known by me. Draw me into a deep and satisfying friendship with you. Amen.

Reflection Question: How does knowing that God wants a friendship with you change the way you experience him?

Jesus Brings Us into His Light

KRISTEN HATTON

If you've ever poured oil into a cup of water, you know they don't mix. Their molecular makeup causes them to form two distinct layers. No part of the oil will combine with the water. Similarly, it is impossible for any darkness (or sin) to be in God. It is contrary to his nature.

Of all the things John could say about God here, he describes God as *light* (1 John 1:5). John is emphasizing God's holiness, his spiritual and moral purity. We cannot fully understand God's love unless we first see God as holy, the One in whom no darkness can be found. And so it seems that if darkness cannot abide in God's presence, he would not invite sinners to come to him.

This is where Jesus, our Advocate, comes into play. John says Jesus invaded the darkness of our world to take our sin upon himself and experience God's judgment and wrath in our place. Our sin is so offensive that apart from Jesus' dying for us, we could not be in relationship with God. But he died the death we deserved because God's heart is for us to be rescued out of darkness and come into the light and into eternal fellowship with him.

Jesus has removed the darkness within Christians so that nothing can separate us from his love. Jesus not only paid for your past sins; your present and future sins have been wiped away forevermore as well. God now sees you as he sees his Son—righteous.

This truth may lead some to think it isn't a big deal to go on sinning. But sin is *such* a big deal that Jesus had to die to redeem us from it. But while the problem of sin within us is taken care of, we will continue to fight against it all our lives. John wants believers to know that their sin still won't change God's mind about them. Our right standing with him is secure. When we do sin, we can look to Jesus, our Advocate, whose righteousness we wear.

Prayer: Lord, thank you for sending Jesus into the world to redeem sinners like me. That a holy God like you would want to fellowship with me is astounding. In gratitude, let me live as Jesus lived.

Reflection Question: What thoughts come into your mind when you remember God's holiness and his personal love for you?

How Does God View You?

CARL LAFERTON

How much someone's opinion of you matters is based on two things: what they say and who they are. If you get called a jerk, it matters far less if it's coming from a kid in class who acts like a bully than if it's from your best friend. And if someone says you're wonderful, it's going to mean far more if it comes from someone whose views you respect.

So here's the question: What is *God's* view of you? Many of us live as though God's view of us rises and falls based on how we're doing. When we do well in obeying him, he smiles on us; when we fail and sin, he looks at us with a frown. Deep down, most of us think God blesses us more when we're good. When we're not good, we're just waiting for the divine shoe to drop.

This is not what the Bible teaches. The apostle John sums up the relationship anyone can enjoy with the God who made everything and rules everything: "children of God" (1 John 3:1). We can know God as Father, just as Jesus does.

Maybe your experience of human fatherhood has been great. But the best human father is merely a dim reflection of the fatherhood of God. Maybe, though, your dad hasn't been there for you. I'm so sorry. But please don't look at God's fatherhood through the lens of that experience. Instead, let God's Word reveal to you what kind of Father he is. He is a Father who will do anything for his children even when it costs him dearly, who always knows and always does what is best for his children, who never gives up on his children, who is pleased with his children, and who can't wait to welcome his children to his heavenly home.

If you believe in Jesus as your Lord and Savior, you have been given the right to be a child of God (John 1:12). When God looks at you, he smiles. When God looks at your failings, he forgives. When God looks at your struggles, he is with you in them. One day, God will look at you face-to-face. Until then, know that the God who made this whole world and has it in his hands is your Father who loves you.

Prayer: Father, it's amazing I can call you this. You know what I face, where I fail, and what I worry about. Thank you that through it all, you are my Father, who could not love me more. Amen.

Reflection Question: What difference will knowing that God loves you as a perfect Father make the next time you sin? Struggle to obey? Fight against fear?

God's Love Is Real Love

KATIE POLSKI

I keep a bowl of fake fruit in our living room. One of the apples has tiny teeth marks in it. When my daughter was a toddler, the fruit looked so real that she grabbed an apple and sank her teeth into it—only to recoil in confusion. I offered her a real apple, but she resisted because the taste of plastic still lingered. Eventually, she took a cautious bite of the fresh, crisp fruit. Juice dribbled down her chin as she smiled. The imitation hadn't just been empty; it had nearly robbed her of the joy of the real thing.

The love of the world—often focused on self-interest and personal gain—is a poor imitation of genuine Christlike love. Love that comes from God stands out, not because it's loud or showy, but because it's undeniably different. Loving others isn't optional for Christians; it's part of our identity. But how do we love people who annoy us, hurt us, or make life difficult? The answer is in the second half of 1 John 4:7: *Love comes from God.*

Real love for others isn't conjured up on our own. The ability to love another comes from understanding how deeply Jesus loves us. He willingly died to take the punishment for our sins so we could be completely reconciled to him. And he loves us so much that he chose to make us his children through adoption (3:1).

When we begin to grasp the magnificence of God's love, it transforms the way we love others. It means we forgive even when it's hard; we show kindness even when it's inconvenient; and when we fail, we repent and make things right. This is the kind of love the apostle John is encouraging us toward.

John makes it even clearer later in chapter 4: "Whoever claims to love God yet hates a brother or sister is a liar" (v. 20). When bitterness is in our heart, it's like a weed. Before we know it, hatred takes over and squeezes out genuine love. The way we love others reveals how we love God. Pray that God will keep your heart free from hatred so that it has the room to grow in love with Jesus, and then remember this: Because of God's great love for you, your love for others can reflect the real thing.

Prayer: Lord, thank you for loving me unconditionally. Help me reflect your love by loving others, even when it's hard. Amen.

Reflection Question: Think about someone in your life who is difficult to love. How can remembering God's love for you help you love them in a truly Christlike way?

Feeling "In Between"

DAWSON COOPER

I remember what it was like to officially be a teenager—thirteen years old and no longer a "child," whether it meant ordering off the adult menu at a restaurant or being almost ready to go to high school. But in some ways, my parents still treated me as a child, restricting movies I watched or where and when I hung out with friends. Being a teenager often means feeling in between.

John is writing to a church in the early days of Christianity. Jesus' life, death, and resurrection are fresh on their minds, but he has not yet returned. Like a brand-new teenager who still awaits all the benefits and freedom to come with more age and experience, the congregation awaits the fullness that will come when Jesus Christ comes again. In 2 John verse 5, John reminds the believers to follow Jesus' direction, which he gave in John 13:34: "Love one another. As I have loved you, so you must love one another."

Like this congregation, we live in what theologians call the "already and not yet." We live in light of the good news that Jesus lived the perfect life for us, died for our sins on the cross, and rose again to defeat sin and death. But because Jesus has not yet returned, the world we live in is still marred by sin.

The most loving thing we can do for our brothers and sisters in Christ is point them to the cross and the empty tomb. The cross reminds us that it's not up to us to save ourselves. The work has already been completed on our behalf. The empty tomb reminds us that Jesus has won the battle against sin and death, and so the brokenness of the world will not last forever.

As we live in the already and not yet, we will face trials and troubles, whether from outside deceivers or from conflict inside the church. Equipped with the example of love in Jesus and in the power of his Holy Spirit, we can persevere and encourage one another as we eagerly await the fullness of life to come when Jesus returns.

Prayer: Lord, help me rest in the hope of the gospel and remind my brothers and sisters in Christ to do the same.

Reflection Question: How have you already seen God's grace in your life? What do you look forward to when Jesus returns?

Walking in the Truth

KATIE POLSKI

The Christian hip-hop artist Lecrae called himself a Christian during his teenage years. He knew Christian lingo and occasionally went to church, but he says now that his life looked no different from his unbelieving friends. After a serious car accident, Lecrae became convicted for a lack of real faith. He realized that *knowing about* God was not the same as *following* him. He repented, and over time, his actions began to reflect sincere faith as he used his platform to point people to Jesus, even when it cost him popularity.

John's third letter describes a man named Gaius, whose sincere faith reminds me of Lecrae—faith that shows up in the way he lives. John writes to Gaius about Diotrephes, an influential man in the church who does not like John. When John sends the church a letter, Diotrephes rejects it. John then sends missionaries to convey his message and encourage the church, but Diotrephes rejects them as well. Diotrephes's actions reveal a lack of true faith.

Gaius, on the other hand, knows Diotrephes but doesn't feel threatened by him. Gaius welcomes the missionaries with love and hospitality. They return to John and give a positive report about the church and especially about Gaius, whose faith is seen through his kindness and generosity. John responds, "I have no greater joy than to hear that my children are walking in the truth" (v. 4).

Having sincere faith in God isn't just knowledge *about* God; it's a way of life. We see that in Gaius's example, in people like Lecrae, and in other faithful Christians who live out their faith through their actions. What does walking in the truth look like for you? Here are just a few examples: Living out your faith means standing up for God's truth even when it conflicts with the culture (Acts 5:29). It means standing up for someone who is regularly made fun of (Micah 6:8). It means walking away from gossip that causes hurt (Proverbs 16:28). It means not being ashamed to say you're a Christian (Romans 1:16).

Walking in the truth also means recognizing when you fall short and knowing that God forgives completely when you turn from your sin. By God's grace, aim to align your whole life—not just your words—with Jesus. You, too, will set an example as one who walks in the truth.

Prayer: Lord, help me walk in your truth. Give me courage to follow you and grace to start again when I fail.

Reflection Question: When is it hardest for you to walk in the truth?

God Keeps Us

JENNIFER M. KVAMME

Some seasons of life are encouraging for our faith, and others can feel dark and isolating. I remember, in the span of a few months, news headlines told of multiple prominent Christian leaders who failed, while at the same time, several of my friends were walking away from the church. Others who claimed to be Christians were advocating values contrary to God's Word. The weight of it all was disheartening.

This is the backdrop to the book of Jude. Jude writes to urge believers to contend for the faith in a culture of opposition. He warns them about people in their own churches who are twisting God's grace into an excuse for all sorts of sin. They are turning away from the truths of Scripture in favor of material gain, sexual perversion, and rebellion against authority, and they think they're following God in doing so.

Jude warns us to guard against persuasive arguments and to contend steadfastly for the faith entrusted to us. At the same time, he wants us to show mercy to those who doubt. He encourages us to care for our own souls in the process. Build yourself up in the most holy faith, he says, by saturating yourself in God's Word, listening to trusted teachers, and living in community. Pray in the Holy Spirit, nurturing a close connection with God as you bring him all your concerns. And keep yourself in God's love as you wait for Jesus to return and live forever with his people. As we contend for the faith and fight for holiness, we can't neglect keeping ourselves in God's love.

You know what makes this command even more beautiful? Jude talks about being "kept" multiple times in this short letter, and it's almost always God who is doing the keeping. We are *kept* for Jesus (v. 1) by him who is able to *keep* us from stumbling (v. 24). So we can make every effort to *keep* ourselves in God's love (v. 21), knowing that he is the one keeping us there, and he is strong even when we are weak.

Prayer: Father, thank you for keeping me in your love so that no one can snatch me out of your hand. Help my faith grow as I study your Word, pray in your Spirit, and wait for your Son. Amen.

Reflection Question: What can you do this week to build yourself up in the faith and keep yourself in God's love?

Worshiping the Hero of Heaven

MIKE MCGARRY

When I was growing up, I envisioned heaven as a church service that went on for eternity. Since I liked church, this wasn't off-putting, but it made me wonder if it was possible to find it satisfying forever.

I've come to realize that Revelation 4 wasn't written to describe daily life in the heavenly realm, but to highlight Jesus Christ, the glory of heaven. In verses 2–5, John describes a vision of the throne of God and the radiance of Jesus, who is seated on it. John compares Jesus to precious jewels and a shining rainbow, magnificent and beautiful. Then he describes four living creatures around the throne who, along with the twenty-four elders (representing the twelve tribes of Israel and the twelve apostles), all bow down before the throne and worship King Jesus.

John's vision reveals Jesus as the hero of heaven. Every knee will bow before him. Every mouth will declare his praise and confess his reign. He is the Creator, Sustainer, and Savior who is worthy of all glory and honor and power. Here's what we sometimes miss: Worshiping Jesus fills the worshipers with eternally satisfying joy.

Knowing how prone we are to forget the worthiness of Jesus, the apostle Paul reminds us that after Jesus "made himself nothing," "God exalted him to the highest place." And now "every tongue [will] acknowledge that Jesus Christ is Lord" (Philippians 2:7, 9, 11). Today's passage describes this fulfillment!

Maybe you struggle to envision Jesus as more than what you see in a children's Bible. Or maybe he seems so distant that you can't sense his nearness or so familiar that you forget his majesty. Perhaps you're wondering if Jesus is worth sacrificing worldly treasures to follow. Let Revelation 4 raise your eyes to behold the glory and power of the One who gave himself for you on the cross. Worshiping Jesus fills heaven with eternal joy. Let's not wait to begin! When we see the Lord for who he truly is, our response will match the cry of the four living creatures and elders: Jesus, "you are worthy, our Lord and God."

Prayer: Lord Jesus, you have created and sustained all things, and you are my only Savior. When my heart grows cold, lift my eyes to see you for who you truly are. I praise you because you are worthy.

Reflection Question: How can you praise Jesus today as the One who is worthy of your worship?

Jesus' Victory Is Our Victory!

KEVIN YI

I love a good movie, and I get excited when a film goes deeper than just its plot. Marvel movies are fun to watch, but what keeps me coming back are the themes of courage, sacrifice, and redemption.

Revelation 12 is full of cosmic imagery, such as a pregnant woman, a red dragon, and a war in heaven between angels. God shows us the spiritual reality of the Christian life and how Jesus has already secured victory for his people. In the first of the symbols, we see a woman clothed with the sun, and a crown of twelve stars on her head, representing the twelve tribes of Israel (Genesis 37). The prophets often describe the nation of Israel as a woman, so she represents the people of God. Then we see a great red dragon—Satan—with his seven heads and ten horns, symbolizing kingdoms that have persecuted God's people (Ezekiel 29; Daniel 7). The dragon waits to devour a child, but the child is caught up to God. This child is Jesus, and this moment represents his resurrection and his ascension.

As God's people wait for Jesus' return, we are like the woman, accused by Satan but sustained by God. God nourishes us with his grace and truth even as the spiritual battle continues. Jesus defeated Satan through his death and resurrection. When Jesus comes again, we will hear the cry of triumph: "Now have come the salvation and the power and the kingdom of our God." Not only does Jesus triumph, but his people do too. Christians overcome by the blood of the Lamb and the word of their testimony (Revelation 12:11). Our strength comes from holding on to what Jesus has already done and sharing that truth with others.

You may not feel like a conqueror today. Maybe you're overwhelmed by anxiety or discouragement, questioning whether your faith is real. Revelation 12 reminds us that we are part of a much bigger story. The battle is real, but the victory is already won. Satan still deceives and accuses, but the cross has already defeated him. Cling to Jesus, the Conqueror.

Prayer: Father, thank you for making me part of your redemption story. When life feels like a battle, help me remember that Jesus has already won.

Reflection Question: What are some ways Satan tries to discourage you? How does remembering Jesus' victory help you respond?

Reigning with Christ

KEVIN YI

Born and raised in Los Angeles, I've been fortunate to get backstage access for concerts and television shows. It's special to witness crews do their magic behind the scenes. Revelation 20 feels like that. It's as if God gives us a backstage pass to the final act of the story.

Satan is bound and thrown into the pit for one thousand years, which is symbolic of the time between Christ's resurrection and his return. Then the vision shifts to people on thrones in heaven, only they're not celebrities or influencers; they are those who remained faithful through trials. They said no to the world and yes to Jesus. They held tightly to the word of God when it cost them everything. They are not spectators; they are co-heirs who reign *with* him (v. 4).

Many Bible teachers view the "first resurrection" (v. 5) as a spiritual resurrection—the new life we receive through salvation. This parallels Revelation 12, where believers overcome by "the blood of the Lamb and by the word of their testimony" (v. 11). These Christians may not have had much in the eyes of the world, but in the kingdom of God, they are priests and rulers.

As a student, you may not have much authority. You probably live under a lot of it—parents, teachers, and coaches who constantly tell you what to do. But Revelation 20 declares that when you walk faithfully with Jesus, you already reign with him. You do not just survive this world; you represent a better one. When you say no to compromise, when you love others, when you live with integrity, you live as a citizen of heaven. God uses your quiet faithfulness to make an eternal impact.

Prayer: Jesus, help me remember that, even when I feel weak, I already reign with you. Give me courage to say no to the world and yes to you.

Reflection Question: When has following Jesus made things harder? How might the challenges reveal that you are reigning with him even now?

No Longer Any Sea

MARK HOWARD

I remember feeling disappointed when I read that "there was no longer any sea" in eternity (Revelation 21:1). I love the beach! I now understand that Revelation isn't a description for an Airbnb or a travel post for eternity. It's filled with symbolic imagery drawn from Scripture, and "the sea" is a key theme in the Bible.

Humans cannot thrive in the sea. We can't drink saltwater. If you use the sea for farming, your plants will die. So the sea becomes a symbol for evil and death. It was human evil that caused the chaotic waters to cover the earth with death in Noah's time (Genesis 6). Psalm 65:7 compares the "roaring of the seas" to the "turmoil of the nations." And by Jeremiah's time, the "rolling" and "roaring" of the sea represent evil's attempts to thwart God's plan (Jeremiah 5:22).

In the New Testament, when Jesus drives out a legion of demons, it makes sense symbolically that they enter pigs (an unclean animal in Jewish law) and rush headlong into the sea (Mark 5). When Jesus stills the raging sea with a word (4:29) and walks on the waters without sinking (6:49), he is displaying his authority over evil. On the cross, when Jesus takes our sin and evil on himself, he drinks the sea to its fullness, disarming the spiritual rulers and authorities (Colossians 2:19). In Jesus' resurrection, "death has been swallowed up in victory" (1 Corinthians 15:54). Now, rather than this world's saltwater, it is living water—the Holy Spirit—that Jesus offers for our thirsty souls (John 7:38–39).

It may look like the waves of evil still rage and crash in all their power. But before the throne of God, the sea is as calm and transparent as glass (Revelation 4:6; 15:2). God is not threatened. The victory is won. One day, when Jesus returns to bring to fullness the new creation that began in his resurrection, the sea will be no more. Evil will be undone. "There will be no more death or mourning or crying or pain, for the old order of things has passed away" (21:4).

So take courage, evil will not have the final victory because Jesus sits on heaven's throne. Evil will attempt to win the day, but its end is certain. Illness and pain will come, but they will not last forever. We will die, but death is not the end. Jesus has overcome the sea.

Prayer: God of glory, renew me today in the hope of your new creation and the power of your Spirit.

Reflection Question: How does the reality of the new creation challenge you to respond to evil in the world?

Come, Lord Jesus

CHELSEA KINGSTON ERICKSON

"Fifteen minutes with Ms. Moxie will change your life."

I was skeptical, but the fellow youth leader who said this was onto something. Ms. Moxie lived in an AIDs camp near Nassau, Bahamas, after having contracted the virus from a blood transfusion after a car accident. Her husband left her. Her children rarely visited. Yet Ms. Moxie displayed the joy of the Lord. She raised her arms in praise, read psalms to my students, and reminded us that she would soon be with Jesus. She understood what I too easily forget: *God will renew this world, and we will be with him.*

The final scenes of John's vision point to this glorious future. The life-giving river from the Garden of Eden flows from God's throne in the midst of a city. God's people eat from the tree of life, which provides healing for the nations of the world. The curse of sin is gone forever because Jesus has absorbed it by his death and resurrection, thereby conquering Satan. God the Father and Jesus the Lamb are in the midst of God's people, who all serve the Lord, fulfilling his calling for human beings. There is no darkness because God's light fills the city. And his people reign with him over an eternal kingdom.

John gives a glimpse into what eternity will be like when we experience all we were made for: Life in the awesome presence of God, with no sin or shame to separate us from him. God's blessings poured out without measure. Purpose and mission, as we joyfully serve God together. No darkness, no sin, no curse. A kingdom of perfect righteousness and peace in which we share an inheritance with Jesus, the Lamb of God who was slain for us.

As you walk in this world with all its heartache, remember the glorious future that awaits those who trust in Jesus. One day soon, we will be with him forever.

> He who testifies to these things says, "Yes, I am coming soon."
> Amen. Come, Lord Jesus. (22:20)

Prayer: Lord, I sometimes feel weary of this world, and other times I feel attached to it. Give me hope in your good plans for me and for the world.

Reflection Question: In what part of your life do you most need to hold on to the hope of *forever* in God's presence?

How Can I Know Jesus as "God with Me"?

The words of the Bible are true and without error, convicting and encouraging. They're not just a story. They tell of the offer of salvation—deliverance from sin's penalty. Yet you might find yourself wondering if you do indeed belong to Jesus. In God's graciousness, the Bible gives believers clear assurance. Let's walk through some passages that will help you know you are secure in God's presence and love.

Our Need and Jesus' Rescue

John 3:16–17 reads, "God so loved the world that he gave his one and only Son, that whoever believes in him shall not perish but have eternal life. For God did not send his Son into the world to condemn the world, but to save the world through him."

Through the work of the Holy Spirit, we recognize our sin and thus our need for rescue. Once we understand this, we do as anyone does who needs rescue—we look to a rescuer. A drowning person cannot save another drowning person, nor does a drowning person need just a little bit of help. John 3:16 says that God sent Jesus so that we "shall not perish." Through prayer, we call on the name of Jesus, acknowledging our sin and our need of him as our Lord and Savior.

Salvation is through grace alone. There is nothing you can do to deserve salvation, and there is nothing you can do to lose it (Ephesians 2:8–9).

What Salvation Means for Christians

When Jesus died on the cross, he achieved salvation for all who would trust in him once and for all (Hebrews 7:27). In a similar way, you only need to receive that salvation once. You do not have to ask Jesus into your heart or ask God for salvation on multiple occasions. You do not need to fear that the first time didn't take (Romans 10:9–13). Although you will struggle with the temptation to sin throughout your life as a Christian, once you believe in Jesus as your Savior, you are kept and marked as his forever (Ephesians 1:13).

Salvation means a relationship with the God who created you, called you, knows you, and loves you. Because of Jesus, the Christian's relationship with God is restored. In fact, we are adopted as sons and daughters and receive the full benefits of such status (Galatians 4:4–7). Salvation also means that death, illness, shame, guilt, and other aspects of this broken world do not have the final say over your life. In fact, a greater, fuller restored life awaits all Christians eternally and at Jesus' return (John 16:33).

Now, like any relationship, it can take time to become closer. Christians grow in relationship with God through prayer, reading Scripture, and fellowship with other believers through the church. Spiritual growth often looks and feels uncomfortable because it is when we are in greatest need that we cling ever closer to the Lord and thus get to know him more deeply. So in the times of trouble that Jesus promises will come, do not be discouraged or think you are messing it up. Lean even more into God (John 16:33; Philippians 1:6).

Confessing Jesus as Lord

When you become a Christian, you submit all of your life to God—this is what it means for him to be *Lord*. He is a loving, gracious King over all parts of your life. If you haven't yet acknowledged your need for Jesus' atoning life, death, and resurrection and asked him to be Lord over your life, here is a prayer to do so. Remember, it's not the prayer itself that saves us. Instead, the God to whom you call holds the power and promise to redeem your life.

> *Dear God, I confess that I need to be rescued from my sins. On my own, I cannot save myself. I pray that through the atoning life, death, and resurrection of your Son, Jesus, you would save me and come into my life. God, I place my trust in you for both my salvation and my sanctification—make me more like Jesus, I pray! Please be Lord over all of my life. Draw me near to you by your grace and through the Holy Spirit that I may know and love you more with each day. Thank you for creating, loving, and calling me. Amen.*

We encourage you to share with a parent, a pastor, or a trusted believer that you have confessed your need for Jesus and asked him to be Lord of your life. We grow as Christians by encouraging, teaching, and praying for one another in community, and it's important that you share this exciting change with a fellow believer who can help you plug into a church community.

If you have already professed belief in Jesus Christ as your Lord and Savior, then rejoice that you are a child of the one true King and that his Holy Spirit lives in you. Offer thanks for the ways he is working in your life, whether you see it or not.

Heavenly Father, I thank you that I am seen, known, and loved by you, the sovereign and gracious God. Thank you for sending Jesus to rescue me and for giving me the Holy Spirit as a seal over my life in and with you. Thank you for calling me your child. Help me to grow to look more and more like your precious Son every day. Amen.

Reader, we pray for you as you grow in your relationship to God:

> For this reason I kneel before the Father, from whom every family in heaven and on earth derives its name. I pray that out of his glorious riches he may strengthen you with power through his Spirit in your inner being, so that Christ may dwell in your hearts through faith. And I pray that you, being rooted and established in love, may have power, together with all the Lord's holy people, to grasp how wide and long and high and deep is the love of Christ, and to know this love that surpasses knowledge—that you may be filled to the measure of all the fullness of God. (Ephesians 3:14–19)

What Now? How Can I Live as a Christian?

Once you've come to faith in Jesus, you may or may not feel different than you did before. Some people do enjoy a huge sense of relief, happiness, or gratitude, and that's wonderful. Many of us don't experience a lot of dramatic emotion, and that's okay too. No matter what, when Jesus has given you faith in his saving work on the cross, you have been reborn into a whole new life of faith (John 3:3), and we want you to know just how wonderful this new life is.

You were *chosen* for salvation before you were ever born—before the world was even created! And never forget this: God chose you because he loves you. That's the only reason. He loved you then; he loves you still; he will love you always (Deuteronomy 7:7–8; John 15:16; Ephesians 1:4–5).

The Holy Spirit has made you *alive* in Christ! You were "dead" in your sins, but you have been "resurrected" with Christ—awakened to a whole new spiritual reality that you could not see before but do see now. In the same way a branch grows out of a grapevine, receiving water and nutrients to grow grapes, you are united to Christ, receiving his love and power to grow spiritual fruit. You will spend the rest of your life learning the riches of your new relationship with God—Father, Son, and Holy Spirit (John 15:1–17; Galatians 2:20; Ephesians 2:1–6).

Now the Holy Spirit *lives in you*. The Spirit, whom Jesus calls the Helper, fills you with love for God and neighbor, helps you believe you belong to God, teaches you what the Scriptures mean, strengthens you to obey God. No matter what you need for life and godliness, the Spirit is there to give it to you. His permanent presence comes to you as a gift (John 16:7–15; Acts 2:38).

You have been given the *righteousness* of Christ. This big word conveys a simple and astounding truth. Because our sin separates us from our holy God, we need to be sinless in order to be close to him. But human beings cannot *not* sin. As both divine and human, Jesus lived a sinless life, obeying God in everything. When we come to faith, he gives us his record of perfect obedience—he *imputes*, or "sticks," his righteousness to us—so that we can come close to God and God can come close to us. If you are in Christ, then right now, as far as

God is concerned, you have a record of perfect obedience because Christ gave you his (Romans 5:1).

This means you *never have to prove* your goodness or worth to God (or to anyone else, for that matter). Jesus already counted you worth dying for. When you sin (and you will), you can go to him immediately and receive forgiveness. You can confess your deepest, darkest thoughts and actions to him in prayer (he knows it all anyway), and he will not reject you or stop loving you. The righteousness you've been given will never be taken away. You never have to earn God's approval or pleasure. It is his good pleasure to give you his kingdom (Isaiah 53:5–6; Luke 12:32; Ephesians 1:13; Titus 3:4–5; 1 John 1:9).

You have been *adopted* into the family of God. People often speak as if all people are children of God, but the whole truth is that while all human beings are made in God's image, only those who have come to faith in Jesus become God's children. But now, in Jesus, you are as much a child of God as Jesus is. If that doesn't blow your mind, you are a co-heir to God's kingdom with your big brother, Jesus Christ. You can claim the God who created the universe as your *Abba* ("Daddy"), Father. He loves you with an everlasting love (Jeremiah 31:3; John 1:12; Romans 8:17, 23; Galatians 4:5–7; Ephesians 1:5).

What's more, being adopted into God's family means you now have a *family* that includes brothers and sisters across the globe and throughout history—and of course, in the church you attend on Sundays. (If you don't attend church already, find a nearby church that faithfully teaches God's Word, and go grow in faith with them!) No matter how wonderful or how complicated things are at home, you belong to God's eternal family. You will always have a home in the body of Christ (Matthew 12:49–50; 1 Corinthians 12:12–14; Ephesians 2:19; Hebrews 10:24–25).

You will *grow* to look more and more like Jesus—the Bible calls this *sanctification.* Just like a baby has to learn and grow into maturity, so a Christian learns and grows, and God brings about the progress. As we feed on God's Word through reading our Bibles, going to church, and praying, we will be "transformed into his image with ever-increasing glory" (2 Corinthians 3:18; see also John 17:2; Romans 12:2; 1 Corinthians 6:11; 1 Thessalonians 4:3).

You will *live forever* with Jesus when he returns to fully establish his kingdom on the earth. All suffering will end, and together with all God's people, you will see him face-to-face. God is with you and will always be with you, constant and close, steadfastly loving you through your life, your death, and your own one-day-to-come resurrection (Philippians 3:20–21; Hebrews 12:28; 1 John 3:2; Revelation 7:16–17).

As you progress in your walk with Jesus, amid all the ups and downs of life, remember these words:

> [God] has said, "I will NEVER [under any circumstances] DESERT YOU [nor give you up nor leave you without support, nor will I in any degree leave you helpless], NOR WILL I FORSAKE *or* LET YOU DOWN *or* RELAX MY HOLD ON YOU [assuredly not]!" (Hebrews 13:5 AMP)

This is the truest truth in the world: God is with you!

Glossary

Atone: to both cleanse and pay for sin

Covenant: a sacred agreement between two parties, a binding promise

Curse: universal consequences for sin

Glory: the awesome display of God's character and presence

Grace: unearned, lavish love and favor from God

Holiness: spiritual and moral purity, set-apartness

Impute: the way in which Jesus "sticks" his righteousness on us

Incarnate: in bodily form

Justification: being declared righteous in God's sight

Lord: loving, gracious King (in reference to Jesus)

LORD: the sacred name by which God reveals himself to Moses

Messiah: "anointed one," the long-awaited rescuer of God's people

Reconciliation: reestablishing a relationship after an offense

Repentance: turning from sin

Righteousness: right standing with God

Salvation: deliverance from sin's penalty

Sanctification: becoming like Jesus (through the work of the Holy Spirit)

Sin: rebellion against God

Soul: the deepest part of who we are

Yahweh: the Hebrew name by which God reveals himself to Moses

Acknowledgments

Years ago, when our Rooted staff was dreaming big, we said that one day we'd like to write the classic devotional for teenagers, sharing our love for God and His Word with young people for generations to come. Whether it becomes a classic devotional is in God's hands. We're thankful that at this moment, it's in your hands. May God bless you richly through the reading of His Word. May this book be a help to you too.

First and foremost, we'd like to thank our writers. Without you, there would have been nothing to edit! Your love for Jesus, Scripture, and teenagers is as clear and worshipful as your beautiful words. Thank you for your contributions.

The team at Zondervan Reflective has cheered us on through every page of this project. Truly you are a godly team of encouragers, committed to excellence in serving Christ through books. Thank you to Ryan Pazdur and Dale Williams for believing in this project, Dirk Buursma for helping us shape and hone the entries, Emily Voss for launching it into the world, and Sydney Mathieu for overseeing the audiobook. It has been a treat to work with you.

God with You was an all-hands-on-deck project for the staff at Rooted Ministry. We are forever grateful for the innumerable ways each of you has supported and contributed to the book. Special thanks to our executive directors, first to Emily Heide for her steadfast commitment to seeing this dream come to pass, and then to Hannah Dow for cheering us across the finish line. Your godly leadership made all the difference. We are so grateful to you both. Many thanks to Rebecca Lankford, who managed the many moving parts of this book. And to Dawson Cooper, our project manager, who juggled and directed and kept things straight, doing it all with good humor and grace—you are a godsend, a joy to work with, and a joy to have as a friend.

Contributors

Akash Ahuja is the director of high school ministries at Grace Chapel in Lexington, Massachusetts. Akash swam for his high school for all four years and was on the first-ever men's volleyball team. You can now find Akash baking a loaf of bread every week.

Alexis Andre is a middle school English teacher in Nashville, Tennessee. She wrote a book about living for Christ in high school. Alexis has since started a Christian clothing brand called Shema Streetwear, with products centered around biblical Hebrew. Her favorite food is Prince's Hot Chicken.

Chelten L. Carter is director of youth and teens at Progressive Baptist Church in Chicago, Illinois. As a teenager, he played competitive soccer. He loves Swedish Fish and has lived in five different states.

Faith Chang is a writer in Staten Island, New York. When she was a teenager, she took four types of transportation every day as she commuted to high school—bus, subway, ferry, and train. She can stop her hiccups on command (but she can't start them).

Cameron Cole is director of adult and NextGen discipleship at St. Peter's Anglican Church in Birmingham, Alabama. When he was a teenager, he started a music festival modeled after Woodstock. Cameron looks a lot like Buddy the Elf and reenacts a scene from *Elf* with his kids each year out in public.

Kendal Conner is director of Sunday schools at Redeemer Kansas City in Kansas City, Missouri. She used to sing the national anthem at her high school softball games when she was a teenager. Her favorite food is a BBQ pulled pork sandwich with coleslaw on top. She has lived in nine states, in four countries, and on three continents.

Dawson Cooper is the publishing manager for Rooted Ministry. She lives in Birmingham, Alabama, with her husband, whom she met when she was thirteen, and her three boys. She loves to prank people—neighbors, friends, and even her children's school principals.

Hannah Dow is the executive director of Rooted Ministry. She lives in Birmingham, Alabama. Her first car was a vintage Jaguar, and she thought she was the coolest in high school. Her favorite food is Chilton County peaches, but only when they're in season. She has a deep and abiding love for Masterpiece Theatre on PBS.

Curtis Dunlap is a family life pastor at Epiphany Fellowship Church in Philadelphia, Pennsylvania. Not only was he voted class clown in high school, but he was also homecoming king. If you visit Philadelphia, Curtis suggests you get a cheesesteak from Del Rossi's. If he wasn't a pastor, he would like to open his own food truck.

Steve Eatmon is an English pastor at Chinese Bible Church of Maryland in Rockville, Maryland. As a teenager, Steve played for his school's football team. His favorite food is Maryland blue crabs, and he has been to thirty-eight states and twenty countries.

Liz Edrington is associate director of care at McLean Presbyterian Church in Virginia. As a teenager, she was a student athletic trainer, and she loved taping the ankles of her teammates and anyone else who'd let her. Her favorite food is pickles of any sort—especially sour ones. Liz can walk on her hands and loves teaching others to do it.

Chelsea Kingston Erickson is the editor-in-chief at Rooted Ministry and a former youth minister. As a high schooler, she wrote and edited for the school newspaper but was more interested in her social life than her grades. She lives in New England with her husband and two young sons.

Skyler R. Flowers is program director for The Carson Center for Theological Renewal and lives in Oxford, Mississippi. Both first days of his freshman and sophomore years of high school, Skyler got into poison ivy and had a terrible disfiguring rash on his face. He loves all Southern food, but Chicago-style deep dish pizza comes in a close second. He has twice been denied service at his local Taco Bell for trying to order while not in a car.

Clark Fobes IV lives in San Francisco, California, where he is an associate pastor at FirstSF. As a teenager, Clark was an avid participant in his school's choirs and musicals. His favorite food is a SF Mission-style burrito, and his friends make fun of him for bringing a coffee maker set whenever he travels.

Christina Fox is an author and speaker from Chattanooga, Tennessee, where she is also on staff at Covenant College. When she was a teenager, she worked at her local library, which to this day is her favorite job. She loves to travel, and her favorite place so far has been visiting Israel.

Charlotte Getz is an author who lives in Birmingham, Alabama. She was a theater kid, and her favorite food is ribs. You can still find her sleeping with her childhood stuffed animals.

Michael Goldstein is a lead pastor / church planter in Denver, Colorado. When he was a teenager, he spent an afternoon in an ER in Mexico while on a spring break trip after getting stung by a Portuguese man o' war. In 2024, he biked up a 14,000-foot mountain (Mount Blue Sky) from his front door.

Vince Greenwald lives in Nashville, Tennessee, where he is an assistant pastor at Immanuel Nashville. When he was a teenager, he loved rollerblading through the McDonald's drive-through with his friends. He enjoys Nashville hot chicken and a good, nerdy board game.

Anna Meade Harris is a contributing editor at Rooted Ministry. She lives in Birmingham, Alabama, where she is living her teenage dream of being a writer. Her favorite food is fried chicken, and she is known for her Zumba skills.

Mac Harris is a youth pastor at Hope Community Church in Charlotte, North Carolina. In high school, he ate a frozen pizza and drank a chocolate milkshake after school (almost) every day. If given the choice today, he'd pick barbecue or Bojangles as his favorite meal. He enjoys golf, ultimate frisbee, and long walks with his wife (Connor) and dog (Huckleberry).

Kristen Hatton is a licensed professional counselor and author. She lives in Dallas, Texas. Kristen was a four-year varsity soccer player in high school. Her favorite foods are chips and guacamole, and salsa on everything. When challenged to a game of pool, Kristen surprises people when they learn that she is a secret pool shark.

Rebecca Heck is a community manager / youth minister in Atlanta, Georgia. As a teenager, Rebecca was the social planner for her friend group—in fact, her friends would call her house at 4:00 p.m. on a Friday to find out what the plans were for the weekend. Today, she loves Grippos BBQ Potato Chips and exploring abandoned buildings (safely, of course).

Emily Heide lives in Birmingham, Alabama, with her husband and three children. She worked for Rooted for ten years, serving most recently as executive director. Emily started a club in junior high called JAM (Jesus and Me). She loves TexMex, and her hidden talent is that she can burp the ABCs.

Kyle Hoffsmith is pastor of family ministry at Old North Church in Canfield, Ohio. As a teenager, he ran cross-country and long-distance races in track and field. Kyle enjoys leading student ministry all-nighter events every year. His favorite food is an appetizer sampler from Sheetz.

Mark Howard lives in Covington, Georgia, where he serves as director of donor ministry for Rooted Ministry. As a teenager, Mark was a drummer in a funk-rock band called SLiCK FiCTiON. His favorite food is doner kebab. He says his kids are jealous of how much he loves his French bulldog, but they shouldn't be. He loves them much more.

Mary Beth Johnston is senior director of programs for Rooted Ministry. She lives in Lookout Mountain, Georgia, where she loves to enjoy a good bowl of duck gumbo. When Mary Beth was a teenager, she drove a manual Jeep Wrangler. No one else her age drove a stick shift at that time. One of her favorite things to do (and a gift of hers) is coming up with parody song lyrics.

Ericson Joubert is pastor of youth ministry at East Cobb Presbyterian Church in Atlanta, Georgia. As a teenager, Ericson was so obsessed with Chick-fil-A sauces that he would literally drink them from the packet after every bite. One surprising fact about Ericson is that he cannot sit cross-legged.

Carol M. Kaminski is a senior professor of Old Testament at Gordon-Conwell Theological Seminary. She is also the founder of Casket Empty. She lives in Topsfield, Massachusetts, and loves dogs—especially her goldendoodle. Carol played guitar in a band when she was a teenager.

Ashley Kim is a writer and editor who lives in New York City. As a teenager, Ashley wanted to be a K-Pop dancer. She enjoys a Taiwanese breakfast and watches *Curious George* for fun.

Matthew D. Kim is a professor of preaching and pastoral leadership, holder of the George W. Truett Endowed Chair in Preaching and Evangelism, and director of the PhD in Preaching program at Truett Seminary at Baylor University in Waco, Texas. During his junior and senior years in high school, Matthew was elected class president. His favorite food is beef brisket, and he still plays basketball every week at "Dad Ball."

Jennifer M. Kvamme is a student ministry catalyst in Blaine, Minnesota. When she was a teenager, she enjoyed playing keys in her youth group worship band and spent her spare time writing novels for fun. She loves road-tripping to national parks and hiking in the mountains.

Danny Kwon is senior director of youth ministry content and cross-cultural initiatives at Rooted Ministry. He lives in Horsham, Pennsylvania. As a teenager, Danny loved driving his Jeep Wrangler with the top down. He loves Korean food but loves the Philadelphia Eagles even more.

Davis Lacey lives in Ellijay, Georgia, where he is a pastor at Autumn Ridge Community Church. Davis was selected to Georgia's All-State band during each of his four years of high school. When he isn't playing pickleball or cheering on the Atlanta Braves, you might find him enjoying Cuban food—beef empanadas and coffee, to be exact.

Carl Laferton is publisher and co-CEO at The Good Book Company. Carl lives in London, England. When he was a teenager, he was a history nerd and a member of an English Civil War Reenactment Society. Carl married his wife in a real cathedral, and his favorite food is apple crumble.

Carolyn Lankford is an elder at Church of the Cross in Birmingham, Alabama. She was voted "Most Involved" during her senior year in high school. She enjoys local Alabama summer tomatoes. She is learning how to play Mahjong and is hooked.

Rebecca Lankford is a former youth and young adult minister who now works in corporate America in Birmingham, Alabama. A true Southerner, her favorite foods are biscuits, summer tomatoes, and fried okra. As a teenager, she was really, really, really bad at math. As an adult, she is still really, really, really bad at math.

Huey Lee is the pastor of worship and young adults at Christ Central Presbyterian Church in Centreville, Virginia. He learned how to play the guitar in eighth grade in youth group, which has been a lifeline ever since. Huey has also met Shaquille O'Neal while attending a Rooted Ministry conference.

Jonathan Lilley is senior pastor at The First Chinese Church of Christ in Honolulu, Hawaii. When he was a teenager, he was a deejay on the Christian radio station in his hometown. His favorite food is poke. He is learning to surf and bodyboards with his kids every weekend.

Isaiah A. Marshall lives in Nashville, Tennessee, where he is director of ministry development at Rooted Ministry. He was an All-American track athlete. His favorite snack is just about any type of fruit. He is a Christian spoken word artist and created a spoken word event called Beautifully Imperfect.

Mike McGarry is director of Youth Pastor Theologian and lives in Norton, Massachusetts. As a teenager, he had four pet turtles (not at the same time). His favorite food is a fluffernutter sandwich. A unique fact about Mike is that he doesn't dream when he sleeps.

Emily Menendez is mom to three teenagers and currently pursuing a master's in Christian counseling. She is also part of Rooted Ministry's steering committee. While her teenage years were wonderful, when Emily felt anxious, her favorite escape was water skiing. She loves to hike and hopes to visit as many national parks as possible.

Jalyn Porter Mikell is Rooted Ministry's marketing manager. When she was a teenager, she broke her nose playing basketball with her cousins the week before school picture day, leaving her with a swollen nose in her junior-year photo. She is a native Mississippian who hates sweet tea and barbeque sauce but does love a good crawfish boil.

Connie Leung Nelson is a teacher for the high school and college groups at her church, Edmonton Christian Community Church, in Edmonton, Alberta. A trombone player in her teenage days, Connie still loves vintage Polly Pockets and will choose a bowl of pho for a meal any day.

Peter Ong is ministry director at Living Faith Community Church in New York City. Peter skipped freshman year and began his high school career as a sophomore. He has performed off Broadway and has been featured as a spoken word artist. His favorite food is shaved ice with salted plum.

John Onwuchekwa is an author, a storyteller, and a speaker from Atlanta, Georgia. His first flight ever was at age six to Nigeria. His favorite food is pizza, and he once spent a summer visiting coffee shops on five different continents.

Luke Paiva is a middle school history teacher and Sunday school teacher in Franklin, Tennessee. Luke attended four different schools in two states for sixth, seventh, and eighth grades. He is the first-place meme exchanger in his work chat by a mile. When it comes to his favorite food, Luke picks steak from any region for any meal.

Katie Polski is the music director and special events coordinator at Trinity Church Kirkwood in St. Louis, Missouri. When she was about thirteen, she played a duet with the baseball legend "Stan the Man" Musial. He played the harmonica while she played the piano for an on-air Christmas celebration. Katie tends to get songs stuck in her head all. the. time.

Michelle Reyes is a professor of cultural engagement at Wheaton College and the author of *Becoming All Things*. She lives in Birmingham, England, where her favorite food is samosas. During her senior year of high school, she broke the record for most soccer goals scored in a season for the state of Minnesota. In her spare time, Michelle enjoys reading detective novels.

Anne Sanford is the senior director of development at Rooted Ministry. She lives in Prattville, Alabama, with her husband and two boys. She is teaching her boys to appreciate live music and her favorite sports teams. In high school, Anne played year-round volleyball.

Karishma Sriram is a pediatrician in Salt Lake City, Utah. When she was a teenager, she got interested in theater and was in her first musical. She enjoys Trader Joe's chili lime tortilla rolls and still hopes one day to become a stand-up comedian.

Katherine Precht Stine is director of sales and marketing for Rooted Ministry. She lives in Birmingham, Alabama. Her favorite food is boiled peanuts, and her favorite pastime is planning and decorating for parties. One summer in high school, she went to both economics and piano camp.

Syler Thomas lives in Lake Bluff, Illinois, where he is pastor of community life at Christ Church Lake Forest. As a teenager, Syler went on a snorkel cruise with Ozzy Osbourne. His favorite meal is a deep dish pizza at Lou Malnati's. He is a two-time champion of the ESPN Chicago Holiday Song Parody Contest.

Joey Turner is pastor of mission and adults at Patterson Park Church in Beavercreek, Ohio. He had a near-death experience in front of the entire student body of his high school. His favorite food is buckeyes, and he has yet to break a bone.

Kevin Yi lives in Los Angeles, California, where he is a producer on *Armorsaurs*. As a teenager, he taught himself how to play the guitar, bass guitar, drums, and synthesizer drums. He enjoys BBQ chicken pizza, but for Thanksgiving, his ideal meal includes both Korean short ribs and a good lasagna.

Curtis Zackery lives in Franklin, Tennessee, where he is a pastor at New River Church. As a teenager, Curtis was part of a hip-hop group called Project. His favorite food is New Jersey pizza, and he once played a perfect game of Phase 10.

Historical Timeline

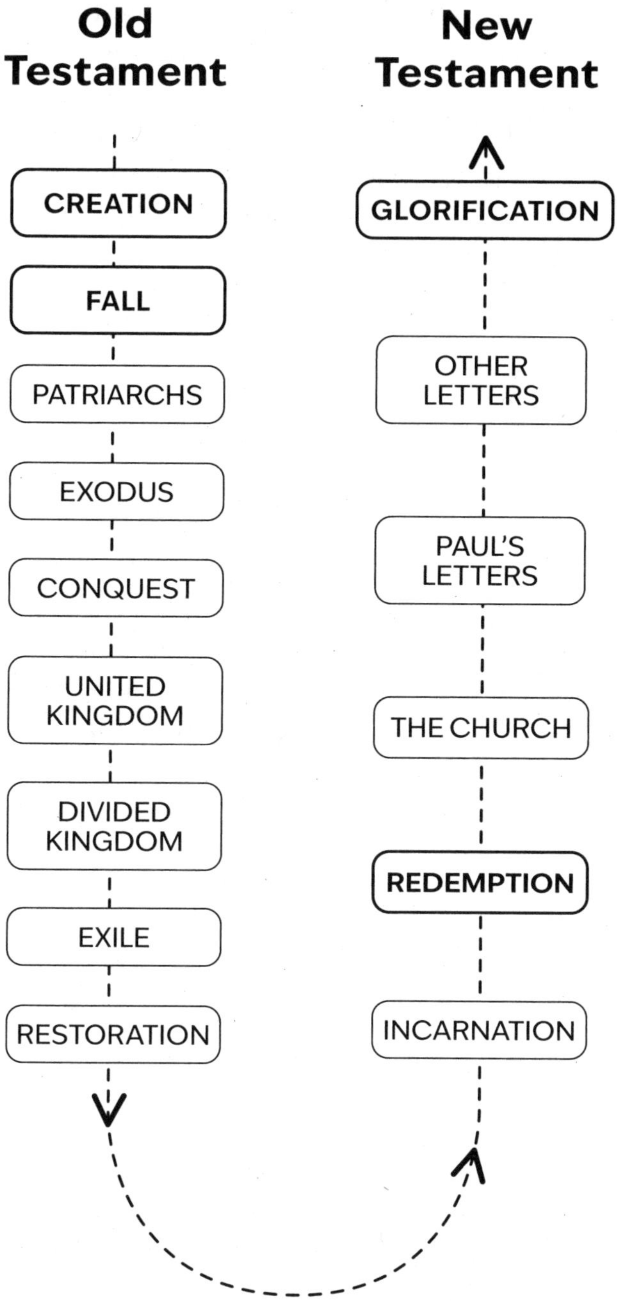

Creation

Books Included: Genesis 1–2

As the Bible begins, God creates the world out of nothing by his spoken word. At first, the world is just empty space, but God shapes it and fills it with life, declaring each part of his creation "good." After making various creatures, God makes human beings uniquely for relationship with him, calling them "very good." The first people enjoy perfect relational harmony with God, each other, and the physical world. God calls them to fill the world and cultivate the life of his creation, reflecting God himself.

Fall

Books Included: Genesis 3–11

The first human beings, Adam and Eve, disobey God's good command. The Bible calls this "sin." As a result, death, pain, and separation enter the world. The fallout from sin is the central problem of the whole Bible and all of life. Now all relationships are broken—between people and God, between people themselves, and even between people and the rest of creation. But God does not leave things in this sad state. Instead, he determines to make all of it right by his grace, promising to send a Savior. As people continue to sin, God repeatedly points to the solution that will come through his grace.

Patriarchs

Books Included: Genesis 12–50

Following the devastating results of human sin, God chooses a man named Abram (later renamed Abraham) and makes a covenant, or a sacred, binding agreement, with him. God promises Abram a family, a special land, a personal relationship with himself, and a significant role in the redemption of the world. Through Abraham's family, the Lord will bless all nations. Abraham and his descendants Isaac, Jacob, and Joseph are known as the "patriarchs," because they are the first of God's people, the Israelites (also known as Hebrews or Jews). God's people are deeply flawed and continue to sin, but God's promise remains intact.

Exodus

Books Included: Exodus, Leviticus, Numbers, Deuteronomy

After the time of the patriarchs, the Hebrew people are enslaved in Egypt for more than three hundred years by an oppressive Pharaoh. The Lord appoints Moses to lead God's people out of slavery, revealing his power to save through many miracles.

Once the people arrive in the wilderness, the Lord gives them the Law, which reveals God's goodness and shows them how to live in relationship with him. God also establishes the sacrificial system in order to deal with the people's sin so they can be near his presence. During their time in the wilderness, the people frequently disobey the Lord and demand to return to Egypt. The Lord often disciplines the Israelites but also extends great mercy and forgiveness to them, as he still plans to do through his promised Messiah.

Conquest

Books Included: Joshua, Judges, Ruth

The Israelites finally enter the promised land under Joshua's leadership. With the Lord's guidance, they conquer Canaan but continue to fall into sin. The people enter a cycle of rebelling against the Lord, following foreign gods, and being conquered by other nations. In those moments, they cry out to the Lord, who raises up leaders (called judges) to deliver the Israelites from their enemies. During this period, the Lord is the only ruler of Israel; there is no human king.

United Kingdom

Books Included: 1 and 2 Samuel, 1 and 2 Kings, 1 and 2 Chronicles; also includes the books of wisdom: Psalms, Proverbs, Ecclesiastes, Song of Songs

Israel pleads with God through the prophet Samuel to give them a human king. The Lord eventually agrees, although he warns his people of the new difficulties a monarch will create. Saul becomes the first king of Israel, followed by David and then Solomon. God promises King David that he will build David's "house," bringing an everlasting kingdom through his family line. During this season, Israel is a united nation that grows in power and prosperity. David, Solomon, and others write the Wisdom Literature (like Psalms and Proverbs). Through their writing, God promises the coming of a Messiah who will sit on David's throne—King Jesus.

Divided Kingdom

Books Included: Starting at 1 Kings 12 through the end of 2 Kings and 2 Chronicles 10 to the end of 2 Chronicles. Many of the prophets fall in this section (Isaiah, Jeremiah, Hosea, Jonah, Nahum, Amos, Zephaniah, Micah, Habakkuk)

Following Solomon's rule, his son Rehoboam is overthrown, and the kingdom is divided in two. This division of the monarchy is a key to understanding much of the Old Testament. The rebel leader, Jeroboam, takes ten of the tribes of Israel and establishes the Northern Kingdom, often referred to as Israel or Ephraim. Meanwhile, Solomon's son Rehoboam continues to rule over the tribes of Judah and Benjamin, forming the Southern Kingdom, known as Judah. Kings from the family line of Judah continue to rule over the Southern Kingdom, just as God promised David.

Essentially, the Northern Kingdom has no faithful kings and commits great evil in the eyes of God. Judah, the Southern Kingdom, has more faithful kings and remains loyal to the Lord for longer, but ultimately Judah's kings also fail to trust God. Throughout this chaotic part of biblical history, God repeatedly raises up prophets to speak his words to the people. The prophets issue warnings but also proclaim God's goodness and grace as they promise a coming Savior from David's line who will rescue God's people.

Exile

Books Included: Books of history: Esther; Prophets: Ezekiel, Daniel, Obadiah, Lamentations

God allows his people from both the Northern and Southern Kingdoms to be taken into exile (removed from the land) by the surrounding nations. The Assyrian armies conquer the city of Samaria in the Northern Kingdom in 722

BC, and the Babylonians conquer the city of Jerusalem in 586 BC, destroying the temple and carrying off many of its sacred objects.

The prophet Jeremiah has warned God's people that God will allow them to be exiled (removed from the land) for seventy years (25:9–13), and this is what eventually happens. The stories of exile focus on the Southern Kingdom, Judah, and the promise of a future king, descended from David. God's people live in Babylon for seventy years, fulfilling Jeremiah's prophecy of the Lord's discipline for their unfaithfulness to him. Being removed from their land is a great tragedy and trauma in Israel's history. Several prophets continue to speak God's words of warning and hope during this time of grief and confusion for Judah.

Restoration

Books Included: Books of History: Ezra and Nehemiah; Prophets: Joel, Zechariah, Haggai, Malachi

The Lord moves in the heart of Cyrus, king of Persia, who releases the Jews from exile. They return to Jerusalem with the charge of rebuilding the city walls, the temple, and the land. While this period begins with excitement and hope, God's people return to their old ways. They neglect the temple and proper worship of the Lord. The Old Testament ends on a low note, with Israel in disarray, but God points forward to the future King, his long-anticipated Messiah. God's people will wait for roughly four hundred years before Jesus arrives on the scene.

Incarnation

Books Included: Matthew, Mark, Luke, John

The New Testament begins with the coming of Jesus, or the Messiah, born to a humble couple in the extended family line of David. All of the promises of the Old Testament are fulfilled as God comes to earth as a human baby, who is also the Son of God. Jesus performs miracles to confirm that he is, in fact, the promised Messiah who has come to save God's people from their sins. He proclaims the arrival of the kingdom of God, the Lord's visible rule on earth. He teaches God's law in truth and in grace. He demonstrates that God himself has come to earth to deliver his people and the world from the effects of sin.

Redemption

Books Included: The endings of Matthew, Mark, Luke, John

The life, works, and teachings of Jesus all culminate in the focal point of his ministry—to die for the sins of God's people. All four of the gospels record how Jesus journcys to Jerusalem where he is arrested, betrayed, beaten, and ultimately crucified on the cross, dying a criminal's death. He takes the penalty—God's judgment—for the sins of mankind, serving as a sacrifice. After Jesus dies and is buried, he rises from the grave, still in his physical body! The end of each gospel includes accounts of Jesus' interactions with his followers in the forty days following his resurrection.

The Church

Books Included: Acts

Forty days after his resurrection, Jesus ascends into heaven to sit at the right hand of God the Father. He sends the Holy Spirit to live in the hearts of believers and to be the presence of God on earth. Jesus promises that the Spirit will give his apostles power to share the gospel and do miraculous works. In doing so, Jesus establishes the Christian church. The apostles travel throughout Judea (the land of the tribe of Judah) and other places across the Roman Empire and beyond. Speaking to both Jews and Gentiles (non-Jews), they spread the *gospel*, or the good news, of God's forgiveness of sins through Jesus' life, death, and resurrection. As people receive the gospel and begin to follow Jesus, local churches are formed, leadership is established, and people mature in faith.

Paul's Letters

Books Included: Romans, 1 and 2 Corinthians, Galatians, Ephesians, Philippians, Colossians, 1 and 2 Thessalonians, 1 and 2 Timothy, Titus, Philemon

Following the beginning of the early church (God's people in their many locations), the rest of the New Testament is composed of letters. The apostle Paul writes many of these to different churches and church leaders, instructing them in the truth of the gospel. He explains what Jesus' coming means for the joy, hope, and salvation of Christians. He also explains the significance of the Holy Spirit in the lives of believers. Paul talks about how we should live in response to the good news of Jesus' life, death, and resurrection and also teaches churches how to operate in a godly manner. While his letters are written to churches from long ago, the message in his letters remains relevant and true for believers today.

Other Letters

Books Included: Hebrews; James; 1 and 2 Peter; 1, 2, and 3 John, Jude

There are eight books that follow Paul's letters. Like Paul's, these letters are written to churches to educate Christians on the meaning of Christ's coming and the gospel. These letters also provide practical instruction about living the Christian life.

Glorification

Books Included: Revelation

The final book of the Bible, Revelation, speaks to the ultimate hope of God's people as they look to Jesus. The term *glorification* means the final stage of salvation, when God completes his work to finish bringing his kingdom through Christ. This book offers a glimpse into the spiritual realm, where God is moving history toward its end: Heaven comes to earth, and the full glory and presence of the Lord dwells with God's people. As Christians, we are living in the middle of the Bible's story as we wait for Jesus to return and make all things new. By the Spirit, we say, *Come, Lord Jesus!*